WORK *together* ANYWHERE

LISETTE SUTHERLAND
and K. JANENE-NELSON

foreword by JURGEN APPELO

WORK *together* ANYWHERE

A HANDBOOK ON WORKING REMOTELY —*successfully*— FOR INDIVIDUALS, TEAMS & MANAGERS

WILEY

Published by John Wiley & Sons, Inc., Hoboken, New Jersey.

Published simultaneously in Canada.

Library of Congress Cataloging-in-Publication Data:

ISBN 9781119745228 (Paperback)
ISBN 9781119745259 (ePDF)
ISBN 9781119745242 (ePub)

Cover and interior design by Erin Seaward-Hiatt (www.erinhiatt.com)
Photo of Lisette Sutherland by José Ignacio de Juan
Photo of Kirsten Janene-Nelson by Jeremy Lindston Robinson

Library of Congress Control Number: 2020938122

Printed in the United States of America

V10018404_051420

Contents

PART I *Extras*

PART II. INDIVIDUALS WORKING REMOTELY 67

PART II *Extras*

PART IV *Extras*

RESOURCES 271

How to Use This Book

GENERALLY stated, to work remotely successfully calls for a particular combination of tool set, skill set, and mind set. More specifically, different settings and contexts call for different combinations of tool set, skill set, and mind set. To help you determine which combination best suits your needs, this book is organized into four parts to guide you—be you employee or employer—straight to the information that will help most now, whether you're just considering working remotely, ready to start out, or perfecting your game.

If the concept of working remotely is new to you, begin with Part I, which relays the primary reasons why both employees and employers have opted to go remote. The Part I EXTRAS are geared toward those uncertain of just how to be effective in the virtual realm; there you'll find both answers to frequently asked questions and an at-a-glance view of some essential benefits of working on-site—as well as how to replicate them online.

Part II focuses on the details applicable to individuals working remotely. For those just contemplating the leap into remote work, chapter 3 begins with a section on deciding for yourself—after which it addresses what you need to get started. The Part II EXTRAS further the exploration with a questionnaire to help you determine if you're ready to work remotely—the results of which specify what you'd need to do to get ready. There is also guidance on taking your decision to the next level, be that convincing your boss (or team) or seeking remote employment. Chapter 4 expands the scope to discuss wider concerns: how to work well for yourself, as well as how to work well with others.

Part III begins the consideration of the remote option from the managerial perspective. For companies or departments first venturing into the virtual realm, chapter 5 shares how to prepare for the expansion, while chapter 6 and the Part III EXTRAS cover how to hire remote employees.

Part IV outlines the full range of what it means to manage remote teams. It walks you through how to make the experience productive, effective, and fun for everyone—from assessing how to translate your on-site needs to the online realm to crafting a team agreement on how everyone will work together. Chapter 10 also includes guidelines on running effective meetings, how to experiment in iterations—even how to scale up when the time comes to grow. Among the Part IV EXTRAS is the Manager's Action Plan, which consolidates the action steps discussed in the individual chapters.

Following the conclusion chapter, the extensive RESOURCES section identifies where to head next, whether you seek details on the plethora of technology & tools available or need more ideas on a wide range of topics, from etiquette and HR to icebreakers and Retrospectives.

Another note: because much of the material relayed here applies to a variety of readers and situations, there is some necessary overlap. So, some information appears in more than one spot and in more than one way. As it happens, those points of overlap emphasize the most important aspects of how to work together well, and so are worth repeating.

Join me in exploring the wonderful world of remote working!

Foreword

TODAY'S meeting with my Agility Scales team was a good one. In the first five minutes, we discussed the most fashionable carnival costumes for our kids. (This season, it's LEGO ninjas, apparently.) The discussion was part of our mandatory chitchat ritual, which both forbids us from immediately diving into work mode and challenges us to be more human and personal with each other. For five minutes.

After the chitchat, we had a vigorous discussion about how to describe the nature of our online product, as well as what terminology to use to best explain it to our customers. We also talked about the priorities of new product features, the role of our user community, and several important decisions we had to make. It was a delightful conversation, one in which everyone participated equally and which felt like a strange mix of marketing and existentialism.

We finished the meeting after precisely one hour, which is how we like it. As usual, we finished with our return on time invested (ROTI) ritual. At the count of three, everyone signals how useful the meeting was by holding up between one and five fingers. Everyone rated the meeting a five—except Kirill, who offered a four. An almost-perfect rating! We joked that we'd never invite Kirill again, and he joked back that he hadn't been invited; he had just shown up to annoy us. A big laugh followed, and then I clicked the LEAVE MEETING button.

I took off my noise-canceling headphones, put away my Android tablet, looked around the airport café to see if anyone had stolen my stuff during the meeting, and then gathered my belongings to go and find my departure gate.

I am a remote worker. I can do my work anywhere.

In my opinion, work is something you do, not a place where you go. This attitude requires a particular way of thinking, a different approach to organization, and a bit of planning.

Where do you keep your documents when your office is wherever you happen to be? How do you work as a team when you rarely get to see each other face-to-face? What are the best tools for online meetings, schedules, workflows, design, and development? And how can you do your work when you're in an environment that's not conducive to focused, creative thinking?

The world of business is not used to this style of working. In fact, the terms that people in "normal" companies use for my kind of work life are all inept, in my view. Why do they call it "remote" working? My company has no office, so there's no central place for me to be "remote" from. And what's the deal with "virtual" teams? Is our team not "real" because we're not physically colocated? And don't get me started on IRL (in real life). I think I enjoy more of a real life than do most office workers, who are slowly dying between four gray walls.

Speaking of both "virtual" and "office" workers, in 2013 I hired Lisette Sutherland to be the virtual team manager for Happy Melly, a global professional happiness association dedicated to helping people be happier at work. Considering that I wanted to build a company without a physical office, and since Lisette was a pioneer in this realm, it made sense to let her do all the learning and exploration and then ask her to show us all the tips and tricks. It turns out that was a great decision. Now Lisette has done the same all over again: she's done all the learning and exploration about virtual work life and teamwork—and now she can teach you everything you need to know to also be a success in this arena.

I started writing this text at Toulouse–Blagnac Airport in France. I'm now completing it in one of my favorite coffee bars in Rotterdam, the Netherlands. In between, I've been writing to you from Düsseldorf, Brussels, and Amsterdam. At the same time, I've also been remotely managing distributed teams spread out over a dozen or more countries on four continents. I'm sure you didn't notice all the smooth transitions.

Does it all sound unfamiliar or challenging? Don't worry. Lisette is here to tell you how you can organize this for yourself and for your teams. So stop going to work; start doing the work!

—Jurgen Appelo, author, speaker, entrepreneur

Introduction

In 2006, I lived in California and belonged to a social community interested in technology, the future, and staying healthy. Every Sunday we went hiking together. One person in the group particularly interested me because he was working on a peculiar start-up idea: he wanted to eradicate death.

I learned there are a lot of longevity devotees out there experimenting with and researching anti-aging: rocket scientists, theoretical physicists, entrepreneurs, software developers. Some practice calorie restriction. Some research cryonics. Some work on nanotechnologies. Through his networks, my death-defying hiking friend was introduced to others working toward the same goal—but no one was talking regularly or sharing data. So he dreamed of building an online project-management tool to enable longevity scientists from all over the world to collaborate and solve the problem of aging.

It was an aha! experience for me. For centuries, employers have hired the most qualified workers who were able to convene at a central location. The location was by necessity the constant; the variable was the most qualified workers able to convene. That didn't necessarily mean the team was populated by "the best and the brightest"—just the best who were nearby or willing to relocate. Of course, that's the employer's view. From the employees' view, the job offers they accepted were the best they could get at the time—whether or not those jobs made them excited to get up in the morning.

But if instead we found a way to make location the variable—indeed, immaterial—then we could have the constant be the far more important concern: qualification, including enthusiasm. Employers could hire the best, the brightest, and the most dedicated—wherever those workers happen to be.

I love this concept. I've held a job that I took on because it was a "good job"—despite the fact that it didn't excite me. And every day, when I arrived at what I called my gray cube (a cubicle like in a *Dilbert* cartoon), a part of me thought, *Ugh. This is not the life I envisioned for myself.* After several years, being rather young and naive, I quit my stable, good-paying job and pursued work that allowed greater self-expression, work that made me feel more alive. It wasn't glamorous and it didn't pay well for a long time, but I eventually found my niche and my own version of success.

It just thrills me to think that technology could make it so that everyone can engage in work that jazzes them. So I started talking to others who were thinking this way too, and I found a lot of people to talk to. I've interviewed directors and managers from more than eighty companies whose business models *depend* on successfully bridging distance—companies that, for example, provide consulting services, outsource work, and offer training courses. In addition I've talked with hundreds of people—from software developers to HR directors to neuroscientists. Everyone had a lot to say about how they make working remotely work for them or their teams. Some things I already knew or had guessed, like the need for regular contact and team building. Some things really surprised me, like how much connection can be created just by turning on the video camera, as well as how reluctant we all can be to try new things.

One of the biggest takeaways I got from all those conversations is that there is no "one solution fits all" for remote working, no single formula to follow. Each person, each company, will need to experiment with various tools and processes to find what makes him, her, or them most productive. But what are the tools available? What processes are effective for different kinds of remote teams? I rustled the virtual bushes to learn everything I could about how to make working remotely not just workable, but undeniably productive—and, in some cases, even preferable. All that and more has been collected in these pages.

To best help you navigate this terrain, this book is divided into parts and chapters suited to different kinds of readers at different stages in the going-remote process. (Please forgive this repeat if you've already read "How to Use This Book.") If all this is completely new to you, start with Part I, which offers a bird's-eye view of the current landscape of remote working, detailing some of the who, what, where, and why of it all. Part II is for individuals, whether you're considering going remote or you're ready to start out (chapter 3), or you're perfecting your game (chapter 4). Parts III and IV are for team leaders and managers/owners: those transitioning to the remote option (chapter 5), those hiring remote workers (chapter 6), and those looking to perfect their game (chapters 7 through 10). Following the chapters in each part are Part EXTRAS: additional resources particularly applicable to that group. After Part IV is the RESOURCES section, which includes additions applicable to many—especially "Technology & Tools." And for those who would benefit from more personalized guidance, you'll also find information about the Work Together Anywhere Workshop, which is available both online and in person.

Be sure not to miss the conclusion, where I wax poetic about how people from all corners of the globe have figured out how to flourish working remotely—and how in so doing have achieved marvels previously thought impossible. And, finally, I want to give a shout-out to the remote-working experts I interviewed for the Collaboration Superpowers podcasts—which as of this writing has aired its 175th unique episode. In the "Interviewees" section I share a bit of what each professional has to offer—as well as information on how to further your acquaintance should you wish to learn more.

ONE of the premises of this book is that to be better informed is to be better prepared. So I strongly recommend that you at least skim the portions written for those you'll be interacting *with*. The more you understand their perspective, and they yours, the better you'll be able to forge something undeniably productive together. This broader perspective magnifies everyone's understanding of how to make it all work well.

For those who haven't yet made the leap, the prospect of going remote can feel daunting—but it doesn't have to. Whether you're an individual, a manager, or an owner, in the pages that follow you'll find all you need not just to get started but also to get ahead. The information collected here paints a bright picture of the possibilities available to us today. Plus, given that businesses are constantly adapting, and the technology of remote collaboration is always improving, the future looks even more promising.

As I continue to interview people who work remotely, I meet ever more people from all over the world who actively pursue work they love. When I think back to my gray days in that cubicle, I think about all the people who currently view their work equally dimly. But they don't have to—the technology exists to bridge distance between a dedicated worker and a job worth getting up for in the morning. In the pages to come, I'll share how to do just that.

By the end of our journey, it's unlikely we'll have eradicated death, as my ambitious colleague aspires to do. But with the tips, tools, and to-do lists that follow, I hope to open your eyes to the possibilities that exist right now for working remotely—and to inspire you to do great things too. Just think of what we could accomplish when we get the right people working together!

PART I
SETTING THE SCENE

Some of the Who, What, Where, and Why of Remote Working

As noted earlier, Part I aims to succinctly convey the terrain in which remote workers and employers find themselves—as well as a bit of what brought them there. Chapter 1 takes the viewpoint of the worker, sharing just what makes the remote option so appealing. (In a word: flexibility.) Chapter 2 demonstrates what a win-win for employers that flexibility can be. And for the more skeptical readers—or those who answer to more skeptical figures—that chapter shares both some common concerns about the remote option and possible solutions. The Part I EXTRAS section continues that discussion with "Frequently Asked Questions," whose answers cross-reference where in the book more information can be found. And "At a Glance" encapsulates some of the many ways to replicate online the benefits of working on-site—material covered in detail in chapter 8.

As for further down the road, individuals ready to move forward can head to Part II—Individuals Working Remotely. Managers ready to move forward can head to Part III—Successful Remote Teams 101: Transitioning and Hiring. Those managers already in remote waters can seek out Part IV—Successful Remote Teams 201: Managing Remote Workers and Teams.

CHAPTER 1

Why Are Individuals Going Remote? Workplace Flexibility

"A lot of what we're looking at is not new. It's just that technologies make working from anywhere possible for a lot more people."

—Pilar Orti, *director, Virtual not Distant*[1]

Most of this book tells you how you can make a success of working remotely, whether you're a team member, a team leader, or flying solo. But before we get into that, some—especially managers—might wonder how it's possible to get *valuable* work out of unsupervised employees. The answer to that question has multiple aspects, the most significant of which hinges on why workers seek remote employment options in the first place. We'll return to both questions later in this chapter. But to best understand the full picture, let's take a look at what kinds of people work remotely.

Some Terminology on Remote Working

Individuals who work remotely can be full-time telecommuting employees, contract freelancers—even digital nomads. [Note that all terms identified by bold italics are included in the glossary.] They typically fall into one of three "employee" types: telecommuter, self-employed, and business owner.

A ***telecommuter*** is someone who works remotely (usually from home), either full time or part time, on a fixed team for one company. According to research firm Global Workplace Analytics, a typical telecommuter in the United States is forty-five or older, college educated, and works as a salaried, non-union employee in a professional or even management role. He or she earns about $58,000 a year and most likely works for a company with more than one hundred employees. (In addition, 75 percent of employees who work from home earn more than $65,000 per year, which puts them in the upper eightieth percentile of all employees, home or office-based.)[2]

Many remote workers are ***self-employed freelancers***. They run mainly service-based businesses and usually work with more than one remote client, whether simultaneously or consecutively. (As noted in the sidebar to follow, Upwork and Freelancers Union define ***freelancers*** as "individuals who have engaged in supplemental, temporary, or project- or contract-based work within the past twelve months."[3])

Some self-employed freelancers are also small business owners, whether ***solopreneurs*** or entrepreneurs (with a few remote employees or contractors).

Any of the above could also be a ***digital nomad***: those who use portable technology to maintain a nomadic lifestyle.

The Five Types of Freelancers

Originally, the term "free-lancer" described a medieval lancer for hire, one not sworn to defend a particular lord. Today there are five main types of freelancers, defined by Upwork and Freelancers Union as "individuals who have engaged in supplemental, temporary, or project- or contract-based work in the past twelve months."

INDEPENDENT CONTRACTORS (40 percent of the independent workforce/21.1 million professionals): Rather than having a steady, full-time employer, these "traditional" freelancers do project-based freelance, temporary, or supplemental work.

MOONLIGHTERS (27 percent/14.3 million): Professionals with a primary, traditional job might also moonlight doing freelance work—perhaps for lower-paying non-profits whose missions they support.

DIVERSIFIED WORKERS (18 percent/9.3 million): Some cobble together a living from a mix of employers. For example, someone who works steady hours as a part-time receptionist might also wait tables, drive for Lyft, and write freelance articles on the side.

TEMPORARY WORKERS (10 percent/5.5 million): This category includes those with a temporary employment status, whether that be one day as a film shoot makeup artist, several weeks as an office or warehouse temp, or several months as a business consultant.

FREELANCE BUSINESS OWNERS (5 percent/2.8 million): A freelancer can also be a solopreneur (with no employees) or an entrepreneur who employs others (usually between one and five employees or subcontractors).

Source: Upwork and Freelancers Union, "Freelancing in America: 2017."[4]

Though working on-site is still the norm in certain sectors, not all telecommuters are seen as an anomaly in their department. Indeed, some companies have turned the concept of "normal" employee on its head, and have teams partially—or even entirely—made up of remote workers.

Remote teams are groups of people who work together on a project: sometimes for the same company, sometimes as a group of freelancers, and sometimes as a combination of both. They typically fall into one of the four following categories, often determined more by location than by function. In some teams several members work together in the same location ("***colocated***"), while others work remotely; this is what's meant by the term "***partly distributed***." In some teams everyone works remotely, regardless of location; this is also known as being "***fully distributed***." Expanding to the company level, some companies are made up of several teams in different locations. And, of course, there are global organizations with offices in different locations. To follow are some examples.

IN PARTLY DISTRIBUTED COMPANIES, SOME WORKERS ARE COLOCATED, AND SOME ARE REMOTE. Targetprocess is a company of about eighty people. The majority of the team—90 percent—works together at the company headquarters in Minsk, Belarus; the remaining 10 percent is spread across the world. For Suitable Technologies it's more of a 40/60 split: roughly 40 percent of its staff commutes to the headquarters in Palo Alto, California, while the other 60 percent beams in to drivable robots.

IN FULLY DISTRIBUTED COMPANIES, ALL WORKERS ARE REMOTE. Happy Melly is a global professional happiness association that provides access to resources promoting job satisfaction and professional development. The members of its remote team—myself included—work from Belgium, Canada, Finland, India, the Netherlands, Russia, Slovenia, Spain, South Sudan, and the United Kingdom.

StarterSquad develops software for start-ups, all care of their international team of highly skilled developers, designers, and "growth hackers." Their team has an interesting "How did you get together?" story. A client with a software development project hired various freelancers using the online working site Upwork (formerly Elance). Though they didn't know each other before the project started, over time the team clicked—so well that, when the client unexpectedly ran out of money, the team members weren't ready to part ways. They've operated as a self-organized team of entrepreneurs ever since.

SOME COMPANIES WORK WITH SEVERAL TEAMS IN DIFFERENT LOCATIONS. Before starting his own company, Ralph van Roosmalen worked at an office in the Dutch city of 's-Hertogenbosch, where he managed three teams based in three countries: the Netherlands, Romania, and the United States. The partners at Radical Inclusion also live and work from three different countries: Belgium, Brazil, and Germany.

Geographic and Cultural Definitions

Geographically speaking, remote teams can be in the same location, near-located, or far-located. ***Near-located*** generally means that team members are within driving distance of each other. ***Far-located*** teams include one or more people who are far enough away that getting together in person requires planning. (The farthest far-located prize goes to the six people who work on the International Space Station, which orbits the Earth once every 90 minutes at a distance of 250 miles from our planet. Back on Earth, a team works to support them remotely at NASA—the National Aeronautics and Space Administration—themselves working from all over the world.)

Another aspect of remote working involves different cultural characterizations, which are often referred to as "near-shoring" and "off-shoring." When people from countries with a similar language and/or culture work together, it's called ***near-shoring***, such as a team with members in Europe, Scandinavia, and the United States. When people from countries with rather different languages and/or cultures work together, it's called ***off-shoring***, such as a team with members from Colombia, Europe, Pakistan, and the United States.

The Face of Remote Working

What about the individuals working in these capacities and configurations—what kind of people seek work outside the traditional office setting? A wide range, actually. Since working remotely usually requires some sort of technology, one might imagine such workers are mostly members of the millennial/Gen Y generation or younger (namely those born after 1985). Globally this is likely true; according to the 2018 Payoneer Freelancer Income Survey, more than 50 percent of respondents—21,000 people in 170 countries—are under age thirty.[5] But in the United States the average skews higher. According to 2017 State of Telecommuting in the U.S. Employee Workforce report, half of telecommuters are forty-five or older.[6]

In August 2017, the online employment resource FlexJobs, which specializes in professional flexible employment, published the results of its annual survey of those in the United States seeking flexible employment—5,500 respondents. Baby Boomers and "Gen-Xers" (together, those born between 1945 and 1984) comprise nearly three-quarters—72 percent. And the survey pool self-identified as a diverse group of working parents and entrepreneurs, students and retirees—the vast majority of whom (81 percent) sought to telecommute for their entire workweeks.[7] (See the sidebar to follow.)

Stats from the 2017 FlexJobs "Super Survey"

RESPONDENTS (5,500) SELF-IDENTIFIED AS

- Working parents (35%)
- Freelancers (26%)
- Entrepreneurs (21%)
- People living in rural areas (15%)
- Stay-at-home moms (14%)
- People with chronic physical or mental illness (14%)
- Digital nomads (12%)
- Caregivers (9%)
- Students (9%)
- Retirees (8%)
- Super-commuters (8%)
- Military spouses (2%)
- Stay-at-home dads (2%)

AGES/GENERATIONS

- Gen X (41%)
- Baby Boomer (31%)
- Millennial/Gen Y (21%)
- Silent Generation (6%)
- Gen Z (1%)

QUANTITY OF WORK SOUGHT

- Telecommuting 100% of the time (81%)
- Flexible schedule (70%)
- Telecommuting some of the time (46%)
- Part-time schedule (46%)
- Alternative schedule (44%)
- Freelance contract (39%)[8]

Such a diverse group has numerous reasons for preferring to work remotely. For many it's about schedule—specifically, the ability to maximize the time spent with their families. Indeed, a separate 2017 FlexJobs survey found that parents rank work flexibility (84 percent) ahead of even salary (75 percent).[9]

For some, the answer concerns their SITUATION, such as stay-at-home parents or adults caring for their parents, and military spouses—who appreciate not having the family's next deployment disrupt their own employment. Retirees are also keen remote workers. Entrepreneur, speaker, and author Leslie Truex notes that "a lot of people are looking at how they can supplement their retirement. Or they are already retired or want to retire sooner—and know they need an income to do that."[10] Writer and career development expert Brie Reynolds agrees, sharing: "Both my parents are in retirement now. They want to stay active, but they don't want to commute every day—and they don't want all the office politics. What they *do* want is to apply the knowledge and the skills they've learned across their lifetimes to something meaningful in retirement."[11]

But one of the biggest reasons remote working is on the rise derives from sheer opportunity. With the proliferation of online work websites (like Freelancer.com, SimplyHired, and Upwork), there are ever more opportunities for contract work. The survey "Freelancing in America: 2017" notes that "71 percent of freelancers say the percentage of work they have obtained online has increased over the past year," and that 77 percent of those "who have found work online" start projects "within a week." Indeed, at the "current growth rate, the majority of the U.S. workforce will be freelancers by 2027."[12] As for the income from that work, in early 2018 annual freelancer earnings on Upwork.com reached the $1.5 billion mark.[13]

An additional factor within sheer opportunity is how working remotely allows an employee to test out a new position *before* relocating. As financial services executive Jeremy Stanton puts it: "There's a lot of risk taking a job, especially when you have to uproot your family and move. What if you get six months in and it doesn't work out? That's an awful conversation to have with your spouse. If you start remotely, there's more room to ramp up into the company, and everybody gets a chance to see if it works out."[14]

And many seek remote employment in the face of insufficient in-office opportunities. Leslie Truex reports: "Though some people are scared to become freelancers because they want the salary and benefits they're used to, we're seeing that more and more employers are cutting benefits, even if they aren't going out of business. The idea that the in-house job is the safe route isn't necessarily true anymore."[15] In other words, many freelancers feel they have more stability working for themselves—because they don't rely on one company for their income. I faced this scenario myself. One company I worked for went out of business overnight because their one and only investor was involved in a scandal. I was at my next job for two years until the company was sold, leaving me unemployed again. That inspired me to stop looking for "regular jobs" and instead take things into my own hands; essentially, I switched to full-time freelancing for job *security*.

An additional, widely shared reason for preferring the remote option concerns COMMUTING. For some, it isn't so much that they don't want to work on-site—it's the getting there that's the problem. As SourceSeek cofounder Dave Hecker puts it, "The world is changing. A lot of people don't want to come to the office anymore."[16] Among my own interviewees, the number-one reason people want to work remotely is to end the dreaded commute. Around the world, commuting times vary, from a few minutes to a few hours per day. According to the 2016 "PGi Global Telework" Survey, the majority of surveyed "non-teleworkers" commuted thirty to sixty minutes round-trip per day; the figure exceeds an hour for one-third of those in the Asia Pacific region.[17] Every minute we commute is a minute we aren't working or doing something we love—or being with someone we love. On top of that, the journey itself is often stressful, rife with traffic jams, crowded buses and trains, delays, smells, and noise. The world over, a large number of workers feel a bad commute can ruin a great job.

Another factor about commuting concerns expense, both of the commute itself as well as the cost of living within a decent commuting distance from work. Several of the people I interviewed appreciated being able to enjoy a metropolitan income while also residing in a region with a low cost of living.

PRODUCTIVITY

As for the time when people are working on-site: while some benefit from the nose-to-the-grindstone atmosphere of an office, a significant majority find they're least productive in that setting. Why? Many find it too distracting. Meetings, side conversations, noise, celebrations . . . all these and more get in the way of productivity. Citing several years of FlexJobs survey data, career development expert Brie Reynolds relates how people want to work remotely "to get away from office distractions. They don't want the office politics and the quick pop-ins to their cubicles. They want to be able to focus and actually get work done."[18]

FlexJobs's 2017 Survey: Productivity Outside the Office

To follow are the top reasons respondents said they would be, or are, more productive working remotely:

- Fewer interruptions from colleagues (76%)
- Fewer distractions (76%)
- Reduced stress from commuting (70%)
- Minimal office politics (69%)
- Quieter noise level (62%)
- More comfortable clothes (54%)
- More personalized office environment (51%)
- Less frequent meetings (46%)
- More efficient meetings (31%)

Source: "Workers Are More Productive at Home," FlexJobs, 21 August 2017.[19]

Entrepreneur and author Leslie Truex agrees: "The reality is we've all been in a workplace where our colleagues are present but they're not getting things done. Lots of studies show that productivity among telecommuters is actually high. They get a lot done in less time."[20] For example, in 2017 *Forbes* reported that, "according to the 'State of Work' productivity report, 65 percent of full-time employees think a remote work schedule would increase productivity. This is backed up by more than two-thirds of managers reporting an increase in overall productivity from their remote employees."[21]

In 2014, *Harvard Business Review* interviewed the authors of a half-remote, half-in-house productivity study at a call center of the Chinese travel website Ctrip. The study found that "people working from home completed 13.5 percent more calls than the staff in the office did—meaning that Ctrip got almost an extra workday a week out of them." As Nicholas Bloom, a professor of economics at Stanford University, reported: "One-third of the productivity increase, we think, was due to having a quieter environment, which makes it easier to process calls. At home people don't experience what we call the 'cake in the break room' effect. Offices are actually incredibly distracting places. The other two-thirds can be attributed to the fact that the people at home worked more hours. They started earlier, took shorter breaks, and worked until the end of the day. They had no commute. They didn't run errands at lunch. Sick days for employees working from home plummeted."[22]

Even the technology giant Best Buy "reported in 2006 that productivity had on average increased 35 percent in departments that shifted to working from wherever they wanted, whenever they wanted." And though Best Buy famously ended that option, it was apparently because "working together, in person, has a different set of benefits."[23] (This point gets revisited in the FAQ section in the Part I EXTRAS.)

Productivity When Working Remotely

The title of this 2016 Hubstaff article says it all: "Are Remote Workers More Productive? We've Checked All the Research So You Don't Have To." Based on "a number of different studies, conducted by both big companies and civil society organizations," they conclude that the option to work remotely yields greater productivity. In sum, the findings suggest the following:

- Remote workers PERFORM BETTER AND FASTER the same type of jobs as those of office workers.
- Remote workers LOG MORE HOURS. This happens in part because they TAKE LESS SICK LEAVE, since it's possible to work from home without infecting the office. The fact that they "also show better engagement with the work and report higher levels of personal satisfaction and happiness" (as noted below) likely adds to their productivity.
- Remote workers are MORE ENGAGED.
- Remote workers are HAPPIER WITH THEIR JOBS.
- Remote workers are BETTER AT COLLABORATION.
- Remote workers REDUCE EMPLOYERS' COSTS.

Hubstaff cites the following among their sources: ConnectSolutions (now CoSo Cloud), Gallup's 2017 "State of the American Workplace" report, GlobalWorkplaceAnalytics.com (based on analysis of 2005–2015 U.S. Census Bureau data), *Harvard Business Review*, and Remote.co.[24]

Given that the working world of today has in many cases outgrown its former cookie-cutter mold, there is no longer a singular approach to working. And for many workers, in many industries, the most productive workspace is not the office.

> **My first aha! moment was when I was on a holiday and had to do some work. And I noticed that the work was some of the best I had ever done, and I had done it faster than when I was in my office. That's when I realized that by changing where I worked, I could improve what I did.**
>
> —TEO HÄRÉN, creativity expert, interesting.org[25]

> **Everything is in the cloud. I'm as effective from home or when I'm traveling abroad as I would be if I was in the office.**
>
> —NICK TIMMONS, director of sales, Personify Inc.[26]

> **Without question I'm more productive when working at home—at least when it comes to tasks that require almost no collaboration. Focus is best achieved when I'm isolated, and at work I'm constantly interrupted. Often for work-related stuff, which is fine, but I'm also drawn into conversations about non-work-related topics.**
>
> —Abraham Heward, senior engineer at Carvana[27]

The plain fact is that different people thrive in different environments, and we appreciate being free to choose a location and setup that works for us. But this concept of choice extends beyond just one work environment: quite a few of my interviewees opt for a different workspace depending on the task at hand.

> **Where I work depends on the job I'm doing. If the job requires thinking and designing and needs concentration, I like coffee shops. I concentrate best when there are a lot of people around me. When the job is routine and I just need to check something, I stay home.**
>
> —Yegor Bugayenko, CEO, Zerocracy.com[28]

> **A *hybrid model* is my preferred situation, because efficient pair programming and training happens when I am colocated, but focus is best achieved when I'm isolated.**
>
> —Abraham Heward, senior engineer at Carvana[29]

> **Personally, I don't define an office. I look for the office I need to solve my task. I find it very boring to do invoicing, so I want to do it at a very beautiful place. I save invoices for two or three months, and then go to the ocean and sit at a café, and do that boring stuff at an inspiring place. My twin brother hates invoicing as well, but he solves it in another way. He likes to sit in a room with no windows to make things so boring that he works as quickly as he can.**
>
> —Teo Härén, creativity expert, interesting.org[30]

There's a psychological aspect to this too. It's undeniable that the freedom to choose one's workspace is a boon for the worker—and a boost to the worker's mood. But note that that opportunity, that autonomy, translates back to benefit the *employer* as well as the worker. Employees who have a positive association with their work and work environment can't help but produce better work. As Troy Gardner, CTO of Cloud9 Brewing Systems, puts it: "I love not being in a 72-degree, noisy, fluorescent-lit room. . . . I love my sit-stand desk, my comfy chair, and my gazillion monitors."[31] (We'll return to this point later on.)

Of course, some endeavors require participation on-site. Workers don't begrudge that; they simply appreciate some flexibility regarding other aspects of their responsibilities. For example, when employees of the headquarters of Gap Inc. were given the option of choosing their work hours, many still came into work—they just chose to commute during off-peak times, reducing their commute time by as much as an hour or more each day. And they usually spent that additional time working. Ultimately, the flexible option made them *more* productive.[32]

Remote Solutions Provide the Best of Both Worlds

Putting aside for the moment the legitimate need for in-person meetings and face-to-face collaboration, some don't know how they'd get ahead on the job—let alone cultivate a successful career over time—if they didn't work in a central workplace. Many can't imagine working without being able to easily find their teammates to ask a quick question. Many cite the importance of being privy to the unplanned benefits of working together—notably in overhearing conversations. As interviewee Laura Rooke puts it: "What you miss out on when working remotely is what you would overhear if you were in an office. Sometimes the conversations you overhear are just as valuable as the conversations you have with somebody."[33] Plus, of course, there are the social benefits of working in an office—the spontaneous moments at the water cooler, the shared lunches and drinks after work, and the simple fact of being with others as opposed to working in isolation.

Fortunately, both technology and ingenuity have produced numerous means of addressing all these valid concerns. And, since the whole point of this book is to share them with you, you'll find specifics about all of them throughout these pages, especially in "Technology & Tools" in the RESOURCES section and in the chapters concerning teams (Part IV). For now, here are just a few of the many solutions available to the points mentioned above.

EASY ACCESS TO COLLEAGUES

First, just plain-old digital communication: phone, email, text, and ***instant messaging (IM)***—combined with informing one's colleagues on how best to be reached when—solves the problem of getting a quick answer to a question. Second, more advanced visual communication, such as video chat (see next entry), as well as the communication capabilities of ***virtual office*** technology, offer more meaningful interaction. Note that some studies suggest that these digital communication options are necessary for even those who work on-site; an internal study conducted at biotechnology giant Genentech found that employees were not at their desks for 80 percent (!) of the standard workday.[34]

THE BENEFITS OF "FACE TIME" INTERACTIONS

The following anecdote demonstrates how effective digital face time—video chat—can be. While working on a six-month special project in London, England, associate professor and neuroradiologist Marion Smits needed to maintain high-quality interaction with her PhD students back at Erasmus MC in Rotterdam, the Netherlands. Before she left, her students were concerned that they wouldn't have enough contact and would lose touch. However, thanks to Skype calls replacing their in-person meetings, they found that they worked together just the same, especially since they already used email to communicate and Dropbox to share files anyway. In fact, when Marion returned from London the students joked about the inconvenience of having to walk the fifteen minutes across campus to meet her in her office.

THE UNPLANNED BENEFITS OF WORKING TOGETHER

The solution to this concern fuses digital-age technology with modern-day methodology in a practice known as "***working out loud***." (This is covered more in chapter 4 and throughout Part IV.)

THE SOCIAL BENEFITS OF WORKING IN AN OFFICE

Since humans are so enterprising, it's not surprising that quite a few digital solutions address our needs as social creatures. For example, workers utilizing a company's virtual office can identify if they're available to chat—if their digital door is "open" to virtual pop-ins. And as Stephan Dohrn, Managing Partner at Radical Inclusion, puts it, "Group chat makes a great virtual water cooler."[35] Video chat also enables spending time together over lunch—or over drinks after work.

THE DOWNSIDES OF WORKING IN ISOLATION

For those who simply prefer to not be the only human in the room during the workday, thanks to ***portable technology*** (such as cellphone, laptop, and cloud-based software) there's always the option of snagging a corner table at a café or renting a spot at a coworking space—the latter available on-demand or year-round.

THE BENEFITS OF ACTUAL FACE TIME

As for the endeavors that require more than just digital face time, even far-located employees can schedule in-person interactions when such is preferable. In fact, most remote-working experts encourage making a habit of getting together in person when possible.

The point bears repeating: we love having options concerning both our schedule and our workspace. And we love getting to choose work that's meaningful to us—with colleagues who also love their work, who also take pride in the work they do. It was said over and over in my interviews: while salary is important, there came a point when people valued working on interesting projects with people they liked more than they valued their pay package.

> **I enjoy programming and I like to work with people who share the same passion for writing high-quality code. My work is not just about making money. It's not just a job, it's a pleasure for me. Every day I get to work with people who care about the same things I do.**
>
> —Yegor Bugayenko, CEO, Zerocracy.com[36]

In my company, we are working on defending people against all kinds of security threats. It feels good to work on something that makes a difference in some of the not-so-pleasant things of online life.

—Mark Kilby, Agile coach, Sonatype[37]

There's a certain wonderful feeling when you are doing something that you are passionate about and making money with it. There's nothing better than that.

—Gerard Beaulieu, cofounder, Tornadosedge.com; and founder, Virtual Ice Breakers[38]

Workplace Flexibility: Results-Oriented vs. Hours-Oriented Work

"There's a presumption that people are slacking off [when working outside the office]. What we've found is that people don't want to get fired. . . . They know they can't slack off."

—Eric Severson, *former co-CHRO, Gap Inc.; Appointee, National Advisory Council on Innovation & Entrepreneurship*[39]

This chapter began by noting that those of a managerial mind set might wonder how—or even if—it's possible to get valuable work out of unsupervised employees. The quick answer to "if" is yes. The larger context of "how" is to be found in the philosophy of ***results-oriented working***.

There's a quiet, steady revolution taking place in the work arena regarding worker autonomy. For hundreds of years, workers came to a central workplace during set hours. Today, technology has made it possible to produce valuable work at any hour, from any location. This capability could make some managers nervous, thinking that it takes a supervisory eye to keep workers productive. But that concern is an artifact of ***hours-oriented work***: work where, if you put in your time-clocked hours, your work is done.

In 2003, Cali Ressler and Jody Thompson created a workplace strategy that focuses not on hours but on results. They trademarked their creation Results-Only Work Environment, or ROWE. As Ressler and Thompson put it, ROWE is a "management strategy where employees are evaluated on performance, not presence."[40]

Web-developer agency 10up Inc. offers:

> **How do businesses measure productivity of colocated workers? By how busy they appear to be when you walk by? By whether they enter the office at 9:00 AM and leave around 5:00 PM? Any business that effectively measures employee productivity surely isn't relying on anything having to do with physical location.**
>
> **In truth, well-managed distributed teams are often far more productive than colocated teams, because, indeed, you're *forced* to measure productivity by far more objective metrics than things like "time in the building."[41]**

This isn't to say that hourly workers don't track their time; the difference concerns the company's expectations of those workers. ROWE-minded organizations often break down larger work into "granular" or very-short-time-frame work phases that employees commit to delivering. By this means, any potential obstacles to the long-term project can be identified and resolved much more quickly.

According to the CultureIQ website, the ROWE "strategy puts the role of working directly into the employees' hands. They become more empowered at their ability to contribute to the greater good, which builds their passion and willingness to strive for greatness in the workplace. As employees' performance is ultimately their responsibility, they have more of a drive to get things done well and expediently."[42]

Put simply, giving workers the flexibility they want is good for the bottom line. For more on present-day employee preferences, see the following sidebar. In the next chapter, we'll revisit the issue with additional data identifying how remote-working options ultimately benefit the employer as much as they benefit the employee.

Big-Picture Reasons Individuals Favor Remote Working

Of the 5,500 respondents in the 2017 "FlexJobs Super Survey," the percentages below indicate how many regarded the following as the "most important factors" when considering a job:

- Work-life balance (72%)
- Flexible schedule and salary (tie) (69%)
- Telecommuting (60%)
- Meaningful work (57%)
- Work schedule (48%)
- Location (45%)
- Company reputation (40%)
- Health insurance (37%)
- Professional challenge (36%)
- Company culture (34%)
- Career progression (30%)
- 401(k)/retirement benefits and vacation time (tie) (29%)
- Skills training and education options (28%)
- Amount of travel required (25%)

In addition, when assessing how much flexible options in the workplace would impact their quality of life, 45 percent identified such would be a huge improvement. More specifically, 78 percent of people believed they'd be healthier; 86 percent said they'd be less stressed.[43]

To bring the discussion back to the beginning: one of the secrets to successful remote working is going from a nine-to-five, time-oriented mind set to a results-oriented one. More and more, work is not a place we go, it's something we do—and what matters is that we deliver by the deadline.

Remote Reminders

- Advances in technology have made working remotely easier and more affordable than ever before.
- Remote workers worldwide are a diverse group: young and old, working parents and entrepreneurs, students and retirees. They include full-time telecommuting employees, self-employed freelancers, solopreneurs, and freelance business owners.
- The top reasons workers wish to telework include schedule, commuting, family situation/caretaking, preferred work environment, increased productivity, increased opportunities, even "trying out" a position or role. Additional people who seek remote work include those wishing to supplement their income, retirees wanting to stay active, military spouses, and the disabled.
- Many seek the remote option just for the flexibility of not commuting a few days a week.
- Embracing the remote option calls for shifting from a mind set of hours-oriented working to results-oriented working or ROWE.

CHAPTER 2

How Remote Working Benefits Employers

"Once we got our remote team running smoothly, we had a fantastic work experience. These days, I would say that remote teams or distributed teams are at least as capable as colocated teams."

—Lucius Bobikiewicz, *trainer for distributed Agile teams at SpreadScrum.com*[1]

Chapter 1 conveys that it's absolutely possible for unsupervised employees to make essential contributions to their employers' objectives. Expanding on that concept, in this chapter we'll look at the many ways offering employees the option to work remotely benefits *employers*. We'll also identify some concerns about the potential pitfalls of the remote option—as well as the means of avoiding such drawbacks. Ultimately, growing evidence indicates that, for many companies, in a wide range of industries, the pros of the remote option far outweigh the cons.

Reasons to Offer the Remote Option

The trend is undeniable: more and more companies are offering flexible work options to their established employees and/or are hiring remote staff. For example, according to a joint 2017 Eurofound/ILO (International Labour Office) report, in 1995 just 9 percent of global workers telecommuted; by 2015, that figure had grown to 37 percent.[2] And in the United States, a Gallup poll in 2012 found that 39 percent of employees worked away from the office at least some of the time; by 2016 that figure was 43 percent.[3]

The Legal Right to Request Flexible Hours

The Institute for Women's Policy Research examined the flexible-working laws of twenty "high-income" countries, including Australia, Belgium, Canada, Denmark, Finland, France, Germany, Italy, the Netherlands, New Zealand, Norway, Portugal, Spain, Sweden, the United Kingdom, and the United States. The subsequent report released in 2007, "Statutory Routes to Workplace Flexibility in Cross-National Perspective," notes the following among its findings: seventeen countries "have statutes to help parents adjust working hours; six help with family caregiving responsibilities for adults; twelve allow change in hours to facilitate lifelong learning; eleven support gradual retirement; and five have statutory arrangements open to all employees, irrespective of the reason for seeking different work arrangements."[4]

This trend strongly suggests that companies that *don't* offer the remote option endanger their long-term viability, especially given that reasons to welcome remote working are steadily advancing. Some would go so far as to say that "remote work is the future, [and] those who push against it are on the losing side of history."[5]

The companies I interviewed shared the following reasons for going remote: to stay competitive, to retain and attract talent, to grow and shrink the company as needed, and to reduce costs and increase profits.

STAY COMPETITIVE—RETAIN AND ATTRACT TALENT

> *"You have companies that have distributed teams as a means for flexibility. But you also have companies that are doing it because they're in a city where it takes some people two hours to get to the office."*
>
> —Robert Rogge, *cofounder and CEO, Zingword; cofounder and advisor, Managing Virtual Teams*[6]

Let's take another look at the 2017 "FlexJobs Super Survey" discussed in chapter 1. (See the sidebar to follow.) For many employees, the option to work remotely isn't just a desirable perk—it's a necessity. So only the employers who provide that option will be able to retain those employees.

How Flexible Working Options Benefit Employers

Of the 5,500 respondents in the 2017 "FlexJobs Super Survey," 62 percent have left or considered leaving jobs that offered no work flexibility. (That figure broken down: 32 percent have left a job; 16 percent were looking at the time; and 14 percent have considered leaving.) The flip side to this is what respondents would offer flexible employers in return:

EMPLOYEE RETENTION: 79 percent of respondents said they would be more loyal to their employers if they had flexible work options.

WORKING RELATIONSHIPS: 73 percent think remote work is conducive to having strong work relationships.

REDUCING EXPENSES: 29 percent of respondents said they would take a 10 percent or 20 percent cut in pay; 22 percent are willing to forfeit vacation time; and 19 percent would give up employer-matching retirement contributions.

EDUCATION AND EXPERIENCE: Work flexibility appeals to highly educated and experienced workers: 79 percent of respondents have at least a college degree, and 31 percent are senior manager level or higher.

HIRING STRATEGY: 97 percent of respondents are interested in being a flexible worker in the long-term. Offering flexible work options can help attract well-educated professionals with solid experience who come from diverse backgrounds.[7]

Given that numerous sources—such as the Center for American Progress, *Forbes*, *The Huffington Post*, and the Society for Human Resource Management—state that it generally costs a company (much) less to retain an employee than to hire and train a new one,[8] the remote option is a wise consideration.

As for attracting new talent, in some cases the "right person" for the job is simply not to be found in a company's immediate vicinity. For example, Formstack is a data management solution company in Indianapolis, Indiana. In 2013, though their client base was growing, they couldn't find the talent they needed nearby. So they transitioned the entire company to what's known as ***office optional*** in order to incorporate new hires from outside the area—a solution that's worked well ever since. As of early 2018 they have a staff of around eighty people, only thirty-five of whom are near Indianapolis.

Ralph van Roosmalen had the same experience. He worked with a company that needed to increase production, but they couldn't find enough software developers locally in the Netherlands. So they looked beyond their borders—and hired teams in Romania and the United States.

This scenario is one that Hugo Messer knows well:

> **In some parts of Europe, there is a scarcity of talent, and it's hard to find people with the right skills. We help companies from Europe find people in India and the Ukraine. The European companies can grow and become more profitable by adding people at a lower cost. At the same time, they create jobs in another country.**
>
> —Hugo Messer, distributed Agile expert and founder, Bridge Global and Ekipa[9]

Another angle to this is the high cost of living in many metropolitan areas. As freelance project manager Fernando Garrido Vaz relates: "It can be difficult and expensive to put together a good team in certain locations. It's either very expensive to hire people, or there's a lot of competition in that geographical area. Many companies have chosen to be remote because it was the only way to gather a good team."[10] One such organization is NanoTecNexus, which requires experts in nanotechnology in its mission to accelerate advances in the field. Not surprisingly, nanotech experts are not concentrated in any one city. But given that founder Adriana Vela embraced the remote option, she's been able to assemble an effective, specialized team—whose members happen to span the United States and Canada. To Adriana, "The right person is what matters first, regardless of where they are."[11]

Hassan Osman expands on that stance:

> **One benefit of virtual teams is the access to talent. Competition in large organizations is cutthroat, and you need to stay ten steps ahead to survive. At Cisco, we can hire anyone in the world who has access to an internet connection. That gives a huge competitive advantage. Having that sort of access to talent keeps us nimble, and at the forefront of technology.**
>
> —HASSAN OSMAN, PMO manager, Cisco Systems (note, these views are Hassan's, not Cisco's)[12]

But there's an additional angle to this too. The flip side is that more and more workers value the option of working remotely—and those workers will favor the *employers* who give them that option. In some cases the benefit is purely gain. For example, Peter Wilson runs a company that connects Australian businesses with talent in the Philippines. Since the Philippines is commonly plagued with heavy traffic jams, it's a big incentive for Filipinos to work from home; that incentive translates to remarkable loyalty. In other cases the benefit more pointedly avoids a loss. As the authors of the U.K.-based Timewise Flexible Jobs Index state: "Employers are cutting themselves off from a proportion of the candidate market by not stating their openness to flexibility in their recruitment advertising. These 'lost' candidates include some of the very best available talent."[13] The same sentiment resounded amongst my interviewees as well.

> **We're going to see that companies will need to become a lot more flexible. The "you should be glad that you have a job with us" attitude doesn't work anymore. Companies have to start meeting the needs of the employees to get the best-quality work out of them.**
>
> —LUIS SUAREZ, data analytics adviser, panagenda[14]

> **In the beginning working remotely was about tightening the budget to increase productivity and efficiency. But now it's much more of a business imperative. The millennials are coming into the workforce, and they have a different view on working where and when they like—rather than working in a fixed place and being paid for the number of hours they put in.**
>
> —Chris Ridgewell, director, Wisework Ltd.; principal and owner, Charterhouse Consultants group[15]

Finance executive Jeremy Stanton puts it the most bluntly: "Companies that can support remote working will outperform companies that don't."[16]

GROW AND SHRINK THE COMPANY

> *"For the company that doesn't need a full-time person, employing remote staff on an as-needed basis is incredibly useful. The company doesn't need to pay someone if there's not enough work, and they don't have to pay for office space."*
>
> —Laura Rooke, *customer support specialist, GoLightly, Sgrouples, and AgileBits Inc.*[17]

In yet another hiring angle, the flexibility of hiring remote workers—specifically, project-based hiring—gives companies the freedom to expand and contract depending on their current needs. For example, Marc Hughes and Ajay Reddy are cofounders of ScrumDo, a platform that helps teams organize, manage, and collaborate. (For more, see "Technology & Tools" [*p. 301*] in the RESOURCES section.) The pair scale their business up and down depending on the projects they're working on.

Teamed.io does the same. As founder and former CTO Yegor Bugayenko describes: "We build distributed teams for every project. Every time we want to develop software, we gather people from different parts of the world who know particular technologies, and we put them together on a virtual team. This team creates a piece of software, delivers it to the customer, and then we let these people go. And we start another project."[18]

REDUCE COSTS, INCREASE PROFITS

A major factor in considering the remote option is assessing the potential return on investment. Indeed, all the companies I interviewed cited cost savings as the biggest factor behind going remote. Allowing employees to work remotely saves costs in a number of ways.

We've already mentioned the often significant savings of KEEPING A VALUABLE EMPLOYEE rather than hiring a new one.[19]

Another savings often cited concerns OVERHEAD—the physical station that the in-house employee requires. Of course, if you have few remote workers, a few empty desks won't have much impact. But on a larger scale, the savings on real estate could be significant. (See the sidebar to follow.)

In addition, THE COST OF HIRING PEOPLE OFFSHORE CAN BE SIGNIFICANTLY LESS than hiring local talent. The difference in salary between a programmer in San Francisco and one in Hanoi or Santiago is vast. As financial services executive Jeremy Stanton points out: "Working remotely, you can get great people at a reduced rate without it feeling like a reduced rate to them. The employees can get a premium salary for their location—and they have the added benefit of not having to move."[20] Freelance consultant and Agile coach Mario Lucero adds: "Many U.S. companies prefer to work with South American software developers and testers because we are a lot less expensive. My salary in Chile is about 30 percent of what the same Agile coach would make in the U.S. That kind of cost savings is something that companies can't ignore."[21]

But even some who benefit from reduced costs nonetheless consider such to be only of secondary importance. For example, Victor Ingalls, VP of world service for American Express, shares: "Some companies view a remote workforce as a means of reducing operating cost. We view it as an investment in finding the very best talent—so we can deliver the superior service our customers expect."[22]

On the other hand, one argument some make against offering the remote option is the cost of doing so. As gets covered in later chapters, the companies that make the greatest success with remote workers take care to invest in high-quality equipment. And since coming together in person can be at times preferable, even necessary, there are costs associated with travel and local hospitality. In addition, some would say that the distance between team members can lead to a reduction in productivity—though note that most others claim remote working often increases productivity. (See the sidebar to follow for some potential figures.)

Since all those costs can add up, many view the remote option as an unattractive expense—even if it's one they ultimately take on. Management consultancy director Chris Ridgewell points out: "In the U.K., lots of managers in traditional organizations see flexible working as a cost. We're implementing these flexible work options to appease the employees because they demand it, but that's a cost to us."[23] And yet, that view can change when it becomes clear that the ability to attract and retain staff isn't the only financial benefit. Many of the company leaders I've interviewed cited additional plusses, like hitting targets earlier and increased productivity. Increased client satisfaction is another advantage; clients in other time zones benefit greatly from working with employees in their same time zone—or workers equipped to work in their time zone. As start-up technologist Tiziano Perrucci notes: "I'm often up in the middle of the night working online with a client in another time zone. I can do that comfortably because I'm working from my home office."[24]

Positive Sum Gain: The Costs—and Cost Savings—of Remote Working

Though each situation is different, the following are some of the potential costs and cost savings of companies offering the remote option.

POTENTIAL COSTS

- High-quality technology: the in-house hardware, team-wide software, and infrastructure changes that support telework (though see also UNMEASURABLE COST SAVINGS below).
- Travel and local hospitality for in-person meetings.
- Home office setup costs or coworking space rental.
- Remote technical support.

» UNMEASURABLE COSTS

- Delays in getting answers to questions or information.
- Possible lowered productivity; unfortunately, that's a factor that is often difficult to measure.[25]
- Some note a lessened ability to assess if an individual or even an entire team is struggling.

POTENTIAL COST SAVINGS

- Retaining valuable employees: saving the cost of replacing workers.
- Overhead: in-house technology, workstations, square footage, utilities.
- According to Global Workplace Analytics, the average real-estate savings with full-time telework is $10,000 per employee per year.[26] (See also REAL ESTATE* entries below.)
- Salary: access to top-talent workers who live in regions with a lower cost of living.
- Ability to grow and shrink the company as needed.

» UNMEASURABLE COST SAVINGS

- According to Global Workplace Analytics, infrastructure changes that support telework improve efficiency for all employees, whether on-site or off-site.[27]
- Hiring the best talent increases competitive advantage and company viability.
- Several factors increase productivity. Many spend their previous commute time working. Happier, healthier workers can be more loyal, more engaged, and more effective. And, since remote workers need to demonstrate their productivity more tangibly than by how long they're in the office, they're more likely to produce demonstrable results.
- Many cite increased client satisfaction, especially when clients get additional same-time-zone interaction with workers who are generally more engaged.

* REAL ESTATE: Chris Ridgewell specializes in helping companies consolidate and reuse properties. He shares: "One client went from sixty-eight

buildings down to three campus sites by adding flexible work options. That was clearly a property-driven business decision to save on costs."

He continues: "If you can't sell your legacy buildings, you can consider making better use of them. For example, we have a fifteenth-century stone barn that we converted into a coworking space. Another client transformed fifty redundant schools in mainly rural communities into work hubs and local business start-up centers."[28]

If you're ready to learn more about how to get started, head to Part III—Successful Remote Teams 101: Transitioning and Hiring. Or, if you seek more lay of the land first, keep reading.

Common Concerns About the Remote Option—and Their Solutions

What about productivity?

There's no denying the fact that managers who want to offer flexible work options are taking a risk. If offering the remote option hits a snag, the responsibility falls on their heads. So, many find that keeping the status quo is a safer course. For example, Judy Rees recalled working as a manager at Teletext. "I gave someone permission to work from home for one day a week. But I remember that sinking feeling of, 'This is a risk. If this goes wrong, it's on my head. If I say no, there is no risk to me.' A lot of managers are judged on *not* losing—rather than on winning."[29]

This view is widely shared:

> **As a manager, you want to know that you're getting your money's worth, and that people are working as you expect them to.**
>
> —Marcus Rosenthal, self-employed senior business consultant[30]

> **The key issue still is trust. If I can't see you at your desk, you're not working.**
>
> —Chris Ridgewell, director, Wisework Ltd.; principal and owner, Charterhouse Consultants group[31]

The concern about unsupervised workers has led some to utilize monitoring software to serve that purpose. Indeed, one of my interviewees recommends companies consider this option. But many others advise against that approach; see the sidebar to follow.

Some Thoughts on Monitoring Software

It's noted earlier that Peter Wilson runs an offshoring company that connects Australian businesses with talent in the Philippines. Peter states: "It's a big step for some companies to work with people outside their office, or from another country. Using software that monitors the screen or keystrokes can help alleviate those fears."[32]

But others have a different take. First, the more practical standpoint, as relayed by Marissa Lang in the *San Francisco Chronicle*: "The more popular these tools become . . . the greater the need to have a conversation: about regulation, privacy, and the interests of workers and their employers."[33] And then there's the personal angle. As software engineer Piero Toffanin points out: "There are all these tools that can be installed on computers, which I find creepy. Somebody will look at what keystrokes you're typing or watch your screen and make sure you're actually working. It's unhealthy. A healthy client relationship means there is mutual trust that you're going to do the work and they're going to pay you."[34]

Entrepreneur Bart Van Loon agrees: "You have to start with a decent level of trusting each other, which can then go up or down. Companies tend to err on the side of controlling too much. For example, we've had clients put up a permanent camera in the room where a team is working. Or constantly record screens, so that they can see what employees are working on. We always discourage this, because in the long run, these techniques give bad results. People who are overcontrolled tend to become overdependent. You shouldn't see controlling your workforce as a problem to solve; it's really a problem you should avoid."[35]

So how can managers be assured that workers are working? One answer can be found in replacing a time-oriented mind set (like being at the office during set hours) with a results-oriented mind set.

> **Managers have a fear of people not being productive when they work from home, that they're just going to slack off and watch TV. That fear only exists before people start working from home. Once they do, and they are actually productive, managers can see that they are getting their work done. So it's just a fear of the unknown.**
>
> —Brie Reynolds, career development expert and senior career specialist, FlexJobs[36]

With a results-oriented mind set, work is the results we deliver. As such, results-oriented managers are tasked with holding team members accountable. Workers know this; we know we need to demonstrate our productivity. In exchange for being allowed out from under a command-and-control workplace, we gladly take on a share of the responsibility of meeting our shared goals. As Agility Scales CEO Jurgen Appelo often says: "Management is too important to leave to the managers."

In other words, we all have some responsibility for ensuring our teams and projects thrive, no matter where we are.

Plus, keep in mind that productivity results from engagement. According to a worldwide study conducted by Towers Watson, "the single highest driver of engagement is whether or not workers feel their managers are genuinely interested in their well-being." In 2012, "less than 40 percent of workers felt so engaged." As for more recent assessments, according to the 2017 Gallup "State of the Global Workplace" report, "worldwide, the percentage of adults who work full time for an employer and are engaged at work—[meaning] they are highly involved in and enthusiastic about their work and workplace—is just 15 percent."[37] But an employee granted—indeed, entrusted with—the remote option has every reason to be engaged, involved, and highly productive.

We'll look at many productivity solutions in the chapters to come.

What about effective collaboration?

> *"Soon we won't be talking about virtual teams anymore. We'll just be talking about teams."*
>
> —Pilar Orti, *director, Virtual not Distant*[38]

It can't be denied: in-person collaboration can be extremely effective. But that doesn't mean we can't find a way to replicate that efficacy remotely without feeling that we're cutting corners. Indeed, many technologies and methodologies have long demonstrated their importance in the virtual setting. As software executive Marc Hughes notes: "A lot of people prefer being colocated and organizing their tasks on a giant board on the wall with the sticky notes and everything. And that's great if you're all there. But as soon as you have one person who's not in the office every day, you need some kind of virtual tool that everyone can see and manipulate."[39] Fortunately, there are many tools for running effective virtual brainstorming sessions. (For more, see "Technology & Tools" [*p. 301*] in the RESOURCES section.)

In an article on Medium.com, Karolina Szczur points out that a lot of colocated work already utilizes remote-friendly means. "Coworkers can be effectively asynchronous while sitting in the same office—when working on multiple projects or taking extended amounts of time to reply to messages. Lack of synchronicity is part of every workday." She continues: "Some, especially bigger organizations, don't realize they're already doing remote. From outsourcing to specialists to daily communication happening without face-to-face interaction at all—a plethora of emails, messages, and discussions conducted online. Oftentimes the amount of actual in-person work boils down to a minimum."[40]

Keep in mind that developers have been collaborating online for years now—which means we can benefit from their perfected software and processes. When two programmers, whether colocated or remote, work together on the same code, they call it "pair programming"; one person codes while the other simultaneously reviews the work. In person, two developers will sit at one workstation together; but remotely, using video and screen sharing, they can collaborate more easily, comfortably, and efficiently—especially if others want to add to the conversation. As you can imagine, a video call sharing screens is much more feasible and productive than what is called "mob programming," when several workers huddle around one computer.

Continuing on the topic of communication, product director Christina Ng expresses a common concern: "What's hard for companies who are going remote is that there's not enough culture established about documenting things, because it's so much easier to just walk over to the next cubicle, talk to your coworker, and make a decision right there and then. This is especially true for start-ups, when things move so fast that you just need to get things out as soon as possible. It takes a different kind of culture to include those who aren't there in the day-to-day decisions."[41] Fortunately, that "different kind of culture" doesn't require reinventing the wheel; we simply need to be deliberate in establishing new processes. We'll revisit this at length in chapters 8 and 9.

> *"Take the time to learn new ways of working. It's only strange until we get used to it."*
>
> —AgileBill Krebs, *coach and founder, Agile Dimensions*[42]

What about the camaraderie aspect of working together?

Another product executive, Sumant Kowshik, notes an additional concern shared by team leaders and members alike: "Even though we've made rapid strides in collaboration, I think we still struggle with the idea of being together. What's missing are the hallway conversations, or where you can just turn around to the person next to you and ask a quick question. Plus of course going out and having coffee or lunch with people, or having ad hoc brainstorming sessions. All of that is still missing—though I also think that technology will continue to bridge the gap."[43] Indeed, cultivating a sense of closeness is an essential element of effective teams. As it happens, technology and practices can address this important concern as well—which we'll discuss at length in chapter 8.

That said, some forms of social bonding or collaboration simply call for in-person face time, such as the start-up or brainstorming phase, which can require more back-and-forth interaction. In such cases we can schedule those meetings—just like companies have always done.

> **Let's rewind maybe twenty to forty years. For a brainstorming session with the heads of a division, everyone had to fly in—and that was quite expensive. They'd be together for a couple days for a big company summit, but with only forty-eight hours of time together.**
>
> —Vanessa Shaw, workplace innovator, Human Side of Tech[44]

An additional benefit of remote-working strategies is the ability to extend the collaboration and camaraderie of in-person interactions well beyond the two-day summit mentioned above. As more and more businesses embrace the remote option, and report their success in doing so, larger companies are starting to recognize that distributed teams can be as professional and successful as traditional on-site ones—often even more so. This is possible because the tools and strategies that enable successful remote working are beneficial regardless of each member's location. (We cover this more in the *Reasons to Try Out Remote Working Now* section lower down.)

What about technical challenges?

As technologies advance, it's becoming easier to engage productively with remote colleagues. Gone are the days when our only option was to crowd around a spider phone, yelling to an invisible coworker over a crackling connection. And advanced communication capabilities are getting more affordable and more accessible every day. As Andrew Montalenti, CTO of tech company Parse.ly, puts it:

> **Fully distributed teams are only going to get better—and more common—over time. Our tools are simply getting great at this stuff. For example, Google Hangouts [now Google Meet] offers group video conferencing for large teams for free. At Parse.ly we use Google Hangouts to hold full team meetings. So, face time is now distributed too, and multi-computer collaboration is getting easier even in asynchronous modes. I also think some technology will enable collaboration methods that were simply deemed impractical in the age before distributed teams. So, technology—and, in particular, audio/video technology—will help distributed teams along in the next ten years.**

> **We're moving away from one-on-one conversation as the primary way to collaborate and toward many-to-many. I also think that the world has not fully internalized the degree to which technology systems impact collaboration approaches. I'm quite excited about the future.**[45]

(For more, see "Technology & Tools" [*p. 301*] in the RESOURCES section, both the *Collaboration* and the *Communication* portions.)

Of course, that's the big-picture portion of tech. As for the individual, tech-support angle, booking software company Timely recommends connecting with "dial a tech" services.[46]

What about security?

One concern regarding the swift pace of technological development is the challenge of keeping up with it all. To enable their productivity, team members (remote or in-house) will want to try out new applications for keeping them connected, oftentimes using company computers. But for many companies, adopting a remote-working doctrine calls for revisiting security protocols. As management consultancy director Chris Ridgewell points out, "Many large organizations use fixed technologies, and so they don't allow things like 'bring your own device' because of concerns about security, data protection, and legal ramifications." But the trouble is, "because of that, technology is leaving these companies behind. Whereas the smaller businesses [that embrace technology] are moving fast."[47] To again quote Jeremy Stanton of Amino Payments: "Companies that can support remote working will outperform companies that don't."[48] That translates to: if you don't attract top talent, others will. In some contexts, companies resist the remote option at their own peril.

And so the solution is to address security concerns from the perspective of striving to make virtual technologies both safe and effective. And some very large, very security-focused employers have embraced the remote option, as demonstrated in FlexJobs's "100 Top Companies with Remote Jobs in 2018" list (*p. 122* in the Part II EXTRAS). A few players there include ADP, American Express, JPMorgan Chase, the Hartford, UnitedHealth Group, and Wells Fargo. The point is, it can be done.

Reasons to Try Out Remote Working Now

> *"Things that seemed fantastical six years ago are commonplace today. All of us in this emerging field are pioneers looking for traction, ground, and a common language."*
>
> —Howard B. Esbin, *CEO, Playprelude.com*[49]

RETAIN THE STAFF YOU ALREADY HAVE

It's worth reiterating: the remote option isn't just about attracting new talent. As HR consultant Dirk-Jan Padmos points out, remote working is more and more a benefit that companies offer their employees. As such, companies are realizing the importance of retaining their established workforce. So even if you're not ready to take on new remote hires, you'd be wise to take steps to retain the talent you already have. As this new way of working becomes standard, more workers will come to demand the benefits of work-life freedom.

REMOTE-FIRST: EMERGENCY BACKUP PLAN

Whether or not you plan to fully allow flexible work options at your company, it's good to have the processes in place that make it possible to work outside the office in case it's unexpectedly necessary. Consider various unavoidable events that can keep workers from their desks: traffic jams, public transit delays, sick children, inclement weather. With a minimal amount of preparation, your workforce won't have to grind to a halt on account of a sudden contingency. This concept is called "remote-first."

> **There are many situations where someone needs to stay home, like to wait for the plumber who will be coming somewhere between 9:00 AM and 3:00 PM. My employees were perfectly capable of working from home. The benefit to them was that they didn't have to take a day off for the plumber. And the benefit to me was that they didn't go away for a day in the middle of a project with impending deadlines.**
>
> —Maarten Koopmans, owner, Vrijhed.net[50]

So, what kind of preparation are we talking about? In a word: access. At the minimum, employees would need to have:

- access to reliable technology, such as phone, computer, and high-bandwidth internet connection;
- access to necessary contact info; and
- access to the files they're currently working on.

Again, this is just the bare minimum. Making a company fully resilient to the unexpected calls for a bit more—details of which can be found in Chapter 5: Transitioning Toward the Remote Option.

REMOTE TOOLS AND STRATEGIES ARE BENEFICIAL REGARDLESS

> *"Companies don't have to have remotes. But if they have communication processes that make it easy for a remote team member to work with them, they're going to be better off. All the things that make it possible for a remote team to work are things that you'd want anyway."*
>
> —Jeremy Stanton, *SVP of engineering, Amino Payments*[51]

The checklist of what makes remote working successful is equally applicable to running an efficient company:

- effortless and fast communication;
- shared, designated place to store files;
- ready means of conversation and collaboration;
- having everyone on the same page; and
- working toward a common vision.

Many of my interviewees emphasized: companies would be wise to ensure the above items are securely in place before trying out the remote option.

It just so happens that the flip side of what it takes to go remote well also serves as a caveat for *not* going remote, or at least not just yet. HR consultant Dirk-Jan Padmos offers: "Working together in an office forces a certain tie between people. Colleagues are forced to interact with each other, and that keeps things relatively organized. If you add remote working to teams who don't already communicate well, it will only amplify the problems."[52] (Since good communication practices are particularly important, we cover communication at length in the chapters to come.)

Agile coach Ralph van Roosmalen takes it further: "Working remotely makes structural problems very visible in an organization. If you lack vision, communication, team building, etc., those insufficiencies will be a real issue when working remotely. You could blame distributed working, but in most cases the glitches are the result of a deeper problem."[53]

This is not to dwell on the prospect of "deeper" concerns plaguing the consideration of trying out the remote option. This is just to say the better informed you are, the better off you'll be. Of course there are organizations—or particular roles in those organizations—that simply aren't in a position to embrace the world of virtual work. But unless that's a given in your situation, just as a remote-first company is resilient in the face of emergencies, a company or department or team willing to *examine its capacity* for remote working is well on its way to improving its in-house operations—even if no one actually goes remote.

One last point: the remote-work resource Remote.co asked 135 "***remote-friendly***" companies a series of questions, including what advice they would offer a group considering the remote option.[54] Quite a few said: "Go for it!" Now, the more conservative and/or unconvinced readers might think, *Well, that's fine for you to say, but our configuration/industry probably wouldn't work with the remote option*. But if you whittle past the enthusiasm of those for whom remote working is a great setup, even the more sober respondents ultimately give similar advice. In essence, give it a try. While it might be that it's truly not for you, the preparation required to give it a decent chance will make you stronger in the long run. And if you make it work—and nearly every respondent thinks any company can make it work if they're diligent and smart about their choices—well then, you'll have expanded your horizons beyond what you previously thought possible.

> **The benefits of remote employees far outweigh the costs and obstacles you will face. Overcoming and mastering the differences in culture and language allows your company to appeal to a vastly wider audience. Take these challenges and make them your company's strengths.**
>
> —Deven Bhagwandin, Work Afar[55]

So, in summary: if you haven't thought about remote collaboration options in a while, you might be surprised by what's possible. We've come a long way, and it's getting better all the time.

Remote Reminders

REASONS TO OFFER THE REMOTE OPTION

- Offering the remote option allows employers to retain and attract the talent they need to remain competitive; this benefit can be essential when a project calls for specific expertise.
- Retaining strong employees costs less than the cost of replacing them.
- Hiring project-based remote workers enables growing or shrinking a company as needed.
- Many companies find that remote staff enable them to reduce costs and increase profits.
- The global talent pool allows for a more diverse workforce, whose greater breadth of worldview can bring about fresh ideas, greater innovation, and better solutions.

COMMON CONCERNS ABOUT THE REMOTE OPTION—AND THEIR SOLUTIONS

- There are many ways to address concerns about off-site productivity—starting with replacing an hours-based perspective with a results-based one. The simple fact is that studies show that remote workers are often even more productive than their on-site colleagues, in part because they work during the time when they would have otherwise been commuting.

- Various tools and practices are remarkably effective at enabling both productive collaboration and essential team bonding among distributed teammates.
- Large, very security-focused employers have demonstrated both the viability and the benefit of embracing the remote option. When set up by expert hands, virtual technologies have proven to be both safe and effective.

REASONS TO TRY OUT REMOTE WORKING NOW

- It's worth repeating: offering the remote option is a prime means of retaining the talent you already have.
- At the minimum, establishing the office as "remote-first" enables work to continue unabated regardless of whatever traffic, weather, or other city-wide emergencies may occur—not to mention employees needing to stay home on account of family illness or awaiting the ever-elusive plumber.
- It just so happens that the tools and strategies of successful remote working are beneficial to all teams, regardless of where they work.

PART I *Extras*

FREQUENTLY ASKED QUESTIONS

Part of what can make remote working seem so daunting is the element of the unknown—from a manager wondering if a remote employee is working to a team member wondering if a terse email reflects annoyance or haste or neither. As a result, many have questions about just how a company or team can function effectively when one or more workers isn't on-site. To follow are answers to a series of such questions—from team member concerns such as career advancement, income, and social isolation to team leader concerns such as productivity, trust, and plain-old tech glitches. And while it's true that not every situation has a positive solution, strong evidence suggests that those "no go" situations are in the minority. In most cases, an optimal combination of skill set, tool set, and mind set will prove to be admirably effective.

Individual/Team Member Concerns

APTITUDE

How can I tell if I'm cut out for working remotely?

- Working well remotely is as much about attitude as it is about aptitude. Great team members don't just do their work effectively; truly excellent team members work effectively *with* their coworkers. That calls for regularly striving to build a sense of connection and trust, especially regarding reliability. You can learn all you need to know in chapters 3 and 4.

Isn't it hard to be productive working outside the office?

- It's true that some just work best in an office environment. But for the rest of us, it's simply a matter of trying out different approaches to determine what routine suits us best. For example, consider this quote from "HR champion" Morgan Legge: "I think I was definitely *less* productive when I first started. That's because I didn't know how to work remotely. Once I made that transition I was very productive, but I worked too much. The second phase was understanding how to fit the culture of my workplace into my job and my work. Now I take time during the day to run errands when the shops are empty (huge bonus!) and exercise to break up the day. This makes me even more productive and I work fewer hours."[1]

CAREER DEVELOPMENT

I currently work on-site but really want to work from home a couple days a week—but I'm afraid to ask. Won't my manager think I'm less of a team player and overlook me come promotion time?

- As it happens, just wanting the flexibility of working from home a few days per week is the top reason workers request the remote option: a 2017 FlexJobs survey found that parents rank work flexibility (84 percent) ahead of even salary (75 percent).[2] Since you are by no means in the minority, managers across the world are coming to realize that they need to take the steps necessary to both attract and retain top talent. Also, it's less expensive to retain a good employee than to recruit and hire a new one. In short, you have much more leverage than you think. Check out both chapters 1 and 2 to get a feel for today's work reality—and then turn to Part II, especially "Convincing Your Boss (or Team)" (*p. 115*) in the Part II EXTRAS.

I really want to break into a particular industry, but I can't afford to live where the jobs are—so I'm thinking of applying for a remote position. But what about developing a relationship with my manager—how can someone encourage my development if that person doesn't even know me?

- Many managers express this same concern about their employees—and will go out of their way to ensure everyone feels connected and heard. For more, see the *Strengthen Your Relationship with Each Team Member* section (*p. 241*) in chapter 10.

- The quickest means of building relationship from afar is to connect face-to-face whenever possible—which means turning on the webcam. Your best bet of furthering that connection is to do your end of getting that right, which calls for both a great setup and great video skills. See the *Ensure You're Tech Equipped and Savvy* section (*p. 72*) in chapter 3.

- According to Global Workplace Analytics, "Some employees cite career fears as a reason not to telecommute. Successful teleworking programs overcome the 'out of sight, out of mind' issue with performance-based measurement systems [and] productivity versus presenteeism attitudes. Teleworkers who maintain regular communications (telephone, email, instant chat, even the occasional face-to-face meeting) with traditional coworkers and managers find career impact is not an issue."[3] Plus, all experts recommend that teams meet in person whenever possible. When you're interviewing, ask how often the team gets together; hopefully it will be more than just once per year.

- Of course, there's only so much you can do if your manager takes little interest in you—but then that applies to colocated situations as well.

FINANCE

Won't working remotely greatly reduce my income?

- Of course, the answer to this will differ from industry to industry. But according to the 2017 "Freelancing in America" survey, of those who left a traditional job in order to freelance, nearly three in four said they make the same (10 percent) or more money (62 percent) than they did before they started freelancing—indicating that freelancing can be an even more lucrative career path than traditional jobs are. And of those freelancers who now earn more, 75 percent earned more within their first year.[4]

For those working for online sites, aren't you taking a big risk of not being paid for your work?

- Unfortunately, this approach is not foolproof. The worst statistics, conducted by the Pew Research Center in late 2016, indicate that 29 percent of gig workers have performed work using online working sites for which they did not receive payment.[5] While this statistic is not to be sneezed at, do note that it refers to one in three *workers* not receiving proper payment, not 29 percent of all *work*. And that "proper payment" figure is a large one: the working site Upwork announced in early 2018 that annual freelancer earnings had passed the $1.5 billion mark.[6] Plus, the best news is there are steps you can take to protect yourself. For starters, put your work agreements in writing so the terms and conditions are clearly understood by both sides.

- Some workers request 50 percent up-front and 50 percent upon completion. In some industries—freelance editing, for example—some will invoice for half the total amount once they've submitted half the edit, and then invoice for the remainder upon completion. And many workers in all industries invoice every one to two weeks—which limits the amount of work at risk of being uncompensated. For more, see the *Think Through Your Financial Setup* portion (*p. 77*) of chapter 3, as well as the Freelancer Union's "Freelancer's Guide to Getting Paid on Time" (*p. 320*) in "For Further Reading, Listening, and Consultation" in the RESOURCES section.

SOCIAL ISOLATION

Isn't it unbearably lonely working from home?

- Of course, this will differ from person to person, but many remote workers, even those who live alone, enjoy a surprising amount of social interaction—including virtual face time—without ever leaving their homes.
- That said, isolation can be a concern. Respondents in the 2017 Remoters.net "7 Remote Work Trends" survey cited missing social interaction (29 percent) and loneliness (15 percent) as the biggest disadvantages to working virtually. (An additional 15 percent reported no disadvantages.)[7]
- But there are ways to address the potential for loneliness: via increased social interaction both online and in person. For more, see the *How to Tend To Your Own Needs* section (*p. 85*) in chapter 4, especially the portion about social needs.

Even separate from loneliness, what about feeling camaraderie with teammates? I can't imagine feeling connected to people I'm not in the same space with.

- You might be surprised by the team building that's possible when working remotely. For example, in a global Polycom Inc. study 92 percent of respondents reported that video collaboration technology improves teamwork. This is likely because video restores in the online realm some of the sense of human interaction of on-site work.[8] Also, according to the 2015 "ConnectSolutions Remote Collaborative Worker Survey," "42 percent of remote workers feel they're just as connected with colleagues as if they were working on-premises." An additional "10 percent feel even more connected."[9]
- Chapter 8 conveys a great deal about how managers can facilitate successful remote teams. Check out in particular the *Bonding* section (*p. 183*). Take notes on what might work for your team—and then share that information with your boss.

Manager/Team Leader Concerns

Though some on my team could work remotely, with other roles it's just not an option. Wouldn't those workers who want to work remotely—but can't—resent the ones who can? That would ruin team camaraderie and productivity.

- That concern about jealousy is definitely a part of why some companies don't offer the remote option. But given how many workers seek flexible options, you could lose (or never get to hire) great talent if you refuse that option. You could start by polling the team anonymously, specifically asking if those who couldn't work remotely would resent that others had the option. You might find that they'd vote for the remote option in anticipation of the day when they too could benefit from it. You could also offer a different perk for those who can't work off-site.
- Many recommend creating a flexibility policy that applies equally to everyone in positions for which remote working is viable. Just be sure to

allow the remote option to all who qualify.[10] Global Workplace Analytics recommends clarifying precisely why certain positions are not eligible for the remote option.[11] Since making a "partially distributed" team work well together takes conscious effort, you can require that the remote team members be assiduously responsive and productive—so their colleagues back in the office still feel their presence.[12] This concern is yet another reason why it's highly recommended that teams with remote members mutually craft a team agreement regarding precisely how they will work together. For more, see chapters 8 and 9.

How could I trust that my employees are actually working?

- Many surveys (such as by FlexJobs) indicate that a large percentage of individuals want to work remotely so as to *increase* their productivity, both by getting to choose a more productive workspace and by not having to commute.[13] It's actually far more likely that remote workers will work too much rather than too little.
- Addressing this concern calls for a few changes. One is in how work is assigned. Give employees the opportunity to demonstrate their productivity: break projects into batches that can be completed in a short time frame, and then hold them to those deadlines. This practice falls under the concept of ROWE: Results-Oriented Work Environment. (For more, see the *Workplace Flexibility: Results-Oriented vs. Hours-Oriented Work* section [*p. 22*] of chapter 1.)
- A second change is in mind set. Several managers who successfully transitioned to the remote option have marveled at the positive result of learning to trust their remote employees. The subject of managerial trust gets covered at length in Chapter 7: Commit and Lead, Trust and Succeed. In addition, we discuss how workers can earn that trust in the *Building Trust: Demonstrating Reliability* portion (*p. 93*) of chapter 4.

How do you implement results-oriented work if your industry bills by the hour?

- Hourly employees still track their time; the difference concerns the frequency with which workers are expected to demonstrate their progress.

- Many companies conduct regular check-in meetings to keep on top of how projects are progressing. For more, see the *Productivity and Collaboration* section (*p. 176*) of chapter 8, particularly the STAND-UPS AND RETROSPECTIVES portion.
- Many team members commit to regularly publicizing what they're working on as a means of demonstrating that they're working. For more, see the *Bonding* section (*p. 183*) of chapter 8, specifically the WORK TOGETHER ONLINE portion.

Isn't the productivity claim a lie? Big companies like IBM, Best Buy, and Yahoo have concluded that the experiments of letting employees work remotely failed.

- It can't be denied that there are job roles, even entire industries, that are not suited to remote working. But as for those companies, *The American Interest* offers the following in an article about IBM ceasing its remote option: "Even as remote work becomes normal, IBM isn't alone in placing an emphasis on working together in person. Yahoo made headlines in 2013 when Marissa Mayer made an abrupt decision to end Yahoo's remote work policy, and companies like Reddit and Best Buy have, like Yahoo, formally colocated their teams within the last several years. It's not that remote work didn't have benefits—Best Buy, for instance, reported in 2006 that productivity had on average increased 35 percent in departments that shifted to [letting employees work] from wherever they wanted, whenever they wanted. Rather, it's that working together, in person, has a different set of benefits. Like Best Buy and Yahoo at the points at which they decided to colocate, IBM is a business that needs to do something new."[14]
- Web-developer agency 10up.com states that "well-managed distributed teams are often far more productive than colocated teams, because, indeed, you're *forced* to measure productivity by far more objective metrics than things like 'time in the building.'"[15] It's just a matter of establishing an agreement with your employees wherein it's determined in advance just how they will demonstrate their productivity. For more, see the *Demonstrate Reliability by Working Out Loud* section (*p. 179*) in chapter 8, as well as Chapter 9: Tune Your Team with a Team Agreement.

- In 2016 Hubstaff published an article titled "Are Remote Workers More Productive? We've Checked All the Research So You Don't Have To." The upshot: very much so. For more, see the "Productivity When Working Remotely" sidebar (*p. 16*) in chapter 1.

What about cost? Won't I lose money with the remote option?

- Several sources claim it's less expensive to retain a valuable employee (by offering the remote option) than it is to hire a new one.[16] And losing a valuable employee is a real concern; according to the 2015 "PGi Global Telework Survey," about "60 percent of surveyed teleworkers worldwide would leave their existing job for a similar job, at the same pay rate, if they could work from home full time."[17]
- In addition, the 2016 Hubstaff article "Are Remote Workers More Productive? We've Checked All the Research So You Don't Have To" distinctly claims that remote workers reduce employers' costs.[18]
- All the companies I interviewed cited cost savings as being the biggest factor behind deciding to go remote.
- Some even cite their reduced costs as being of secondary importance. For example, as American Express shared in an interview with Remote.co: "Some companies view a remote workforce as a means of reducing operating cost. We view it as an investment in finding the very best talent so we can deliver the superior service our customers expect."[19]
- For more, see the *Reduce Costs, Increase Profits* section (*p. 32*) in chapter 2, including the "Positive Sum Gain: The Costs—and Cost Savings—of Remote Working" sidebar.

I've heard that making a virtual team work is just too hard—as thought-leader Patrick Lencioni has repeatedly declared. Why shouldn't I just trust him and save myself the trouble?

- For starters, let's name one such declaration: Patrick Lencioni's May 2017 article "Virtual Teams Are Worse Than I Thought." (Pilar Orti and I discuss this in episode 126 of her *21st-Century Work Life* podcast.[20]) In his article Lencioni describes the difficulties he encountered in one virtual team and extrapolates that experience as speaking for all virtual teams—in part because his team members were "genuinely humble . . . and well-intentioned," "some of the most virtuous, kind, and gracious human beings [he's] ever known." As he relates, the team encountered some interpersonal difficulties. They identified that "everything was attributable to not having regular, daily, face-to-face interactions," and redoubled their efforts to stay in touch and assume positive intent should another misunderstanding occur. Although the article specifies he's worked with this team for three years, as written it suggests that all it took was one additional disruption for him to conclude that everyone should "avoid virtual teams" if at all possible.

It's unfortunate that Lencioni chose to broadcast his defeatist conclusion rather than honestly assess what in this team might be at play of his own theory, detailed in his book of the same name, regarding the five dysfunctions of a team: absence of trust, fear of conflict, lack of commitment, avoidance of accountability, and inattention to results. To be fair, his article does name several productive steps those "stuck" in a virtual team can take—but to do so from within such a "good luck with that, guys" attitude does a great disservice to us all. To declare, as he does: "The truth is, virtual teams can work. But they often don't"[21] is an indefensible statement—especially as it's offered without extensive studies to back him up. The real truth is that many, many teams and companies have done the hard work to make it work, and have been amply rewarded for their efforts. If you commit to the guidelines in this book, and don't cry foul at the first impasse you encounter, you could claim the same for your team.

The Realities of Working Remotely (Individuals and Managers)

OFFICE-BASED PRODUCTIVITY

How can you be productive if you're not all together? People need to be in a communal workplace in order to get work done.

- While it's true that some people are more productive when in the presence of others being productive, that's not the case for everyone. Some feel stifled in an office atmosphere but feel freed when they get to choose their own workspaces. For example, in a 2017 global Polycom Inc. study 98 percent of respondents agreed that an "anywhere working" approach makes them more productive—simply because they can choose where they will work most efficiently.[22]

- Many home offices are quieter and less distracting than places of business. Indeed, the book *Remote: Office Not Required* goes so far as to say "the modern office has become an interruption factory."[23]
- Workers in self-tailored work environments tend to do better work.
- If workers are happier in their lives in general (because, say, they can go for a run in the middle of the day), they'll do much better work.
- According to a worldwide study conducted by Towers Watson, "the single highest driver of engagement is whether or not workers feel their managers are genuinely interested in their well-being."[24] Offering the remote option would be a significant gesture regarding employees' well-being. In addition, a remote-friendly employer would be justified in requesting that the gesture be repaid with demonstrable results.
- The following is from Larry Alton's *Forbes* article "Are Remote Workers More Productive Than In-Office Workers?": "The bottom line is that working from home can make a worker more productive, but that isn't a guarantee. However, it's safe to say that, according to studies, as long as the job is one that can be performed from home, *most people are more productive when working from home*, but that productivity is strongly subject to the policies put in place by the employer."[25]

But in an office you can always go talk to someone in person to get a quick answer; you can't do that remotely—right?

- Actually, you can do that remotely in a number of ways—using technology. In fact, being able to virtually walk into someone's "office" and ask a question is one of the hallmarks of "virtual office" apps Sococo and Walkabout Workplace. At many companies workers communicate all day via Slack, where posting a question to one or more people produces quick answers. And one team at Spotify always keeps the video conferencing tool Google Meet open with microphones on mute; those with a question can simply turn the mic on and ask it. For more, see "Technology & Tools" (*p. 301*) in the RESOURCES section.

- Plus, in some companies it's actually *harder* to find someone in the office. A study done at Genentech found that, between 9:00 AM and 5:00 PM, workers weren't in their own seats 80 percent of the time.[26] Whereas remote workers know it's important to always be reachable, so they ensure others know how best to do so.
- And even if colocated workers are at their desks, that doesn't mean they're nearby. As consultant Fredrik Wiik points out: "Even just working on different floors in the same office is a barrier. Many people don't walk upstairs just to ask a simple question. Tools for working successfully remotely can be just as helpful when everyone works at the same address."[27] For many, communicating digitally is already the more efficient option.

What about self-discipline? Don't the kids, the TV, and the household chores prevent getting any concentrated work done?

- For some who work at home, those are valid concerns—but there are also numerous strategies for addressing them. For example, some have a designated office space with a closable door—and strict rules about others respecting their work hours. Others simply don't work at home. (For more, see the *Create a Productive Workspace* section [*p. 74*] in chapter 3.)
- Some don't have any trouble with self-discipline; striving to get ahead is their cue. For others, multiple approaches can address this concern; see the *How to Deliver What Your Employer Needs* section (*p. 80*) in chapter 4.
- Another point: those who don't currently work from home might have trouble associating home with working—and so of course might get distracted by everything but work. But if you do work from home, you very strongly associate your home with working—sometimes to a fault. Most of the individuals I interviewed told me they had a hard time switching *off* work mode, not on.

PRACTICALITIES

Isn't the available tech more glitchy than effective?

- In a word, no—happily. As web technologies advance, it's becoming remarkably easy, even fun, to engage productively with remote colleagues.
- In particular, developments in video conferencing capabilities, which are now readily accessible to many, bring us much closer together. And the newest technologies hold great promise. With telepresence, for example, we can see each other *and* explore another location; with Virtual Reality (VR), we can hang out in a virtual space just like we do in real life. (We'll cover this extensively in chapter 6 and in "Technology & Tools" in the RESOURCES section.)

What about time zone issues?

- Since we can't physically squeeze the world closer together, the reality is that time zone issues are a part of working on a global team. But there are steps you can take to make it work for you rather than against you. We discuss this at length in chapter 9.
- The issues that result from time zone differences can be addressed in different ways. To keep the time difference to a minimum, some teams are structured from North to South rather than from East to West. Other teams simply "share the burden," and take turns working in off hours.
- Of course, not all work requires real-time communication. Plus, in some situations a significant time difference can be a benefit, where for example an overnight turnaround could be the norm.

Don't you need what's physically at the office to get all your work done?

- As Personify Inc.'s Nick Timmons puts it: "Everything is in the cloud. I'm as effective from home or when I'm traveling abroad as I would be if I was sitting right here in the office."[28] More specifically, it's simply a matter of companies allowing for the appropriate files and contacts to be accessed securely via an internet connection.

How can I help my team bond if we don't regularly get together?

- Regular use of video for work-related communication greatly facilitates team bonding. As noted in an earlier answer, the 2015 "ConnectSolutions Remote Collaborative Worker Survey" cites that "42 percent of remote workers feel they're just as connected with colleagues as if they were working on-premises," with an additional "10 percent feel[ing] even more connected."[29]

- Spending social time together via video—even just for a few minutes before or after meetings—is remarkably effective for building camaraderie. Many teams also share virtual coffee or after-work drinks, play games together, even host a regular Trivia Night. For more, see the *Bonding* section (*p. 183*) in chapter 8.

- It's highly recommended that remote team members meet in person regularly. At least once per quarter (or more often) is ideal, though some teams can meet only once per year. Many claim that all time spent in person deepens team bonding exponentially.

What about data security?

- Of course, steps need to be taken to address security concerns; fortunately, the vast majority of companies find that such concerns are easily handled.

- According to Global Workplace Analytics, 92 percent of managers in an IRS pilot telework program claimed to have no problem with data security. In addition, "90 percent of those charged with security in large organizations feel that home-based workers are not a security concern. In fact, they are more concerned with the occasional work that is taken out of the office by traditional employees who lack the training, tools, and technologies that teleworkers receive."[30] As such, part of the solution is to ensure that all employees get sufficient security training.

AT A GLANCE

How to Replicate Online the Benefits of Working On-Site

Note that possible brand-name tools (which are noted in parentheses) are just a few options of many and apply only as of July 2018. Since tool names can change, and new tools are released all the time, be sure to check my regularly updated list at https://collaborationsuperpowers.com/tools.

On-Site Benefit: *Efficiency and Accessibility*

A successful team benefits from the efficiency of working in the same location, where the answer to a question or a copy of a report is just a few steps away.

Facilitating Efficiency and Accessibility Online

GENERAL APPROACH

- Communicate online, regularly. (In chapter 8 AgileBill Krebs equates effective "high-bandwidth communication" with co-located communication.)

SPECIFIC SOLUTION OR DESCRIPTION

- Make communicating easy, especially via great equipment and great internet capability.
- Establish protocols regarding tools and etiquette (especially on how quickly to respond).

TYPE OF TOOL

- Computer, internet, webcam, headset
- Email, text, IM, group chat (such as with Slack)
- Video conferencing (perhaps using BlueJeans, Skype, or Zoom)
- Virtual office (Sococo or Walkabout Workplace)

On-Site Benefit: *Productivity and Collaboration*

A successful team benefits from the productivity of working in the same location, where they can update, report, plan, and brainstorm as a group.

Facilitating Productivity and Collaboration Online

GENERAL APPROACH

- Meet just as often—online.
- Record meetings for those who can't attend.
- Use online communal task board/task-management software.

SPECIFIC SOLUTION OR DESCRIPTION

- Work out loud: make your work visible to your colleagues.
- Hold regular (perhaps daily) "stand-ups": brief status updates.
- Hold weekly or bimonthly "Retrospectives": meetings for feedback and troubleshooting.

TYPE OF TOOL

- Brainstorming software (RealtimeBoard, Stormboard)
- Communal task board/task management (Asana, Jira, Trello)
- Decision-making software (GroupMap, WE THINQ)
- Group chat (Slack)
- Stand-up/Retrospective software (Google Meet, Standup Bot, Standuply, Retrium)

- Video conferencing (BlueJeans, Skype, Zoom)
- Virtual office (Sococo, Walkabout Workplace)

On-Site Benefit: *Trust*

A successful team benefits from the sense of personal accountability of working in the same location—of knowing that others will come through with their commitments. The trust that such reliability develops strengthens the team as a whole.

Facilitating Trust Online

GENERAL APPROACH

- Work out loud.
- Demonstrate reliability with results.

SPECIFIC SOLUTION OR DESCRIPTION

- Post your activities online so everyone can see what you're doing (I Done This, Jira, Salesforce Chatter, Slack).
- Maintain status updates of how you can be reached (IM, Slack, Sococo).

TYPE OF TOOL

- Communal task board/task-management software (Asana, Jira, Trello)
- Virtual office (Sococo, Walkabout Workplace)

On-Site Benefit: *Bonding*

A successful team benefits from the social aspects of working in the same location since the strengthened social ties of face-to-face interactions strengthen the team as a whole.

Facilitating Bonding Online

GENERAL APPROACH

- Communicate often, via video whenever possible.
- Schedule in-person when possible.

SPECIFIC SOLUTION OR DESCRIPTION

- Facilitate social time.

TYPE OF TOOL

- Group chat (Slack)
- Video conferencing (BlueJeans, Skype, Zoom)

On-Site Benefit: *Addressing Conflict*

A successful team benefits from in-person communication because facial expressions and body language convey tone and intention. Without that buffering, interpersonal relationships can erode, and minor annoyances can become extended conflicts.

Addressing Conflict Online

GENERAL APPROACH

- Have a team agreement in place that details how everyone wants to work together.
- Communicate via video whenever possible.
- Practice positive communication approaches.
- Use a communal task board or software to indicate who is working on what—thus avoiding task redundancy.
- Work out loud to avoid miscommunication and task redundancy.
- Have feedback loops in place (such as regular Retrospectives).
- Have practices in place to address conflict.

TYPE OF TOOL

- Various

This material is discussed at length in Chapter 8: Facilitate Their Success with Leadership, Alignment, and a Full Arsenal.

Remote Reminders

- Have high-bandwidth capability.
- Take the time to be savvy with your tools.
- Communicate often.
- Have protocols and etiquette in place, and revisit them regularly.
- Have a forum for raising concerns.
- Continuously try new things.
- Watch out for having too many tools. (Many recommend the occasion of onboarding a new hire as an ideal time to re-evaluate tool choices and etiquette; for more, see Chapter 9: Tune Your Team with a Team Agreement.)

PART II
INDIVIDUALS WORKING REMOTELY

> *"Rather than climbing the corporate ladder for the corner office, I just built one myself."*
>
> —JESSE FEWELL, *speaker, coach, and author*[1]

As stated elsewhere in this book, the key to making a success of remote working is finding your optimal combination of skill set, tool set, and mind set. Of course, some details will be dictated by your position or industry—but there is a great deal that applies to nearly all situations, especially concerning the attitude with which you approach your work.

Chapter 3 lays out what you'd need to get started: fundamental skills and practices as well as physical components like workspace and equipment. These are items that you'd set up, master, and progress from. Chapter 4 addresses what to constantly work at to perfect your game. There you can learn how to deliver what your employer needs (think motivation and productivity), how to tend to your own needs (such as not overworking), and how to be a great team player.

If your getting-started plan includes gauging whether you're suited for the remote route, you'll find guidance throughout Part II, starting with the *Deciding for Yourself* section in chapter 3. In the Part II EXTRAS an extensive questionnaire can help you determine if you're ready to work remotely—as well as what to do next if you're not. Those ready to continue can check out "Convincing Your Boss (or Team)" and "Seeking Remote Employment."

Despite all the detail, what it really comes down to is very simple: to succeed at working remotely, you have to want to succeed. If you can apply that determination to the guidelines that follow, you'll proceed swimmingly.

CHAPTER 3

Remote Working 101: Getting Started

"Remote workers aren't trying to escape doing work. We're trying to escape the day-prison. We want to use technology to make better use of our time. We want to spend more time doing things that matter to us, and less time stuck in traffic."

—LISETTE SUTHERLAND, *"Work Together Anywhere," TEDx talk for Theme: Unbox the Future*[1]

If you're already a remote-working member of an established team, then you'll probably want to jump to chapter 4 for tips on perfecting your game. If you're definitely going remote and ready to get going, then skip ahead to the *Getting Set Up* portion (*p. 72*) in the next section. For those just considering going remote, keep reading—all of what follows is pertinent to you.

Pre-Remote: Deciding for Yourself

"When my role is to be a virtual team member, I need to be self-motivated, focused, curious, flexible, and, above all, collaborative."

—MEGHAN M. BIRO, *"Telecommuting Is the Future of Work,"* Forbes[2]

Part of the decision about going remote—whether it's you who is unsure or you're worried your boss will be (if you have a boss, that is)—concerns both temperament and skill set. We'll cover how to convince your boss later on. For now, let's spend some time thinking about what it takes to work remotely successfully. Even if you're fully convinced this is the path you want to take—or you feel it's your only option—try to approach the following with an open mind. You'd be much better off identifying now what temperament and skill sets you could improve upon before you're actually in the at-home hot seat.

The following sidebar lists the top traits that make for a successful remote worker.

Top Remote-Worker Traits

The best remote workers:

SKILL SET

- are tech-savvy (both their skill set and their equipment);
- are excellent communicators;
- have good work habits: they're organized, and they prioritize and manage time effectively;
- are good at problem-solving/troubleshooting;
- have previous experience working remotely;

MIND SET

- are proactive: they're independent/self-starters;
- have team-focused work ethics: they're reliable, results-oriented, and highly responsive; and
- are good team players: they're pleasant, collaborative, supportive, and receptive to feedback.

SUCCESSFUL REMOTE WORKERS ARE TECH-SAVVY, NOT TECH-AVERSE. This doesn't mean you need to know how to replace your motherboard or hack your registry file. It does mean you're not intimidated by the prospect of figuring out why your audio isn't working on a Skype call—as well as that you know where to turn if your registry file gets hacked.

SUCCESSFUL REMOTE WORKERS ARE EXCELLENT COMMUNICATORS, especially with written communication. HR consultant Dirk-Jan Padmos points out that "remote working can amplify bad communication,"[3] so you'd want to be diligent about how well you phrase what you need to say. Another angle to this is willingness. As is emphasized throughout this book, with remote work overcommunicating isn't just preferable to undercommunicating—it's actually ideal. As Intridea/Mobomo's Kathryn Ottinger puts it: "If you think you're overcommunicating, you're doing it right."[4]

SUCCESSFUL REMOTE WORKERS HAVE GOOD WORK HABITS. In particular they're organized, they're able to prioritize, and they manage their time effectively.

SUCCESSFUL REMOTE WORKERS ARE ABLE TO PROBLEM-SOLVE AND TROUBLESHOOT on their own—and they know when and where to turn if they need extra help.

Employers seek remote workers who are proactive/independent/self-starters. Translating from the HR cheat sheet, that means SUCCESSFUL REMOTE WORKERS ARE BOTH SELF-MOTIVATED AND SELF-SUFFICIENT. As Agile trainer, coach, and advisor Ben Linders puts it: "It takes discipline to do your work when there's nobody there telling you what to do."[5]

SUCCESSFUL REMOTE WORKERS HAVE "TEAM-FOCUSED" WORK ETHICS. That means they are reliable, results-oriented, and highly responsive. (Note that such traits are as applicable to the solopreneur as to the team member.) Since this is such a potent aspect of remote working, these traits are covered extensively throughout the book under different terms and topics, such as building trust (by demonstrating reliability), productivity (producing results)—even transparency (also referred to as "working out loud").

And SUCCESSFUL REMOTE WORKERS ARE GOOD TEAM PLAYERS. That means they're pleasant, collaborative, supportive, and receptive to feedback. It also means they're willing to follow deliberate processes, as might be determined via a team agreement. (For more on the latter, see chapter 9.)

THE ABOVE terrain is viewed with a wide lens. The more thorough assessment comes from considering with a sharper focus the various elements that make for successful remote working. To do that, closely read both the *Ready, Set, Remote* section to follow and the entirety of the subsequent chapter on perfecting your game. Along the way, take careful notes regarding where you see yourself in relation to what's being discussed. After that, the "Are You Ready to Work Remotely?" questionnaire in the Part II EXTRAS can help clarify what to work on from there. (And note, the questionnaire would be much less meaningful if you jump to it without first reading through chapter 4.)

Ready, Set, Remote: Getting Set Up

Getting set up means finalizing where you'll work, using what equipment and tools, and under what house rules. And since it's wiser to try out working remotely for a time before you build a free-standing office in your backyard, we'll cover your tech needs before discussing workspace.

ENSURE YOU'RE TECH EQUIPPED AND SAVVY

> *"When I'm on a call with someone, I always ask 'How's my sound?' Through the microphone, through the internet, through the router, through the cloud, and then back again is a lot of hops. There are a lot of chances for error."*
>
> —AGILEBILL KREBS, *coach and founder, Agile Dimensions, LLC*[6]

When it comes to technology, the advice for individuals is the same as for companies: invest in high-quality equipment. We want crystal-clear, high-bandwidth communication on our remote teams. In order to have that, we need great internet and high-quality accessory tools. The cost of a headset and webcam is a small price to pay for productive conversations.

To follow is the minimum setup you'll need to maintain strong remote-worker relations—after which we'll elaborate on a few items.

- Phone
- Computer (desktop or laptop)
- Internet access, often via modem and DSL/Wi-Fi/Ethernet
- Reliable document storage and back-up system
- Webcam capability (built in to most modern laptops and monitors)
- Access to phone and email contact info
- Access to the files you'll need to work on
- Quiet space for audio calls
- Video-friendly setup

MINIMIZE YOUR BACKGROUND NOISE. Even with a stellar internet connection, background noise can distract everyone on the call. So just as your on-site teammates don't want to hear the cappuccino machine at your local café, they also won't be impressed by your kids squabbling in the background. That means you'll want to know your quiet-space options *before* call time approaches.

MAXIMIZE YOUR VIDEO PRESENCE. Because non-verbal communication is a big part of our interactions, it's important to turn on the webcams whenever possible. That means we have to pay attention to the details of lighting and background. It's all too easy in video calls to be backlit or, worse, in the shadows—and science has shown that when video lighting is poor, the conversation is less engaging.[7] Another concern is background. If the area behind you is messy, or busy with people walking back and forth, it can be a big distraction. So part of having a professional video setup includes ensuring the view behind you doesn't lessen the conversation; some recommend setting up a screen or room divider for this very purpose.

Finally, it's not enough to be set with high-quality tech; you'll want to ensure you're savvy with it too. So TAKE THE TIME TO LEARN HOW TO USE YOUR TOOLS. It's especially important that you're comfortable with video calls. As coach AgileBill Krebs points out: "There's another set of skills that includes mastering your video, your voice, and being able to move in a 3-D web environment. If we work with a team, everyone's got to be comfortable with the technology used."[8]

A few extra tips:

- Choose a mobile phone plan that suits your needs. For example, you might want to not have to worry about roaming, or how many minutes you're using.
- Get a laptop with great battery life, or keep a separate power bank/battery pack (or two) fully charged.
- Make sure you have access to tech support—as well as a plan B should your tech fail during a critical time.

CREATE A PRODUCTIVE WORKSPACE

Our workspaces play a big part in how productive we are, so we need to choose wisely—as well as to adapt when necessary.

Working from Home

According to a number of sources, a majority of remote workers work from home.[9] If you'll be adding yourself to that statistic, there are a few recommendations to keep in mind:

- Establish a dedicated workspace that you can turn to at any time. If you have a family, the dining room table is likely not a good option.
- Many recommend not using your bedroom if at all possible. Ideally your workspace will be somewhat separate from your living space. There's a double benefit to this: being in your workspace will encourage you to work when you need to—instead of being distracted by

the unmade bed or the overspilling laundry hamper; and your living area will remain a sanctuary—rather than serving as an eternal call to crank out ever more work.

- You'll want to set clear boundaries and expectations with your family or housemates, both in terms of workspace and work hours—and then be firm about maintaining those boundaries.

As for your actual setup, of course there is no "one size fits all" optimal office. It can take some time to figure out personal preferences, especially regarding physical setup and ergonomics. I for one love my standing desk; some use an ergonomic kneeling chair. Yves Hanoulle built a home "walking office": an electronic sit-stand desk combined with a treadmill. He says, "It makes my work time more intentional and helps me move more."

Many recommend tinkering with your space until you get it right. When Jesse Fewell first started working from home, he created an office space in his attic. Since he's a tall guy, after a while the low ceilings made him feel hunched over. So he set up a space in a corner of his bedroom—but before long he realized he rarely left that room. So he ended up building a small office in his backyard, which suited him (and his family) perfectly. As he phrased it: "Be prepared for the journey. Don't expect to get things right on the first try. It's a process of small experiments and iterations."[10]

Coworking Spaces

Of course, for some working from home is not an (ideal) option. Those in many major metropolitan areas can rent a station at a coworking space, whether that be a seat at a shared table or a private office, for an hour, a day, or a month. Many remote workers enjoy the amenities of coworking spaces—such as access to Wi-Fi and equipment like printers and scanners—as well as the chance to be around others who appreciate the remote option.

Hybrid Model/Public Spaces

Many find a hybrid model more to their liking—as well as more conducive to certain kinds of tasks.

> **An average day for me is working from my coworking space, which is a couple minutes' walk from my home in Barcelona. On days where I need it to be quiet or I need to take calls, I work from home. I love that I can choose where I work, whether that's my coworking space, my home—or even my mom's kitchen table in California.**
>
> —Vanessa Shaw, workplace innovator, Human Side of Tech[11]

> **For me, being in a coffee house is an enjoyable experience. I get the energy of people around me. Others might want the peace and quiet of their own home. The nice thing about having an anywhere office is that you can go where you need based on your mood. I'm kind of an introvert by nature and a forced extrovert by habit. And so, depending on the day, I may want to be in my house or I may want to be out in a coffee house. I find having that choice very empowering.**
>
> —David Horowitz, cofounder and CEO, Retrium[12]

And Some Find an Office Just Works Best

My entrepreneur husband tried both working at home and working at a coworking space, and he didn't like either. At home, he felt lonely, distracted, and bored being in the same place day and night. In coworking spaces, it wasn't convenient to bring all the equipment he wanted (external monitor, keyboard, and standing desk), and the chairs were uncomfortable. In the end, he rented an office for himself and his colleagues. If renting an entire office would be too much for you, note that some rent an extra room in a functioning office, even one in a different industry.

On the Road

You don't have to be a digital nomad to need to know how to work effectively on the road. Adriana Vela, the founder of NanoTecNexus, travels all over the world for her work. Along the way she has honed her ability to work from anywhere with the right tools, planning, and creativity. She shares:

One of my mantras on the road is "adapt, improvise, overcome": adapt to your environment, improvise, and overcome the limitations. Working while on the go comes down to being disciplined and appreciating change and limitations. Limitations are what make us creative—and it's creativity that's going to help you address your challenges.

She also offers the following recommendations:

- Pack only the essentials.
- Keep an extra power cord and batteries in your travel bag.
- Label your cords and connectors, especially if you speak at events.
- If your laptop doesn't have a backlit keyboard, get a USB LED light.
- Pack single-serve medications or a small first-aid kit.
- Print out your itinerary for when Wi-Fi is inaccessible.
- Categorize your task list based on where you can do certain activities, especially concerning Wi-Fi access.[13]

THINK THROUGH YOUR BUSINESS DETAILS AND FINANCIAL SETUP

If you'll be going remote in your established job or getting hired as a stable employee, your financial setup might not change all that much. But if you'll be setting up shop as a freelancer for hire, there are many self-employment details to attend to—which are well beyond the scope of this book. Such details could include:

- obtaining a business license and the like;
- registering a business name;
- acquiring health or business insurance;
- establishing a separate bank account and/or credit card;
- consulting attorneys, business advisors, career counselors, and the like;

- tax planning (and perhaps making regular tax payments);
- creating contracts and invoices; and
- creating/building an online presence.

This list just scratches the surface. For more, see the FOR INDIVIDUALS category (*p. 319*) in the *Books & Guides* portion of "For Further Reading, Listening, and Consultation" in the RESOURCES section.

Remote Reminders

PRE-REMOTE: DECIDING FOR YOURSELF

- Successful remote workers are tech-savvy, not tech-averse.
- Successful remote workers are excellent communicators.
- Successful remote workers have good work habits: in particular they're organized, they're able to prioritize, and they manage their time effectively.
- Successful remote workers are able to problem-solve and troubleshoot on their own—and they know when and where to turn if they need extra help.
- Successful remote workers are self-motivated and self-sufficient.
- Successful remote workers have "team-focused" work ethics; that means they are reliable, results-oriented, and highly responsive.
- Successful remote workers are good team players; that means they're pleasant, collaborative, supportive, and receptive to feedback.

READY, SET, REMOTE: GETTING SET UP

- Equip yourself with high-quality technology—and be sure you're savvy using it.
- When communicating by voice and/or video, minimize your background noise and maximize your visual presence.
- Ensure you have access to a productive workspace, and set clear boundaries with others regarding how you need to use it.
- Plan ahead for times when you'll be working on the road.
- Think through the financial or business details of your setup.

CHAPTER 4

Remote Working 201: Perfecting Your Game

"As a remote worker, you have to combine working with getting enough rest. You have to know when you're procrastinating and then consciously stop. Sometimes it means powering through, and sometimes it means taking a break. You need the self-knowledge to be able to take care of yourself properly."

—MAARTEN KOOPMANS, *owner, physicist, team lead, and software developer, Vrijhed.net*[1]

In the above quote, Maarten Koopmans touches on the fundamental task at hand: self-knowledge. In the end, rising to any challenge comes down to knowing what you're made of—and constantly striving to improve.

As for the goal of perfecting your game, working remotely falls under three umbrella headings: how to deliver what your employer needs, how to tend to your own needs, and how to be a team player.

How to Deliver What Your Employer Needs

Referring back to the top traits of successful remote workers, our watchwords for this section are: motivation, organization, productivity, prioritization, and time management. First up: starting each workday.

MOTIVATION AND SELF-DISCIPLINE

> *"It takes discipline to do your work when there's nobody there telling you what to do."*
>
> —Ben Linders, *trainer, coach, and advisor*[2]

There's a sense of discipline built into an on-site working environment. When working remotely, we have to come up with our own motivation and discipline. Fortunately, the advice on this is pretty unanimous:

- Have a set routine in the morning.
- Dress like you're going to work.
- Work in a space designated for work.
- Set a schedule and stick to it.

Information systems engineer and IT consultant Andrea Zabala shares: "Don't just wake up and jump on your computer. Take a shower and get dressed like you're leaving the house. This makes it feel like you are about to start something that's different from domestic life. And just like you would take a break at the office, take a break at home too."[3]

Note that this process might call for developing new associations. If you've never worked remotely before, your first remote Monday might feel like a three-day weekend. So you'll want to establish new habits and new ways of perceiving your space. As physicist and software architect Maarten Koopmans puts it: "Cultivate discipline."[4] And don't worry if it's hard at first. Give yourself a chance to adapt to your new working situation.

Some recommend planning your next day the night before, perhaps organizing your tasks so you can't help but tend to them first. If your morning head is anything like mine, you'd likely appreciate not having to figure out the first thing you need to do, at least until the caffeine kicks in.

PRODUCTIVITY

"There is an implicit social convention in an office that is not the most productive. What is productive for you is not productive for me, so the average becomes the least productive for all of us. Remote working is important to me because it allows me to be in control of my own productivity."

—MAARTEN KOOPMANS, *owner, physicist, team lead, and software developer, Vrijhed.net*[5]

In the previous chapter we covered how it's important to choose a workspace where you'll feel the most able to do your work. For example, my home office is a sanctuary where I'm most comfortable and productive. I have complete control over my tools and environment, which I can curate to allow maximum focus with a minimum of distraction—plus the perks of my standing desk, delicious coffee, and the neighbor cat's daily visits.

Though many are able to multitask reasonably well, the plain fact is that our best work is done when we're able to focus on just one task at a time. In a study at Stanford University, researchers set out to determine just what makes multitaskers so productive—and concluded the exact opposite. Their finding: multitaskers underperformed in comparison with those who prefer to focus on their task *and* had the luxury of doing so. The study's authors identified that the subjects "couldn't help thinking about the task they weren't doing" and weren't "able to filter out what's not relevant to their current goal."[6]

So, what can we do to maximize our focus? Minimize our distractions.

One way to do this is to PREVENT INTERRUPTIONS. For example, we can customize our notification settings for email, phone, apps, etc. So, rather than getting pinged every time someone we know breathes on Facebook, we can turn notifications off for tags, comments on posts, friend requests, group posts, and the like. And as for work email, some opt to always finish their paragraph or line of code before looking to see what arrived, let alone replying. Some establish in advance with their coworkers that they respond to messages at only, say, the top of the hour, or every half-hour. For those times when you need to focus for a longer stretch, you could announce that you're working on such-and-such deadline and will check back in three hours' time.

An additional angle on this concerns SETTING BOUNDARIES with our housemates and non-resident loved ones. Though this was said in the previous chapter, it's worth repeating: you'll want to set clear boundaries and expectations with your family or housemates, in terms of both workspace and respecting work hours. It can be surprisingly hard to set our own boundaries—and even harder to stick to them. But it's essential that we determine for ourselves what we need, and then communicate that to those around us.

Another tactic is to take full advantage of when you function at optimal capacity. That means knowing when you work best—and then planning accordingly.

Prioritization/Task Management/Time Management

One aspect of planning—and organization—relevant to productivity is just keeping track of all we have to do. Fortunately, several apps designed to manage even large work projects, such as Trello and Asana, can be commandeered to keep us on top of our personal to-do lists as well. So play around with a few such tools to see how they'd suit you. (Note that many apps offer a fair amount of their functionality for free, and charge only if you seek more premium services; others have a free trial period. Note too that, though Asana can be used for very complicated projects, productivity consultant Paul Minors offers at his blog a demo of why it's his favorite personal organization tool.[7])

I mention Trello and Asana in particular because they represent two different approaches to task management. Asana's main interface uses the more straightforward list, while Trello is based on the more visual system of using "boards" or "cards," sometimes referred to as "Kanban." This latter approach was developed because many advocate visualizing your work; some find it makes them more productive. As Personal Kanban creator Jim Benson points out: "Scientists have found that prioritization is the most mentally taxing thing that people do," in part because we can't see each thing that needs to be done. But if we make each task visible, we're better able to determine what should be done and when, or in what order.[8]

It so happens that Jim's two rules of Personal Kanban are directly applicable to focus and productivity:

- Visualize your work.
- Limit your work in progress to just three tasks at a time.

Why just three at a time? Because when we're able to focus on the task at hand, we're able to not just finish that task, but also to do it well—which pleases ourselves as much as it pleases those we're doing the work for. Whereas when we're rushed and harried, we produce work we don't feel good about, because we know it's subpar. As Jim says, "That doesn't prepare you for doing future work, because you're already disappointed in past work."[9]

An additional consideration is the workload we agree to. So that we can fulfill what we promise to, many recommend not taking on more than we can handle. And note: it can take discipline to sometimes say no to requests. But even so, an honest reply of "I couldn't give it my best until next week" could ultimately be better for everyone—especially if the alternative is submitting mediocre work.

Pace Yourself

Yet another angle on productivity concerns stamina and mental acuity. Numerous interviewees recommend regulating one's energy so as to maximize productivity. For many this calls for taking proper breaks. Affymetrix Inc. developer Ed Erwin offers: "My piano is in the same room that I use for my office. When I need a break from work, I can just turn around and play some music for a while. When I need a bigger break, I go for a bike ride in the nearby hills."[10] For some those proper breaks can include taking (power) naps. Blue Spruce Holdings partner Derek Scruggs shares: "It's important for me to regulate how much energy I have at any given time. Most important, I need to get enough sleep."[11] (I can attest to that myself. While I used to be able to sort of function on insufficient sleep, today I find I'm a better person when I'm fully rested.) We'll return to the important topic of energy regulation in the next section.

But first, note that some swear they're most productive when using the Pomodoro Technique, which advocates working in twenty-five-minute focused stints, punctuated by short breaks. (Italian Francesco Cirillo named his approach after his tomato-shaped timer.)[12] Of course, the best approach depends on the person and the task, so the point is to simply work at your maximum sustainable pace—and then give your brain a chance to rest.

Your Workspace

There's one last item regarding productivity, this time in relation to the physical organization of the home office. The website of home office design consultant Linda Varone points out that "your problems working at home may have less to do with willpower than with the setup of your workspace." She also notes that "a boring office is just as unproductive as a cluttered office."[13] If you need some help in that department, check out either her site (www.thesmarterhomeoffice.com) or her book, *The Smarter Home Office: 8 Simple Steps to Increase Your Income, Inspiration, and Comfort.*

How to Tend To Your Own Needs

Part of the self-knowledge challenge is knowing what we need to sustain in ourselves so as to fulfill our obligations. In this regard, the top caveat cited by my interviewees concerns the high risk of burning out.

THE RISKS OF OVERWORKING

> *"I can do almost all of my work anywhere. And I love my job so it's easy to always work."*
>
> —Marion Smits, *associate professor of neuroradiology, Erasmus MC, Rotterdam, the Netherlands*[14]

> *"Something that typically happens to me in the evening is that I'll go into my office to just quickly check something on the computer. And then three hours later, I'm still at my desk."*
>
> —YVES HANOULLE, *self-employed creative collaboration agent*[15]

In chapter 5 we note that a vast majority of managers contemplating the remote option fear that workers would slack off when out from the watchful eye of the office. The reality is that remote employees are more likely to overwork than underwork.

The more common reason for this is passion and dedication: like Marion Smits quoted above, we've chosen work we love, and we love to do it. The trick is knowing how to balance that. As Jeremy Stanton explains: "It can be extra hard to turn off, simply because we don't want to. If you're the type of person who enjoys what you do, work could just consume you if you let it."[16]

Another reason we might work too much concerns accommodating different time zones. And with that comes the very real danger of never switching off—of working around the clock to serve the immediate needs of colleagues around the globe. WorkAtHomeSuccess.com founder Leslie Truex specifically warns: "Don't work 24/7. You'll make yourself crazy."[17]

So, in order to maintain our best work, we need to keep a watchful eye on our energy levels. That means stopping and relaxing every once in a while. But more so, Information Systems engineer Andrea Zabala recommends doing the things you always wished you could do when you were working in an office, like having lunch on your patio, going for a walk, even just stepping outside for five minutes of fresh air. Don't forget to take advantage of the perks of working remotely that you sought in the first place—which leads us right to our next topic.

Stand Up, Sit Less, Move More

A 2015 study conducted in Australia found impressive health benefits from the following routine: sit for twenty minutes, stand for eight minutes, and move around for at least two minutes. Or, if you usually work standing, you could maintain twenty-eight-minute work sprints followed by a moving break. Of course, if like most of us you have only a sitting desk, you'd have to tailor the recommended routine to your situation. But this study's researchers say it's likely worth the effort, citing high "cardio-metabolic risk"—in particular cardiovascular disease, diabetes, and premature mortality—for those who spend consecutive hours sitting, *even* for those who engage in great cardio exercise in their off-hours.[18]

WORK-LIFE FUSION

> *"Work-life balance is a slippery slope. You can get stuck in this point where you're always on and you never unplug. But that's a matter of self-management. And part of managing ourselves is setting strict boundaries and guidelines for what's okay and what's not okay."*
>
> —PHIL MONTERO, *systems engineer, The Garam Group*[19]

Previously, the supposed goal in the slippery slope of "work-life balance" was to keep work and life from overlapping. But recently the conversation has turned toward seeking "work-life fusion," where the lines between work and life are blurred.

To my mind, this welcome evolution is long overdue. Too many of us have been advised to separate our pastimes from our careers, and have tried in vain to cram our passions into slots around our work. But as it happens, remote-working experts join researchers and stress consultants in advocating that remote workers regularly pursue non-work activities. Indeed, several of the scores of respondents consulted in Remote.co's "remote-friendly company" survey said they look for candidates who have interests outside work, for several reasons. One concerns demonstration of self-sufficiency, and of being a "finisher" as well as a "starter." Web developer SitePen in particular "lean[s] toward people who are active participants in outside communities. This demonstrates leadership, organization, and passion." Another reason concerns the admirable objective of continuous self-improvement; a worker steadily progressing toward besting one's 10K finish time is likely also a worker steadily progressing toward bigger and better work initiatives. And a third reason has to do with plain old burnout. World Wide Web Hosting notes: "It's imperative to find candidates who have a social foundation outside of work, . . . who gain their social side of life from other avenues." This is because those who rely on work for their social fix "tend to be unsuccessful in remote positions."[20] Altogether, this speaks to the fact that outside interests help to alleviate a significant aspect of working remotely: the solitude, and its potential deleterious effects. More on that coming up.

Remote Work-Life Fusion at Its Best

Andy Willis is the director of Working from Anywhere. He shares: "I ran a small company for a few years. One year, I decided to go to France for a month to see if I could ride my bike in the Alps while still working with my colleagues back in Australia. And nothing went wrong. That was life-changing. I realized that I could work from anywhere. As you get older, you see people who defer their life till retirement. But I didn't want to do that. I wanted to work around my life rather than live around my work."[21]

The beauty is that it's possible to do great work *and* enjoy the scenery. In another example: my husband is crazy about mountaineering. Several times a year we go on a "workcation," when we work and explore a new mountain range at the same time. We'll rent an Airbnb with several rooms and great Wi-Fi, and we'll work when we need to and go hiking and climbing when we can. For us, changing the scenery every once in a while gives a new perspective to our work.

Sonatype product owner Jeffry Hesse feels the same: "I find myself happiest when I'm in nature, when I'm in the mountains. Climbing is one of my passions. And since I can work from anywhere, it means I can go to, say, Argentina for two months to climb the Patagonias. Last December, I spent a month visiting my grandma in Alaska. Next week I fly to California to go climbing. And then I'm going back to Alaska for a few months to climb on glaciers. I couldn't live like this if I were working in the office. Don't get me wrong—we work really hard to get everything done. But we make it convenient to do other things in our lives. And that's what's so great about working remote. You can merge work and life."[22]

To wrap up this section, it really comes down to just simple advice: take care of yourself, and take time off when you need it.

TUNE IN TO YOUR SOCIAL NEEDS

"I think people who have never worked remotely might underestimate how lonely it can be."

—Iwein Fuld, *cofounder and lean business hacker, StarterSquad*[23]

In the previous section, World Wide Web Hosting identified a concern about hiring candidates who have no outlet for feeding their social needs outside work. This is because seasoned remote-friendly employers know all too well what Sonatype Agile coach Mark Kilby defines so succinctly: "The isolation can really get to you at times."[24]

When we work on our own, we can easily become disconnected. Many of those I interviewed shared that they struggled with loneliness when they first went remote. Many people simply miss the coffee machine banter.

Fortunately, we have options, and they don't all have to include face time. First, there's no shortage of opportunities (for better or worse) to engage with like-minded people on the internet. Joining groups on social media lets you tap into the breathtaking array of knowledge and passions and projects initiated by people around the world.

Another possibility is working together online. As noted earlier, coworking spaces offer work stations for rent by the hour, day, or month. For many, the chance to be around others is even more appealing than the productive workspace. But for some, like myself, it's just too distracting—the noise, the movement, and the lack of privacy keep me from concentrating on my work. So, as much as I enjoy working with others, coworking is not for me. But virtual coworking? That's another story! With virtual coworking, I can maintain social connections from the comforts of my perfectly tailored home office. How? By using visual technology to regularly check in with like-minded colleagues.

Back in 2012, I wrote a book for a mutual client with Gretchen Wegner, an academic life coach who lives in California. Every day we'd meet for a few hours during the time when our workdays overlapped, using Skype to talk to each other and a Google Doc to write the book. We'd turn on our video for the first five to ten minutes to say hello and check in, and then we'd turn off the video to focus on the writing. Our sessions were extremely productive and a lot of fun, and we became good friends. We liked working together so much that, even once the book was done, we decided to continue our daily sessions with our own projects. To this day we still work together—and we've still not met in person.

Note that this approach isn't limited to just two people; video conferencing technology makes it possible to meaningfully connect with a whole team. For more, check out the WORK TOGETHER ONLINE section of chapter 8, which describes a number of ways to digitally foster the camaraderie of working with a group.

If it's face time you crave, note that social networking services aren't just for the world of the web; sites such as Meetup.com help like-minded individuals spend time together in the physical realm, perhaps practicing a language, or learning to cook. (At the time of this writing, upcoming Meetup events in San Francisco included "Taiji, Xinyi, and Bagua internal strength training" and "serving breakfast at a homeless shelter.")

Of course, if you want to spend more time around other solo professionals, finding a coworking space is ideal. And note: that needn't be a full-time setup; even just renting a spot one day a week could be just what you need—especially if you choose a day (like a Thursday or Friday) when the work day could evolve into drinks or dinner afterward.

To sum up: there are many ways to spark connection from our remote-working posts; we just need to find the ways that work for us. And when we find the trick to tending to all our needs, we'll be better equipped to learn exactly what we're made of—as well as where we can take ourselves next.

> **Always work on improving yourself. Keep experimenting and learning something new all the time.**
>
> —RALPH VAN ROOSMALEN, coach and Management 3.0 facilitator[25]

How to Be a Team Player

I can't stress it enough: for a remote team to work well together, they must mutually decide upon how they will work together. Chapter 9 details the many considerations of such agreements from the group perspective. For now, we'll touch upon certain aspects from the individual perspective. Since the best configuration of any group results when the sum is greater than its parts, let's make sure your contribution meets that lofty standard.

COMMUNICATION

> *"Good communication is key. Working remotely requires more frequent communications at and between all levels of the organization."*
>
> —CHRIS RIDGEWELL, *director, Wisework; principal and owner, Charterhouse Consultants group*[26]

Both chapters 3 and 6 identify how important excellent communication skills are to remote working, especially given how often written communication is called for. But when it comes to being a good team player, it's not just about clarity or a clever turn of phrase; good communication practices involve how much you say, when you say it, and why.

Preferably, each team will collectively craft a team agreement in which they establish their preferred means of fulfilling their many collaborative activities. (We cover team agreements in chapter 9.) One essential agreement item is communication etiquette, wherein it might be decided, for example, that text or IM (or a chat tool) is preferred over email for relaying certain kinds of information; or that it's ideal to respond to emails within a certain time frame. But even before you forge a team agreement, you can still practice recommended etiquette around communication.

To start off, we can strive to make our emails as effective as possible in two main ways. One, when sending messages that request responses to multiple items, clearly identify each item (perhaps by numbering them) to indicate precisely what information you need. If your respondent leaves any items unanswered, request those again—and maybe try new means of emphasizing them in future correspondence. Two, when responding to multi-item messages, offer a reply to each salient point—just as you would in a verbal conversation. The benefit of this latter approach is twofold: you move the project along with your thorough replies, and you build connection with your teammates by leaving no point ignored or disregarded.

As much as it can be productive to convey a lot in one message, it's also true that email can hide information behind imprecise or even irrelevant subject headings, in part because often more than one subject is addressed. So some recommend keeping each message to just one topic. Hassan Osman at Cisco Systems takes it one step further: he changes the subject line of email threads as the conversation changes so that the information can be more easily tracked down in the future. (This is one reason why many teams prefer chat tools over email, since the chat platform documents information in a central hub that's readily accessible to all.)

An additional consideration is how many emails you send, and how often. Independent consultant Peter Hilton shares a guideline borrowed from Morse code etiquette: "My rule of thumb is: don't send faster than you can receive, and then don't send faster than the other person is sending."[27]

Another tip: learn to type faster. I heard of someone who considered it agonizing to IM with a particular coworker because his messages took so long to arrive. But the friend wasn't even a slow typist—he just took such effort to write well that the recipient fell asleep before the reply came through. So if you're a slow typist or a perfectionist writer, you might want to opt against IM—*and* learn to type faster.

One last point speaks to an upcoming topic: the inevitable conflicts that can emerge within any community—and that often begin with simple misunderstandings and incorrect assumptions. As product manager Fernando Garrido Vaz shares: "Each individual has his or her own traits, obviously. But there are patterns in how people in different regions behave and, in particular, communicate about things. So you just have to be aware that this difference exists, and then train yourself to be slower to react."[28] In other words, learn to not jump to conclusions—as well as to not express annoyance (precipitously). We cover this at length lower down.

COLLABORATION

A similar take is relevant to the collaborative process as well. Trainer, coach, and advisor Ben Linders recommends: "Respect other people's processes. They will often be different than yours."[29] Ben speaks from experience. Based in the Netherlands, Ben collaborated with Portuguese management consultant Luis Gonçalves in writing a book, *Getting Value Out of Agile Retrospectives: A Toolbox of Retrospective Exercises*, which they cowrote remotely. They embarked upon this challenge because they respected each other's knowledge, but they soon learned they had very different ways of working. Though it caused friction at first, once they communicated why they chose the approaches they did they came to respect each other's processes—as well as to find a common ground that worked for both of them.

I've had similar experiences in hiring others to work on aspects of my business. At first it was tricky, but once I learned I liked their results, I had to remind myself to let go and let them work in their own way, using the processes and tools that worked for them..

Both communication and collaboration are essential ingredients in the deeper processes of working on a remote team—namely: building trust, and building relationship.

BUILDING TRUST: DEMONSTRATING RELIABILITY

> *"Reputation is the cornerstone of the collaboration economy."*
>
> —Per Frykman, *founder, Reputation Mastery*[30]

When we work in an office, we can see that our teammates are present and engaged with something—in a meeting, say, or typing at their computers. Part of why we're productive in that setting is because the atmosphere of diligence inspires us to demonstrate ours as well. That industrious team effort produces a sense of trust, which binds a team together.

But when we work remotely we don't have that built-in awareness of everyone contributing to the mission. This is in part because remote teams don't have those in-the-flesh visuals of teammate diligence. But the thing is, those visual cues can be misleading; while it's easy to assume that on-site workers at their computers are being productive—they could in fact be updating their Netflix lists. Conversely, the fact that we can't see remote workers working leaves a visual vacuum—one readily filled by images of them kicking back watching Netflix.

But it doesn't stop there. Thoughts like *I bet they're not working* can accumulate, and develop into worsening negative associations. Next comes the fact that we're less likely to communicate with coworkers we don't feel good about, which only exacerbates the issue. And when teammates stop talking to each other, they can end up withholding information—or, worse, gossiping or disengaging. And, just like in the office, alliances can form. All of this can manifest into distrust, on-site or online. The difference is that when we're working online it's harder to detect where and when things start going wrong.

To replicate that positive, "everyone's contributing" on-site mentality in the virtual realm we have to embrace new mind sets. We need to TRUST that others will deliver the results they committed to; we need to be willing to ADVERTISE our productivity; and we need to DELIVER the results we committed to delivering.

The building blocks of trust start with being reliable, consistent, and transparent. Can I rely on you to get your work done on time? Will you deliver high-quality work? Can I find you if I need to?

> **In a typical office, if you go to all the meetings, you're active, and you speak up, then people think you're productive. But if you're working remotely, you have to deliver things. If you don't deliver the things you promised, everyone sees that.**
>
> —MICHAEL SLIWINSKI, founder and CEO, Nozbe[31]

Of course, delivering what we say we will demonstrates a lot, but those of us whose projects take more than a workday to complete need to find additional means of, in remote parlance, being "visible" to our colleagues. For many of us, working on a remote team calls for being willing to advertise our productivity, which we can do by working out loud.

> **I could be working hard all day—but you won't know that unless I share it with you. But if my document is posted to an online space and you're seeing the updates, and you're seeing things getting accomplished on a shared to-do list, then there's no question that I'm working, or what I'm working on.**
>
> —Phil Montero, systems engineer, The Garam Group[32]

Working out loud is a critical part of working on remote teams. Its basic message is, *Hey guys, I'm contributing*. But just how that gets communicated needs to be determined by the team. Since sending an email every morning saying "Hey, everyone, I'm working on such-and-such" could get tedious, many teams opt for using a dedicated app as a central hub: chat tools like Slack, and/or task-management tools like Asana, Jira, or Trello.

Now, one might wonder how the concept of maintaining one's visibility jibes with limiting distractions so we can get our work done. It all comes down to the group's overall makeup. Some teams need to know what everyone is doing, and so they talk back and forth regularly. For some teams, "getting your work done" amounts to completing lots of little tasks. If they're using a task board like Trello, it's fully visible which tasks were assigned to whom. And when a task gets moved from the "doing" category to the "done" category, everyone can see that work has been accomplished—without a group announcement to that effect. Team members can also advertise what they're working on simply by keeping their status up to date (with IM tools or Skype, for example). Regardless of the methods employed, those who need to limit their distractions can always specify in their app settings which notifications will get through in real time and which will be saved for later. Again, these are all details that can be mutually decided on in a team agreement.

To close the topic of building trust is a contribution that leads right to our next topic: building relationship.

We can build trust in a lot of different ways, but showing caring for each other is huge. If people feel like you have their back, you know something about their personal life, and you're respecting that, all of that builds trust. That is the key to teamwork, whether it's virtual or colocated.

—Dave Blum, founder, Dr. Clue[33]

BUILDING RELATIONSHIP

"To build trust, be transparent and be personal."

—Andrea Zabala, *information systems engineer*[34]

We are a better team when we like the people we work with. And to like them, we need to get to know them. We can begin that process by helping others get to know us, by offering a bit of our personality along with our professionalism. The trick is, some will be more open than others—just as some cultures are more open than others.

The good news is there are many ways to build relationships within teams. And the first one is easy: turn on the webcam. As visual creatures, we can't help but feel more connected when we can match a face with a voice and name. So don't just write or call your teammates; initiate video conversations as a regular means of communication, both one-on-one and as a group.

But the webcam is just the start. On remote teams many just show up to meetings, discuss the agenda, and then resume their individual tasks. That doesn't leave a lot of time for getting to know each other. So at Happy Melly—the fully distributed professional association of which I'm the remote team manager—we build personal time into all our meetings. Anyone who feels like hanging out can arrive five to ten minutes early; otherwise, members simply join at the scheduled time. As you can imagine, the more often you participate in that kind of personal time, the better you'll get to know your teammates—and they you. At Happy Melly we also open our meetings with "icebreakers" to facilitate greater connection. These could be naming a favorite food, or bringing something for show-and-tell: say, the mug you got in Tierra del Fuego. I realize that could sound pretty cheesy, but this kind of thing actually gets people engaged and talking to each other about personal things. Whatever the mechanism, the point is to offer some of our personality to the team, however subtly or overtly we go about it. If you've got an interesting collection of T-shirts, wear them; don't opt for the same sweater every day.

In Part IV we cover various ways teams build relationship with scheduled socializing, such as hosting a Friday Happy Hour or Trivia Night. Though many such activities get planned team-wide, or are manager-initiated, that doesn't mean you can't initiate some yourself. In the same way you might grab coffee with a colocated teammate, grab a virtual coffee or lunch with the mates on your virtual team. Get to know them.

Of course, the top-recommended advice on team building is to meet in person as often as possible. For many teams that would have to be initiated by management, but there's no harm in requesting more face-to-face time if you don't feel you get enough. Though you can develop a lot via video communication, the plain fact is that remote bonding works best once in-the-flesh time has sparked a substantial beginning.

Another tip is to maximize face time when you have it. If your team can't get together regularly, don't fill your limited in-person time with activities that you could do online. Take advantage of proximity when you can.

In sum, though much of team building should come from the top, there are still many ways for individuals to make their own interpersonal in-roads.

ADDRESSING CONFLICT

> *"Remember that you're simply working with a person. Stop making assumptions and start asking questions. Be curious."*
>
> —Pilar Orti, *director, Virtual not Distant*[35]

Building relationship doesn't just make for increased fun time; it also helps to keep conflict at bay. Though some conflict is inevitable, you can prevent minor annoyances from brewing into larger disturbances in a number of ways. First up: positive communication.

Practice Positive Communication

When we're remote, we need to take special care in being kind and constructive in how we communicate with each other. This calls for a few ground rules.

For starters, since it's easy to read negativity into written communication, even when none was intended, it's wise to ALWAYS BE FRIENDLY, even overtly friendly.

The flip side of that is to always ASSUME POSITIVE INTENT. If we don't have enough information on why someone said or did something—or why something wasn't done—it can be all too easy to fill that blank with a negative assumption. Instead, make a conscious effort to not jump to conclusions. Even if your correspondent wasn't in any way friendly, try to assume no ill will was intended. Management consultant Vanessa Shaw offers: "When you're not sure how to respond to someone, ask yourself 'What else do I not know?'"[36]

And finally, RESIST THE URGE TO EXPRESS CHARGED EMOTION. Expanding on this point: some of us are prone to express exactly what we feel as soon as we feel it. Of course, as much as that might feel good in the moment, such words can cause permanent damage to our relationships. It's always wiser to keep what we really want to say to ourselves—and instead respond as constructively as possible. (We'll cover these items again lower down.)

Offer Positive, Constructive Feedback

I'll state this up-front: I recently Googled the term "feedback sandwich." The top hits led to several articles published by reputable sources that specifically did not recommend this feedback approach. So, if you're skeptical of the "sandwich," note two things. One, there's a difference between peer-to-peer feedback and boss-to-employee feedback—and the articles were written to managers. And, two, the writers were objecting to what I consider to be faulty or insufficient use of what really can be an effective method.

With the feedback sandwich, one offers constructive feedback sandwiched between two positives. The trick in making this approach effective concerns the sincerity of the positive comments, the relevance of those comments, and the phrasing of the feedback.

To my mind, the point of the positives isn't to use a spoonful of sugar to help the medicine go down. Sometimes the point is to say: some of what you've done works—now let's see how we can bring the rest of the project up to that standard. After all, we can't produce high-quality work if we're not clear on what would pass that test. Also, in some cases we might think the respondent just didn't get what we were trying to do. But if we can see that some of what we did was appreciated, we're more likely to see the critique as relevant. Another point: since many of us don't do our best work when feeling discouraged, the compliment offered with the feedback could smooth our path back to the drawing board.

On the flip side, regarding a lack of positivity: if the critiquer seems overly negative—or is a negative person in general—it's hard to know what part of the assessment is valid and what is simply a reflection of that coworker's current mood, general outlook, or even personal feelings about us.

To follow are some guidelines for providing constructive feedback.

OFFER SINCERE POSITIVES. These could include parts that work of the piece in question; parts that have worked of your colleagues' previous efforts; your respect for their efforts overall; or your positive feeling about them in general.

PHRASE YOUR FEEDBACK IN TERMS OF YOUR OPINION, NOT OF ABSOLUTES. There's not much efficacy in saying that something is poor/slipshod/mediocre/lousy/stupid. Instead, express why something isn't working for you, or why you think said item won't serve its purpose. For example, "I don't quite follow this argument, so no doubt some others won't as well. Can you clarify it more?" Or, "This feels incomplete to me. How about fleshing out this portion?"

CONSIDER THE OBJECTIVE. Above all, don't lose sight of what's really at stake. If everyone benefits from tasks being done well, then do what you can to help your teammates reach that, yes, happy conclusion.

Next: how to request—and receive—feedback that will actually be helpful to you.

Request Constructive Feedback

In her Trello blog article "Avoid the Seagull Effect: The 30/60/90 Framework for Feedback," Lauren Moon talks about the frustrating occurrence of teammates "swooping" in like seagulls giving negative, way-too-late feedback on projects nearing completion.[37] (Medium.com offers a fuller definition: "Seagulling: when someone comes into your work, shits all over it, then flies away."[38]) To prevent this situation, Lauren recommends using the 30/60/90 framework for requesting feedback, wherein one requests specific levels of feedback at different phases in a project. (See the sidebar to follow.)

The 30/60/90 Feedback Framework

Any project that requires feedback from multiple people can be adapted to the 30/60/90 feedback framework. The levels represent advancing stages in the project's development.

30-PERCENT FEEDBACK

At the beginning stages of an initiative, request feedback on direction and scope—basically, ideas, opinions, or tips on the general concept. Specify that you welcome the following types of input:

- impressions of the higher-level concept;
- thoughts about different audiences to target;
- suggestions for scope and ways to expand;
- "go" or "no go" decisions on project elements; and
- alignment on higher-level organizational goals.

In addition, specify that you're not ready for feedback regarding:

- copyediting, sentence structure, or formatting.

60-PERCENT FEEDBACK

With this second phase, you'll have fleshed out the concept much more, but are still open to significant feedback. Lauren notes: "It's critical during this round to get all stakeholders involved, because it is their suggestions that will catapult the piece—whatever it is—from a first draft to a nearly finished product. Plus, if you don't get their feedback now, you're running the risk falling prey to the dreaded seagulling territory down the road." Specify that you welcome the likes of:

- suggestions of different ways to expand;
- nitty-gritty comments on grammar, copyediting, sentence structure, or formatting;
- details of color, graphics, design, etc.; and
- comments on if the feedback from the previous round was implemented effectively.

In addition, specify that you're not requesting:

- impressions of the higher-level concept;
- "go" or "no go" decisions about key project elements; or
- alignment on higher-level organizational goals.

90-PERCENT FEEDBACK

With the final stage the project is nearly done. "Think of this as the 'Is there anything else I missed?' round of feedback." Specify that you welcome:

- nitty-gritty comments on grammar/copyediting/sentence structure/formatting and
- comments on if the feedback from the previous round was implemented effectively.

In addition, specify that you're not requesting:

- suggestions of different ways to expand (unless relatively minor);
- impressions of the higher-level concept;
- "go" or "no go" decisions about basically any part of the project; or
- alignment on higher-level organizational goals.

Source: Lauren Moon, "Avoid the Seagull Effect: The 30/60/90 Framework for Feedback," Trello Blog, 4 June 2018.[39]

And when you receive feedback, do your best to be open to it. Try to put your ego aside and see where the other person is coming from—especially if the feedback is offered with a mind to benefiting the team and/or the organization as a whole. Of course, ideally the feedback itself would be phrased positively. You can encourage just that by ensuring that all feedback you offer is phrased as kindly and as constructively as possible. (Since effective feedback is so important to productivity and team building, we address it at length in chapter 8.)

Don't Try to Resolve Conflict in Writing

It's widely advised: as soon as an interaction starts to get heated, ditch the written word and pick up the phone or turn on the webcam. It's easy to build up a grievance against a shadowy entity; it's much harder to assume—and impose—negative intent when we're interacting with a human face or voice. Resist the urge to hide in the remote bushes; instead, work on building relationships.

Try to Resolve Conflict One-on-One

Similarly, when you need to voice a concern, don't use a team-wide forum, like group chat, as your first option. Communicate one-on-one. If you reach an impasse, rope in your manager. Personal differences can be tricky enough as it is; don't add public embarrassment (or worse) to the mix.

AS THE ABOVE chapter details, a lot goes into being a great member of a remote team. So let's close with a few lines of advice from remote-working experts:

> **Be generous with your information and resources.**
>
> —HASSAN OSMAN, PMO manager, Cisco Systems[40]

> **Focus on doing great work.**
>
> —FERNANDO GARRIDO VAZ, independent product manager[41]

Be willing to experiment and fail.

—Vanessa Shaw, workplace innovator, Human Side of Tech[42]

Push the ball forward every day.

—Jeffry Hesse, Agile coach, Sonatype[43]

Remote Reminders

HOW TO DELIVER WHAT YOUR EMPLOYER NEEDS

Motivation and Self-Discipline

- Have a set routine in the morning.
- Dress like you're going to work.
- Work in a space designated for work.
- Set a schedule and stick to it.

Productivity

- Experiment with time- and task-management methodologies and apps.
- Minimize multitasking; instead, focus on one thing at a time.
- Pace yourself: regulate your energy so as to maximize your stamina and mental acuity.
- Make sure your workspace aids rather than hinders your productivity.

HOW TO TEND TO YOUR OWN NEEDS

- Balance stints of productive, focused work with sufficient breaks that include movement. For example, try out a routine of sitting for twenty minutes, standing for eight minutes, and moving for two minutes.
- Don't forget to allow yourself the perks of remote working that you sought in the first place.

- Consider the ways you can develop work-life fusion that allows time for your non-work interests.
- Combat the risk of loneliness by actively seeking social interaction—both in person and online.

HOW TO BE A TEAM PLAYER

Communication and Collaboration

- Practice good communication etiquette. Some recommend keeping emails to just one topic or item—with a subject line to match, so the information is easily tracked later.
- Practice positive communication: be overtly friendly, and assume positive intent.
- Adopt a virtual-team mind set. That calls for trusting that others will deliver the results they committed to, advertising your productivity, and delivering the results you committed to.

Building Trust and Relationship

- To build trust, be reliable, consistent, and transparent; make sure your teammates know what you're working on and how to reach you.
- Get to know your teammates. Be personable; share a bit of yourself.
- Use video tools to socialize virtually: schedule a virtual coffee or lunch with a coworker, plan a games night.
- Get together in person when possible.
- Be open to feedback.
- When addressing conflict, resist the urge to express charged emotion. Instead, focus on constructively discussing the issue—preferably by phone, video, or in person.

PART II *Extras*

QUESTIONNAIRE FOR INDIVIDUALS

Are You Ready to Work Remotely?

Working remotely requires "tenacity, trustworthiness, empathy, and adaptability. Thankfully, these are traits anyone can strengthen with commitment and a little effort."

—Kristi DePaul, *Remote.co*[1]

When it comes to what makes for an ideal remote worker, the consensus is clear: remote working is not for everyone. Some crave the working-together energy of being around teammates, as well as the sense of connection from in-person interactions. Some need the structure and nose-to-the-grindstone work environment of an office. Some find a predetermined schedule helps them stay on track. Some need extra guidance. And some just need more social interaction than a day's worth of video calls can provide. So whether you're planning to ask your boss to offer the remote option or you're hoping to be a company's newest remote hire, you'll want to find out in advance just how prepared—and suited—you are to being a great teammate from afar. Then, once you know where you currently stand, you'll know what to focus on to become even more prepared—or if you should stick to the on-site option for now.

This questionnaire is available for download, in both MS Word and PDF formats, at https://collaborationsuperpowers.com/extras.

Instructions for section 1: Answer the following questions. (If you like the tangibility of paper, you can print out either of the two downloadable formats noted above.)

Section 1

MOTIVATION

- Are you clear on all the reasons you're thinking of working remotely? YES/NOT YET
- Do you have a clear sense of the potential drawbacks of working remotely? YES/NOT YET
- If yes, do you think your motivation to succeed in working remotely can make up for whatever drawbacks you experience? YES/NOT YET

TECH READINESS: EQUIPMENT

- Do you have more than one reliable means of being reached? YES/NOT YET
- Do you have access to a quiet space for audio calls? YES/NOT YET
- Do you have a fast, well-functioning computer (desktop or laptop)? YES/NOT YET
- If you have a desktop but not a laptop, can you imagine needing a laptop in addition? YES/NOT YET
- Do you have fast, reliable internet access? YES/NOT YET
- Will you need a secure internet connection for your work? YES/NOT YET
- Do you have webcam capability (built in to most modern laptops and monitors)? YES/NOT YET
- Do you have a headset? YES/NOT YET
- Do you have access to a professional-looking setup for video calls? YES/NOT YET
- Might you need to work while traveling? YES/NOT YET

Depending on your situation, additional supplies you might need include an extension cord, external keyboard, mobile router, additional monitor, mouse, power adapter, or power strip.

TECH READINESS: SAVVY

- Do you consider yourself tech savvy in using your phone? YES/NOT YET
- Do you have access to tech support for your phone if you need it? YES/NOT YET
- Do you consider yourself tech savvy in using your computer(s)? YES/NOT YET
- Do you have access to tech support for your computer(s) if you need it? YES/NOT YET
- Are you comfortable sending texts? YES/NOT YET
- Are you comfortable sending Instant Messages (IM)? YES/NOT YET
- Are you comfortable with video conferencing? YES/NOT YET
- Are you comfortable working with online calendars and the like (Outlook, Mac Mail, Google Calendar, etc.)? YES/NOT YET
- According to a Remote.co survey updated in early 2018, the most commonly used apps among scores of remote-friendly companies are: Basecamp, Google Chat, Pivotal Tracker, Skype, Slack [formerly HipChat, then Stride], Trello, and Yammer.[2] Are you comfortable working with these? YES/NOT YET

EXCELLENT COMMUNICATION SKILLS

- Are you an excellent communicator via the phone? YES/NOT YET
- Are you an excellent communicator in writing? YES/NOT YET
- Are you an excellent communicator via video? YES/NOT YET
- What is your normal response time to phone calls?
- What is your normal response time to emails?
- What is your normal response time to texts?

- Are you comfortable communicating asynchronously in groups? YES/NOT YET
- Would you be working in a different time zone from your team members or boss? YES/NOT YET
- If yes, how many hours of overlap will there be?
- Are you in the practice of being aware of coworkers' time zone(s)? YES/NOT YET

GOOD WORK HABITS

- Do you consider yourself to be organized? YES/NOT YET
- Do you consider yourself to be disciplined? YES/NOT YET
- Do you consider yourself to be focused/not easily distracted? YES/NOT YET
- Are you skilled in prioritizing/time-management strategies? YES/NOT YET
- Have you worked with any project- or task-management tools (for yourself, not in terms of working with others)? YES/NOT YET
- Are you good at staying motivated? YES/NOT YET
- If not yet, do you have any preferred tricks to staying motivated? YES/NOT YET

PROBLEM-SOLVING/TROUBLESHOOTING SKILLS

- Do you consider yourself resourceful in solving problems that come up in your work? YES/NOT YET
- If not yet, do you have thoughts on how you could develop that resourcefulness? YES/NOT YET
- Can you describe a time you demonstrated excellent problem-solving/troubleshooting skills? YES/NOT YET

PREVIOUS EXPERIENCE WORKING REMOTELY (OR USING REMOTE-FRIENDLY SKILLS)

- Do you have experience working remotely in any capacity? (That experience could include working while on a business trip or occasionally working from home, such as when sick or waiting for the plumber.) YES/NOT YET

For those with no previous experience:

- Do you have experience working with a remote team member or (short-term) contractor? (Meaning, you worked on-site, but the other person didn't.) YES/NOT YET
- Have you ever worked on-site where you communicated with some colocated team members by phone or email much more often than face-to-face? (This applies especially to large campuses or offices with multiple floors.) YES/NOT YET
- If you don't have any remote working experience, do you have any ideas of where you could get some experience? YES/NOT YET

For those with previous experience:

- Do you have a sense of what are your favorite and least favorite things about working remotely? YES/NOT YET
- Do you have a sense of what's meaningful to you about working remotely? YES/NOT YET

INDEPENDENCE: PROACTIVE/SELF-MOTIVATED

- Do you consider yourself a self-starter? YES/NOT YET
- Do you consider yourself a proactive communicator? YES/NOT YET
- Do you consider yourself a curious person? YES/NOT YET
- Have you pursued some personal development in the last twelve months? YES/NOT YET

- Do you have interests separate from work? YES/NOT YET
- Do you have any long-term pursuits? YES/NOT YET
- Does your work history reflect upward movement within or across companies? YES/NOT YET
- Have you ever been rehired by a former boss? YES/NOT YET
- Can you demonstrate any examples of being resilient in response to setbacks or hardship? YES/NOT YET

WORK-LIFE CONCERNS

- Do you have trouble switching off of work mode? YES/NOT YET
- Are you skilled in maintaining a healthy work-life balance in general? YES/NOT YET
- Do you have any preferred practices for ensuring a healthy work/life balance? YES/NOT YET
- Is loneliness a potential concern for you? YES/NOT YET
- If yes, do you have ready solutions to loneliness already in place—as in regular access to friends and family; or established sports, group activities, or hobbies? YES/NOT YET
- If you don't already have a "diversified social portfolio" as noted in the previous question, can you imagine developing one? YES/NOT YET

TEAM-FOCUSED WORK ETHICS

- Do you have experience working on a team? YES/NOT YET
- Do you know if you prefer to work on your own or on a team? YES/NOT YET
- Are you willing to keep team members apprised of what you're currently working on? (This is also known as make your work visible to others or "working out loud.") YES/NOT YET

- Are you willing to keep team members apprised of how to reach you during established work hours? YES/NOT YET
- Do you have experience working out loud? YES/NOT YET
- Do you have a preferred means of letting others know what you're working on? YES/NOT YET
- Are you practiced in keeping your status updated for others to see? YES/NOT YET
- Are you familiar with the idea of using different means of communication for different kinds of information? YES/NOT YET

GOOD TEAM PLAYER/INTERPERSONAL GOOD FIT

- Do you maintain a positive tone when writing email, texts, or instant messages? YES/NOT YET
- Would you consider yourself pleasant to interact with? YES/NOT YET
- Would you say that you have a collaborative, supportive nature? YES/NOT YET
- Are you open to making constructive use of feedback? YES/NOT YET
- Are you able to keep your temper in check? YES/NOT YET
- Can you describe the last misunderstanding you had with a coworker—and how you handled it? YES/NOT YET

OVERALL

- Are you willing to do what it takes to be an excellent remote worker? YES/NOT YET
- Could you demonstrate to a potential employer that you'd be a great hire? YES/NOT YET

Section 2

Now, let's tease out your replies a bit. For each question where you answered YES, write a sentence that describes or demonstrates that particular qualification. (Instructions for completing this section digitally vs. on paper follow this paragraph.) For example: "I am willing to respond quickly to all communication to ensure our project continues smoothly." For each question where you answered NOT YET (at least of the items that are applicable to you), write a sentence describing what it would take to make your honest reply a YES. This might be as simple as "I will as soon as I buy a new headset, which I'm doing tomorrow." Or, "I don't have ideal space at home right now, but I'll be looking into the pricing at a coworking space later this week." Or your reply could be more complicated, such as "I'm not always great about responding immediately to emails, but this is something I'm willing to work on." Most important, be honest. If an answer falls along the lines of "I'm not willing to let everyone on my team know where I am or what I'm working on all the time," then you should say so rather than pretend otherwise. The goal here is to identify what will work for you, as well as what you're willing to work for.

INSTRUCTIONS FOR SECTION 2: With this part of the exercise we'll want to finish with each answer as its own separate entity, whether that's a physical square of paper or index card, or a digital "card" you can move around on your screen.

If you like the tangibility of paper, you could write on index cards, write longhand on paper, or type your answers and then print them. (For the two paper options, divide a piece of letter paper into halves or thirds [make two or three columns if you want to type], write or type your answers, and then cut the answers into separate pieces.)

If you prefer the digital realm, consider using a board-style task manager such as Trello. (To go this route, create an ANSWERS list, and then answer each question as a separate card in that list; you'll end with a very long list.) An app like OneNote could also work; the idea is just to make it easy for you to move an answer to a different spot in your workspace.

Section 3

Once you've completed section 2 and have provided fuller answers to each question in section 1, identify two "camps" on your digital workspace or physical table: one for YES and one for NOT YET. (For a task board like Trello, create two new lists to the right of your answers list: YES and NOT YET.) Next, review your answers one at a time, and move them to either the YES camp or the NOT YET camp. (Some might even want a third camp, for "Not going to happen!" Again, we're being honest here.)

Once you've completed that, take a look at where you stand. Based on how big each camp is, you'll have a sense of just how ready you are to work remotely. If you decide to pursue the remote option, you've also just created your to-do list, since every NOT YET reply spells out exactly what you need to do to pursue that item. (This is another reason to try out Trello, since it's designed to help you visualize a project from start to finish.)

THUS ENDS the at-the-moment part of this exercise; what follows will take however long it takes. Start working on your NOT YET items. Once each is done, move it to the YES camp by writing an updated sentence about it (perhaps on the back of your paper square or index card if you're employing the tangible method). This time, describe your new proficiency in that item, as in: "I have a local dial-a-tech lined up should I ever need technical support."

One last thing: just why should you write out proficiency statements for your YES replies? Because they make for great interview answers or cover letter inclusions, or could be used in your pitch to your boss, as in: "My preferred means of letting others know what I'm working on is to post a short update in Slack at the end of each day—in part because it helps me identify what to start on first thing the next day." As it happens, the vast majority of traits that employers seek in a remote worker have been addressed in this exercise, so your ready answer to their future burning questions will demonstrate your ample qualification for the position.

Here's to fruitful progress!

CONVINCING YOUR BOSS (OR TEAM)

If your going-remote plan includes the need to convince your boss, then the first step is to complete the "Are You Ready to Work Remotely?" questionnaire just preceding (if you haven't done so already). This is because the ammunition you'll need for convincing your boss will come from your written-out YES answers to the various questions; those answers will demonstrate you've got what it takes to make your remote venture a success. (Ideally you'll have very few items—if any—remaining in your NOT YET camp before you broach the subject with your boss.)

To begin your boss-convincing plan, let's turn again to the Meghan M. Biro comment quoted earlier, this time in full:

> **When my role is to be a virtual team member, I need to be self-motivated, focused, curious, flexible, and, above all, collaborative. When my role is to be an entrepreneur managing virtual teams, I need to be empathetic, emotionally intelligent, sensitive to what others need, and willing and able to provide whatever tools are necessary for success. In either role, I must . . . be self-aware—in tune with my skills, capabilities, strengths, and weaknesses.**[1]

Consider this description in light of your manager. Do you think she or he is "empathetic, emotionally intelligent, sensitive to what others need, and willing and able to provide whatever tools are necessary for success"? Perhaps that's too much to know the answer to right away, but keep it in mind as you proceed.

Regardless of how well received your request to work remotely might be, you'll want to take the time to consider the prospect from your boss's perspective. What about productivity? Reliability? What about team morale? From there, the goal is to decide how best to demonstrate that you'll be fully accessible, responsive, and, above all, productive.

Another major consideration: pretty much every expert says that if one team member works remotely, even just some of the time, then the team needs to function as if everyone were remote. At first blush that sounds like a tall order, but it's also true that the work practices of remote teams are superior to standard on-site practices—because they call for everyone being more intentional. Even just advertising how to be reached when—as well as what one is currently working on—communicates the dedication to the mission that everyone wants to see.

Now, the task at hand, broken down into steps.

> Note that you can download this material at https://www.collaborationsuperpowers.com/extras.

1. So that you'll be well apprised of *all* the concerns your boss or team might have, you'd be wise to read Chapter 5: Transitioning Toward the Remote Option, especially the *Actually Going Remote* section, as well as the entirety of chapters 7 through 9. (Chapter 10 is less relevant to your objective here.) Along the way, take notes on everything that applies to your work situation, as well as what new practices or tools would be called for. (The items that follow share more about what kind of notes you should take.)

2. Draw up a first-draft plan of what you would need to do or acquire in order to work as successfully when remote as you do now. (This task will be well informed by the to-do list you created from your "Are You Ready to Work Remotely?" questionnaire.)

3. Consider how to quantify all that you do. At the very least, you'll want to pitch just how you will demonstrate that you're fulfilling all your obligations. If possible, show how your going remote will *add* value.

4. Draw up a first-draft plan of what you think your team would need to do (or acquire) in order to maintain the team's current level of productivity with you working remotely.

5. Spend some time considering whether your team would be willing to adopt the practices necessary to maintain your productivity level.

6. If you're starting to think this all might be a tough sell, consider getting feedback from your teammates: share what you're contemplating and ask how receptive they might be to your plan.

7. Prepare a proposal and timeline to present to your boss that addresses the following:

    - WHY it's important to you to work remotely; what benefit you will get from it. Don't shy away from admitting that you want to spend more time with your family—or whatever personal reasons you might have. The point isn't to deny your human side; the point is to demonstrate that the impetus is meaningful enough to you to want to make it work. (Though note the sidebar to follow this list.)
    - WHAT you've already done to prepare yourself for this new challenge. (See item 2, above.)
    - HOW you will personally demonstrate you are continuing to fulfill your obligations to the team. (See item 3, above.)
    - HOW this could be done well team-wide—perhaps including mention that your team has already expressed they're willing to try it out. (See items 4 through 6, above.)
    - HOW it would roll out. Propose a trial period so everyone can see how it works in action. For example, some recommend having the first phase of the rollout be everyone starting out your new remote-communicating practices while you're all still on-site. After a week or two of that, try working from home one day a week for two weeks, then two days for two weeks, etc. Most important, schedule regular check-ins to see how the system could be improved.

8. Schedule a time to meet with your boss and present your proposal—perhaps with him or her reading it with you right there, ready to answer any questions. While the shyer ones amongst us might prefer to simply

submit the proposal and wait for a reply, that approach could also lead to some pretty nervous hours, days, or even weeks before your boss gets back to you. Taking the more assertive approach would be one way of demonstrating just how serious you are about making this work.

Parents Working from Home

If you plan to work from home and you have children, specify that you will be setting expectations with your family. Make it clear that you have no illusions that you can work from home and caretake at the same time. As career development expert Brie Reynolds puts it: "As the mom of a two-year-old, there is absolutely no way I can work from home and have him here with just him and me at the same time. . . . This is a real job. You wouldn't bring your two-year-old to hang out with you every day in a traditional office environment. Certainly, you can't hang out with him at home either."[2]

SEEKING REMOTE EMPLOYMENT

"Don't wait for the stars to align. Whatever it is you want to do, start it now."

—LESLIE TRUEX, *founder, WorkAtHomeSuccess.com*[1]

The steps to finding remote employment, though few, are by no means simple. The good news is that if you're really determined, that very determination will get you where you want to go.

To start off: if you have the luxury of addressing the biggest-picture concerns, take the time to FIGURE OUT EXACTLY WHAT YOU WANT TO DO so you can build a career around what you really want. But even if you don't have that luxury, at the very minimum figure out exactly why you want to work *remotely*. That realization will inform both your job search and the application process. Employers need to know that *you* know, first, who you are; second, how well you'll perform; and, third, that you know what you're getting into.

LEARN WHAT EMPLOYERS SEEK IN A REMOTE EMPLOYEE—AND DEVELOP YOURSELF INTO THAT EMPLOYEE. Fortunately, this tall order comes with a full instruction guide: both the *Hiring Strategy* (*p. 137*) and *Interviewing* (*p. 144*) sections of Chapter 6: Hiring Remote Workers and Teams. There you'll find that the number-one trait sought is experience working remotely, for two reasons: employers need people who, one, can work remotely effectively and, two, actually *like* working remotely. The trick is getting that experience; for more, see the following sidebar.

How to Get Experience Working Remotely

It's a classic Catch-22 situation: you need remote experience to get a remote job, but you can't get the job without the experience. Here are a few tips for addressing that conundrum.

- Get savvy with the remote-working tools and apps most widely used on a regular or daily basis by scores of remote-friendly companies. According to Remote.co, those apps are (listed in order of popularity):
  - » for INSTANT MESSAGING: Slack, Skype, Google Chat;
  - » for PROJECT MANAGEMENT: Trello, Pivotal Tracker, Basecamp;
  - » for TEAM COLLABORATION: Slack, Yammer.[2]
- For practice with the inter-team aspects of such tools, especially the chat tools, enlist some friends to help you gain that experience—preferably those who'd also benefit from the practice.
- Connect with other remote workers. Check out Virtual Team Talk (https://virtualteamtalk.com). Rent a spot at the budget table at a local coworking center. Ask for advice.
- Doggedly pursue short-term remote work, perhaps via online sites such as Fiverr.com, Freelancer.com, or Upwork.com.
- Know intimately why employers seek that remote experience (again, see both the *Hiring Strategy* [*p. 137*] and *Interviewing* [*p. 144*] sections of chapter 6); confess up-front that you don't have the appropriate résumé entry; and explain why you're *still* the perfect person for the job. How are you perfect? Because of your self-awareness regarding how you work, and because of all the preparation you've done on your own—added to your absolute dedication to making it work.

WORK UP YOUR BRAND. Next, capture what you offer in words. That means crafting several versions of the pitch you'll use to advertise your value: one that's three paragraphs long, one that's one paragraph, and one that's just one sentence—or even just a few words.

BUILD YOUR ONLINE BRAND. Your online presence is important, so get active on your social media channels, especially LinkedIn, to demonstrate the value you offer. Build a personal website if such feels appropriate, especially if you'd have sufficient content to maintain a blog. Or, at minimum you could post articles on your LinkedIn page.

> **Typically, when you leave a company, the first thing that HR does is delete your mailbox—with the gigs and gigs of data, connections, and knowledge that you've accumulated over the years. But if you use a social network, your legacy will remain regardless: all your contacts and conversations remain available to others.**
>
> —LUIS SUAREZ, digital transformation and data analytics adviser, panagenda[3]

REACH OUT. Get in touch with your network to let them know you're looking for work. As product manager Fernando Garrido Vaz shares: "Word of mouth is the best way to find work. You don't need a large audience; you just need the right audience."[4]

MINE VARIOUS JOB-SEEKING RESOURCES—DAILY. Apply to everything that appeals to you that you can demonstrate you are qualified for. Start at the "How to Find a Remote Job" page on my Collaboration Superpowers website (https://www.collaborationsuperpowers.com/114-how-to-find-a-remote-job).

WATCH OUT FOR WORK-FROM-HOME SCAMS. The old adage applies: if it seems too good to be true, it probably is. You should never have to pay anything in order to apply for a job. Don't give out passwords. And listen to your intuition.

FLEXJOBS LIST

100 Top Companies with Remote Jobs in 2022[1]

A Place for Mom
Accruent
Achieve Test Prep
ADP
ADTRAV Travel Management
Aerotek
Aetna
AFIRM
Alight Solutions
Amazon
American Express
Anthem, Inc.
Apex Systems
Appen
Auth0
BCD Travel
BELAY
Boldly
BroadPath Healthcare Solutions
CACI International
Cactus Communications
CareCentrix
Carlson Wagonlit Travel (CWT)
Change Healthcare
Cisco
Citizens Bank
Concentrix
CrowdStrike
CSI Companies
CVS Health
CyraCom
Dell
Education First (EF)
Elastic.co
Enterprise Holdings
EXL
Fiserv
Gartner
GitHub
GitLab
GovernmentCIO
Grand Canyon Education (GCE)
Grand Canyon University (GCU)
HashiCorp
Haynes & Company
Hibu
Hilton
Humana

Invitae
Jack Henry & Associates
Jefferson Frank
Johnson & Johnson
JPMorgan Chase
K12
Kaplan
Kelly Services
Kforce
Landi English
LanguageLine Solutions
Leidos
Liberty Healthcare
Lionbridge
Liveops
Magellan Health
Motion Recruitment Partners
Novartis
NTT Group
Parallon
PAREXEL
Paylocity
Pearson
Philips
PRA Health Sciences
Red Hat
Robert Half International
Salesforce
SAP
Science Applications International Corporation (SAIC)
Sodexo
Stryker
Sutherland
SYKES
Syneos Health
The Hartford
Thermo Fisher Scientific
Transcom
TranscribeMe
TTEC
Twilio
U.S. Department of Commerce
Ultimate Software
UnitedHealth Group
VIPKID
VMware
VocoVision
Wayfair
Wells Fargo
Williams-Sonoma
Working Solutions
World Travel Holdings

"Go for it. . . . Making the leap won't be without its pains, but clear communication and managing of expectations will make it easier."

—Tabitha Colie, *director of operations, Seeq*[1]

"Do it! There have never been more resources and tools to make remote work less challenging and more effective."

—Alex Turnbull, *founder and CEO, Groove*[2]

PART III
SUCCESSFUL REMOTE TEAMS 101

Transitioning and Hiring

"Invest time and research into the benefits of remote work. . . . Develop a company culture that syncs with remote work. A successfully run remote organization can draw the best team members possible, regardless of where they're located."

—GABRIELLE PITRE, *recruiter, Coalition Technologies*[3]

So, this remote manager walks into a virtual bar . . .

No, seriously: this section is geared toward those who have concluded that the future includes some version of your company or department having a remote option—whether you approach the prospect with unbridled enthusiasm or more than a whiff of uncertainty. Rather than suggesting you jump into the deep end of the pool, chapter 5 starts with how to establish an office as "remote-first"—something like going through the motions before anyone actually works off-site—before detailing how best to actually go remote. And since you'll likely (in time) need to hire remote workers, chapter 6 discusses hiring strategy and offers tips on both interviewing and onboarding. Both chapters include a "Feedback from the Trenches" section gleaned from scores of remote-friendly companies, who share some of their before-the-fact fears about both managing remote workers (chapter 5) and hiring them (chapter 6). Spoiler alert: it's not as scary as it seems. In fact, it can be downright great—if you do it right.

Let the adventure begin!

CHAPTER 5

Transitioning Toward the Remote Option

"A successful remote working environment is a two-way street: the company must prepare for it just as much as the employee does."

—Ka Wai Cheung, *The DoneDone Blog*[1]

For those readers who are unsure about whether to try out the remote option, the straight-up advice comes down to just a few points. Even separate from the benefits of staying competitive and attracting top-notch talent, a company would be wise to develop into a remote-first operation for two reasons. (As noted in chapter 2, "remote-first" indicates that, at minimum, an organization is prepared for employees to occasionally work off-site if the need arose, especially for emergency reasons.) First, with a remote-first setup, your company's productivity need not be lessened by even one day, regardless of what illness or traffic or weather or worse affects your workforce. And second, the unanimous opinion is that a remote-first operation is stronger and more viable. In short, the work you'd need to do to prepare for the remote option will greatly benefit your operation, whether or not anyone actually goes remote.

The term "remote-first" derives from the earlier term "mobile-first." As Ka Wai Cheung describes in a blog post, Luke Wroblewski first presented the concept of mobile-first in 2009 in response to web design at the time when mobile internet use, via tablets and especially smartphones, was proving to be more than just a minor concern—and one that rendered beautifully designed websites anything but beautiful.

> **Because shoehorning a desktop design into a mobile design can often lead to really poor mobile experiences, the mobile-first approach starts with the lowest common denominator and progressively enhances the design on more feature-rich devices. The end result is not just a better mobile experience, but a focus on what features really matter to everyone the most.**
>
> **. . . We are at a similar crossroads with remote working. A company can decide to shoehorn remote employees into a system designed for in-house employees, or they can take a remote-first approach: figure out how every aspect of their organization can thrive with remote employees, and then progressively enhance them for in-house employees.**
>
> —KA WAI CHEUNG, The DoneDone Blog[2]

One Company's Take on Remote-First

In the article "How We Created a Remote-First Manifesto," Balki Kodarapu shares what remote-first is and isn't for the company PayTrace.

> REMOTE-FIRST CULTURE IS:
>
> - when all meetings that we initiate have a Zoom video conference link by default.
> - where all important conversations happen in [Slack], email, or Confluence by default. If they happen elsewhere, we make sure they are propagated back into one of these systems for the greater good.
> - where we invest heavily in bringing the remote team members to our HQ at regular intervals so the entire team can have quality in-person time together.
> - where we trust our employees and leave it up to the individuals when they want to work from home versus in the office. (Note that to keep their dedicated desks employees must work a minimum of two days a week in the office.)

HOWEVER, REMOTE-FIRST:

- does *not* prevent anyone from having in-person conversations. Good organizations thrive on in-person bonding. The only ask is that important conversations and decisions are propagated to the right stakeholders [via Slack, email, or Confluence].
- is *not* our stated intention to always hire remotely by default; on the contrary, PayTrace wants to be an active part of the Spokane, WA, business/tech community.
- is *not* 100 percent automatic flexibility to "work wherever/whenever" by default. Since some departments and roles need in-person collaboration quite often, certain PayTracers are required to be present in our HQ office during scheduled time slots.[3]

Establishing the Office as Remote-First

Making an office remote-first amounts to taking the steps necessary to enable employees to *effectively* work remotely in an anomalous or emergency scenario. As previously noted, the bare minimum calls for employees having access to reliable technology (phone, computer, and high-bandwidth internet connection), access to phone and email contact info, and secure access to the files they're currently working on.

TOOL SET/INFRASTRUCTURE

Those outside the office might need:

- phone
- computer (desktop or laptop)
- headset
- external monitors or keyboard (if necessary)
- webcam capability
- video-friendly setup/space/screen
- modem (DSL/Wi-Fi/Ethernet, etc.)

- access to company email (such as with Outlook or Mac Mail) via the company server
- access to phone numbers and email addresses
- access to the files they're currently working on
- access to a virtual private network (VPN), as applicable

Those in the office might need:

- quiet/private space and technology for video calls
- guaranteed space for remote workers to use on the days they need to work on-site (sometimes called "hot" desks)
- guaranteed space (such as a meeting or conference room) for collaborative working as a group

MIND SET

Off-site, workers need to be willing to follow deliberate processes for ensuring their work remains satisfactory and conducive to company-wide productivity. That means companies need to take the time to *establish* those deliberate processes—so they can set up their remote workers to succeed in the effort. For this we need to delve into the details of the remote option.

Actually Going Remote

> *"Be prepared for the journey. Don't expect to get things right on the first try. It's a process of small experiments and iterations."*
>
> —JESSE FEWELL, *founder and principal coach, Fewell Innovation*[4]

As mentioned earlier, there is no singular ideal setup with remote working—no one formula to follow. Each person, each company, will need to experiment to find what combination proves to be most productive.

The voluminously helpful website Remote.co offers insights from many companies' experiences transitioning to the remote option. Toggl CEO and founder Alari Aho shares: "We put a lot of thinking into it. We laid out the pros and cons, talked to our team members, and did some research. Once we [got] started . . . we had a lot of questions about staying productive remotely, maintaining a company culture, and managing a distributed team[—]and we all learned together to make it work." Ultimately, "Changing mind set is the hardest part. Everybody in the company has to be on board with it."[5]

And from my own interviews, founder Ade Olonoh of technology company Formstack, based in Indianapolis, Indiana:

> **We existed as a fully local company for seven years before making the decision to transition to a remote workforce. In 2011, we decided to hire our first remote employee, a developer based out of Poland. Not too long after, my wife was offered a job in Oklahoma that led me to try my hand at remote leadership. Our official decision to go remote was formally made after several organic discussions about other team members moving out of state. Several of our former Indy employees now live in other states, and some of our early decisions with remote working made that possible. We've had several trial-and-error experiences with technology, communication, in-person meeting best practices, and other remote-working aspects, but we're strengthening our remote team every day.**[6]

Speaking of "trial-and-error" experiences, take to heart a tip resoundingly shared by those in the know: if just one employee works remotely, even just some of the time, then the team would be wise to function as if everyone were remote. Now, that might seem like a tall order, and I certainly don't want to discourage initiating the remote option. Nor will I lie and say that it's a piece of cake, because it's not. Being a successful remote team takes work, from everyone involved. But all the same, it's still true that remote practices are beneficial regardless of how or where they're employed—and when on-site teams are also strengthened in the process, everyone wins.

For example, consider the following from digital creative agency Sanborn: "In a rapid prototyping, tight-deadline environment, verbal communication is key. So we knew that shifting to remote meant that much of the verbal communication would have to be replaced with written communication. When we went remote, we enforced the documented process, and worked to keep it as lean and mean as possible. This communication happens largely in our project-management software and Slack. The advantage is audit trail. It's easy for anyone coming on to the project to jump in, follow the story, and understand where the project is and why. Overall, it's been very successful."[7] And web developer SitePen offers: "Being remote, we spent a lot of time perfecting the best way to convey information so that content remains clear and intact. Our current tools allow for complete visibility for collaboration and agreement in everything we do. Email is no longer a primary communication method for us, and no initiative lives outside of project tools." (Interestingly, though they "attempted having physical office space in the early days, the idea of going into the office never quite took off.")[8]

Another widely shared piece of advice: do it gradually. Virtual team consultant and transitioning expert Pilar Orti suggests: "If a team is thinking about going virtual, start with one day per week. Then move to two days. Or work from another part of the building. It's all about learning from small experiments."[9] And the following from Jobmonkey.com speaks particularly to the reluctant employer's perspective: "Slowly transition[ing] employees from office life to remote work life . . . gives you the ability to oversee an employee's work ethics before you cut them loose or commit to a long-term remote situation."[10]

FEEDBACK FROM THE TRENCHES: *"What Were Your Biggest Fears About Managing Remote Workers?"*

The website Remote.co (https://remote.co) offers a wealth of information and resources. Among the bounty: they asked 135 "remote-friendly" companies questions about their experience—and then shared the results.[11] To follow are the nuggets I gleaned from answers to the question "What were your biggest fears in managing remote workers?"

The vast majority feared the "when the cat's away the mice will play" syndrome, specifically concerning productivity, accountability, even simple reachability. Fortunately, several of the respondents were happy to report that their fears had been unfounded. Nearly all the remainder identified what solutions worked for them, the top one being hiring dedicated, motivated people—and then ensuring those new hires felt "empowered" and part of a meaningful work culture.

> **We've found that if you hire the right people and empower them to be successful, they will work at or beyond what you expect of them because they view remote work as a privilege. There have been some hiccups along the way, but definitely nothing more than the issues I've seen when working in an office.**
>
> —Brian Patterson, partner, Go Fish Digital[12]

Additional solutions included manager initiatives such as setting clear performance goals and constant communication, especially regarding status updates.

Some noted that changing their mind set was the solution.

> **I feared that I'd have trouble trusting people to get their jobs done. That went away quickly when someone taught me to "give people your trust and let them earn your mistrust." Said differently, until they break your trust, expect that they are doing a great job. That was a life-changer for me.**
>
> —Chris Byers, CEO, Formstack[13]

> **When we started out, especially when we had to grow and hire new people, my biggest fear was that they'd not work hard and would be looking to take advantage of us. That classic fear when you can't see what people are doing. That they might not be doing anything at all! That couldn't have been further from the truth, but I think what was key to making that happen was telling myself to stop worrying about holding people accountable and pushing them to be more productive—and to instead focus on the flip side of that: motivating people, supporting them, and trying to make sure they're as happy as possible. With those factors taken care of, productivity has been an almost inevitable side-effect.**
>
> —Jon Lay, founder, Hanno[14]

What were your biggest fears about managing remote workers?

%	REPLIES
70	PRODUCTIVITY, ACCOUNTABILITY (LESSENED OUTPUT RE: QUANTITY AND/OR QUALITY), REACHABILITY
14	TEAM HAPPINESS/CONNECTION/ENGAGEMENT
8	HIRING: ASSESSING VALID CREDENTIALS
5	COMMUNICATION: ESP. RE: EXPRESSING PRIORITY
3	"THAT IT WOULD BE HARDER THAN IT IS"
100	

Compare the results of that question against those of another posed to the same companies. (Note that, though all companies were asked the same questions, not all companies answered all questions.)

What is the hardest part about managing a remote workforce?

%	REPLIES
22	COMMUNICATION: THAT YOU NEED TO BE DELIBERATE RE: THE QUALITY AND QUANTITY OF YOUR COMMUNICATION TO MAINTAIN ALIGNMENT AND BUILD RELATIONSHIPS WITH TEAM MEMBERS (PLUS "READING BETWEEN THE LINES" OF RECEIVED COMMUNICATION)
15	SUPPORT: SATISFYING NEEDS OF WORKERS/GIVING INDIVIDUAL ATTENTION
12	MANAGING TEAM PRODUCTIVITY/MOTIVATION
9	FACILITATING TEAM BUILDING
8	PERSONAL RELATIONSHIPS: MANAGERS BONDING WITH THEIR EMPLOYEES
5	SCHEDULING DETAILS RE: MULTIPLE TIME ZONES

%	REPLIES (*CONTINUED*)
4	HIRING GOOD PEOPLE
4	TAKES LONGER TO IDENTIFY ISSUES
3	DETAILS RE: GROWING LARGER
3	SETTING EXPECTATIONS
3	ENSURING A CONSISTENT COMPANY CULTURE
2	BORDER-CROSSING LOGISTICS: LAWS & REGULATIONS, IT CONCERNS, ETC.
2	ENSURING THAT MANAGERS CAN MANAGE REMOTE FORCE WELL
2	IDEATION
2	MAINTAINING TRUST IN WORKERS
1	EMPOWERING WORKERS TO SELF-MANAGE
1	WORKING WITH LESS EXPERIENCED EMPLOYEES
1	EFFECTIVE PROCESSES
1	LETTING GO OF SEEING DISTANCE AS PROBLEM, FINDING OTHER MEANS
1	ACKNOWLEDGE THE ADDITIONAL OVERHEAD OF LEADING A REMOTE COMPANY
100	

As you can see, though remote worker productivity was the primary fear heading in, only 12 percent of respondents cited such as being the hardest part about remote-team management. Conversely, though communication was a minor concern going in, it turned out to be of top importance once remote teams were well underway. And, as it happens, apparently efforts regarding team building and bonding turned out to be just as tricky as they were expected to be.

Another point: to the "What is the hardest part . . . ?" question, there were a high number of respondents with relatively unique replies; each of the bottom fourteen rows of the above chart—those on this page—represents no more than 4 percent of respondents. This demonstrates that the primary concerns center on four topics: managing productivity, supporting employees, team building, and the all-important communication. The best news is that many respondents shared the solutions they came up with to address the challenges they encountered along the way.[15] Those gems and more can be found in the chapters that follow.

As FOR the road ahead, to fully contemplate if the remote option would be viable for your team or company calls for considering the steps you'd take if you actually were going remote. So the remainder of the book is written for two kinds of managers: those committed, and those still considering. In the Part IV EXTRAS you'll find the Manager's Action Plan, which begins with steps to walk those still considering through the consideration process—followed by action steps for those ready to embark.

Remote Reminders

- Making an office remote-first means enabling employees to *effectively* work remotely in an anomalous or emergency scenario. To do this they need access to reliable technology (phone, computer, and high-bandwidth internet connection), access to phone and email contact info, and secure access to documents and files.
- There is no single formula for successful remote working. Each person, each company, will need to experiment to find what proves to be most productive. That said, a gradual transition will likely be most effective.
- If just one employee works remotely, even just some of the time, then the team would be wise to function as if everyone were remote. As it happens, remote-team practices make any team more effective.
- According to the consensus of nearly eighty companies polled by Remote.co, what's "hardest about managing a remote workforce" is managing productivity, supporting employees, team building, and communication—all of which we cover at length in the chapters to follow.

CHAPTER 6

Hiring Remote Workers and Teams

"Hire the absolute best people you can as early on as you can. Don't hire three okay people. Hire one great person who can really help you. Then continue to keep that quality of the team. Ultimately, that's what's going to allow you to focus on building the business—as opposed to just running the business."

—CARRIE MCKEEGAN, *CEO, Greenback Expat Tax Services*[1]

Expert advice about hiring remote workers, whether adding just one individual or an entire team, is pretty much unanimous. Essentially, have a well-developed hiring strategy; have a stringent interviewing process for identifying the right people—not just those who will best fit the team, but also those who can work well remotely; and then set them up to succeed with effective onboarding.

Hiring Strategy: What to Look For

The best hiring strategy specifies all potential aspects of your dream team, including the characteristics needed of the collective members. As NanoTecNexus.org founder Adriana Vela puts it, "Be savvy about identifying the right sort of profile and mind set for new hires."[2] So, who are the "right sort"? For starters, the best people you can find.

Hiring the wrong person is the worst thing a business can do. One of my clients wanted to hire more people. I looked at the résumés that came in and I could see that the candidates weren't qualified. The company also knew that the candidates weren't good enough. But instead of continuing their search, they said "We need bodies! We can train them." The thing is, when people aren't qualified, you simply can't train them to do what they need to do.

—DIRK-JAN PADMOS, director, Padmos HR Consultancy[3]

From my interviews as well as from research aggregating the views of nearly one hundred different sources, I've identified the eight most important traits to look for in hiring,[4] which fall into the categories of both skill set and mind set. Regarding skill sets, the best people for the job are sufficiently tech-savvy and excellent communicators. They also most often have a few indispensable work habits: they're organized, they're able to prioritize their tasks, and they manage their time effectively. In addition, it helps if they're good at problem-solving and troubleshooting on their own. Ideally, they also have previous experience working remotely.

As for mind set, it's essential that they be proactive. They must also have team-focused work ethics in being reliable, results-oriented, and highly responsive. And they need to be good team players in that they are pleasant, collaborative, supportive, and receptive to feedback.

Top Remote-Worker Traits

The best remote workers:

SKILL SET

- are tech-savvy (both their skill set and their equipment);
- are excellent communicators;
- have good work habits: they're organized, and they prioritize and manage time effectively;

- are good at problem-solving/troubleshooting;
- have previous experience working remotely;

MIND SET

- are proactive: they're independent/self-starters;
- have team-focused work ethics: they're reliable, results-oriented, and highly responsive; and
- are good team players: they're pleasant, collaborative, supportive, and receptive to feedback.

So let's take these one at a time. (In the *Interviewing* section to follow, we'll look at ways to confirm that candidates have all the preferred skills and traits.)

To start, it's important that a worker be sufficiently tech-savvy for the position. While some might think for some industries that could amount to just decent skills with phone and email, note that any position that calls for some level of team spirit greatly benefits from face time. As such, a remote worker with minimal video chat facility could prove to be a drag on the team as a whole. The two worst scenarios cited in my interviews concerned team members who were hesitant to use video or who demonstrated a lack of professionalism when they did. Also, video isn't just highly preferred in active dialogue; some organizations keep the screens on all day just to help the team feel more connected in general—even if they're all just working on separate tasks.

It's also crucial that the worker have solid writing and communication skills. Since much of remote interaction is done via email and instant messaging, a lesser writer can slow down the whole team—whereas a skilled one keeps the lines of communication flowing freely.

There are many good work habits that are ideal in a candidate, but three in particular are important for remote hires. First, they need to be organized. Most on-site offices are designed for organizational efficiency, so remote workers need to be able to assert a similar efficiency in their preferred workspaces. Second, they must be able to prioritize their activities, which applies as much to which work tasks to do first as it does to prioritizing work over non-work distractions. And third, it's crucial that they have excellent time-management skills—in part because meeting deadlines is even more important for remote workers than for those on-site. Why more important? Because everyone needs to know the work is getting done.

The final two skill set items, though not required for all organizations, are important to some. For many it's highly preferable that team members can troubleshoot on their own—at least in the moment. According to Siofra Pratt, writing for SocialTalent: "Great remote workers are also great problem-solvers/troubleshooters. They have an inbuilt initiative to seek the answer to any problems they face and are comfortable doing so. That said, they also know when it's more efficient to troubleshoot on their own and when it's necessary to seek the assistance of someone else."[5] Other sources particularly name the ability to be decisive when called for—such as when a choice needs to be made before the rest of the team is available to weigh in.

As for the mind set category, the most commonly referenced ideal trait is that the candidate be proactive, an "independent" "self-starter."

> **I want people who don't need to be led. That means self-starters who are accountable. I'd rather have the right kind of person than the right kind of résumé. I'll take people who aren't a fit skill-wise as long as I know that they'll fit the culture—and that they'll attack whatever problem I'm hiring them for.**
>
> —Jeremy Stanton, SVP of engineering, Amino Payments[6]

> **Find people who don't need a lot of day-to-day handholding, who are self-motivated, and who will know when to reach out and ask for help versus when they need to figure things out on their own.**
>
> —Carrie McKeegan, CEO, Greenback Expat Tax Services[7]

In a post on Chargify's Bullring Blog, Lance Walley notes that it's not enough for motivated self-starters to be "doers"; they also need to be "finishers"[8]—proof of which you might want to tease out in an interview. Regardless, keep in mind that in most cases a self-starter still needs to be brought onboard properly, not left to sink or swim. (We address onboarding later on.)

The remaining mind set items concern the team dynamic. And though they are characteristics essential to members of any highly functioning team, they are all the more important when even just one member of that team works remotely. Ideal hires will have team-focused work ethics: that means they're reliable, results-oriented, and responsive to communication. And, on the interpersonal level, top candidates are also good team players: they're pleasant to be around (at the least), happy to work collaboratively, supportive of other team members, and receptive to feedback.

As noted in the previous chapter, the Remote.co website shares the answers to a variety of questions posed to 135 remote-friendly companies —meaning they are either partially or fully distributed. When it comes to hiring remote workers, many companies emphasize the importance of a candidate having experience working remotely, for reasons of both efficiency and temperament. Yet some companies prioritize cultural fit. For example, product design studio Melewi cites "values and attitude fit" as more important than particular skills, for which they're happy to offer training. Developer staffing agency X-Team says: "For us, the time investment of training them is worthwhile compared to hiring people who aren't extraordinary but have remote experience. Just remember to have patience and allow people without experience the opportunity to fail and pick themselves back up a few times."[9] AirTreks, a multi-stop travel planning service provider, offers specifics on the HR angle of this. "We added more steps to our hiring process: core value panels, reference checks for specific people, and questions to screen for harmony-breakers."[10] Regardless, many companies recommend a trial period as beneficial for both employer and candidate.

Feedback from the Trenches: Fears About Hiring Remote Workers

Even with a stringent hiring process, some companies may still worry that hiring remote workers is a risky venture. But take heart: of the entire panel of 135 remote-friendly companies in Remote.co's extensive Q&A section, the consensus was positive. And as for the biggest hiring fears . . .

Managed WordPress solutions provider Pagely notes: "Not being able to meet some people in person means we have to rely more on references and our gut to gauge a potential hire." And yet, "the fear of hiring a crook or a fraud has not come true." (This from digital strategist Rod Austin.)

Working Solutions is a remote-worker staffing agency. Most of its clients "fear a lack of productivity, or lack of communication or engagement" in a remote hire. But as it turns out, very few placements didn't work out—over a period of nearly twenty years. Talent management VP Kristin Kanger attributes that happy result to the fact that their "team members value the benefits they receive working remotely."[11]

Of course, this isn't to say that every hire of those 135 companies worked out. But they were all able to find a recruitment approach that suited their particular needs. In a later sidebar we'll cover guidelines for hiring for short-term gigs. Such can be a great way to help determine what recruitment and hiring strategy would work best for you.

THOUGH WE'VE covered the most commonly identified traits sought in remote workers—according to nearly one hundred sources[12]—there's still more we can say to round out the ideal hire.

Another angle on the highly favored trait of self-motivation is the passion that candidates bring to the work. Retrium CEO David Horowitz shares how "people who are passionate, even if they have slightly fewer technical skills, will be better fit for your company than people who are technically brilliant but who think of the work as just a job. I would hire the former over the latter any day."[13] Indeed, it's those passionate about the work who finish the projects they start—and who bring a contagious optimism to boot. (Note that in advocating such dedication David does not lessen the importance of candidates being tech-savvy; he simply referenced "slightly" less than "technically brilliant.")

In that same Bullring Blog post noted above—titled "Hiring *&* Firing for Small Business Success"—Lance Walley applies his twenty-five years working in nine small businesses to identifying additional traits to look for—as well as veer away from—when hiring for "smaller" teams (namely, teams with no more than seventy-five workers). To the passionate category he adds that ideal candidates don't just continue to expand their skill sets to remain competitive; they further their personal development because they *genuinely enjoy learning.* That sort of person brings another necessary element: a positive rather than negative mind set, which goes hand in hand with being an optimist rather than a pessimist. This is because someone who believes there's an effective solution to be found adds creativity and productivity to the team effort, whereas the risk-fearing pessimist shoots down suggestions before giving them fair consideration. This isn't to say seek out Pollyannas for your workforce; this is to say seek out those curious to see what's behind closed doors—rather than those inclined to close open ones.

Lance rounds out his advice with two caveats. First, treat people well. Second: "You can form a great team, but that team needs leadership and alignment if they're going to do great work."[14] We cover leadership and alignment in the chapters to come; first, let's form a great team.

Hiring and Time Zones

If the work you're hiring for calls for a fair amount of either real-time interaction or nearly synchronous feedback—meaning team members needing to rely on input and assignments from other team members—one additional hiring criterion could be choosing someone in the same time zone as those teammates, or at least someone with a considerable overlap of work hours.

As management consultant Johanna Rothman notes: "Geographically distributed teams were originally set up for saving money. The teams were usually set up from West to East, meaning the testers were East, and the developers were West. But this is the wrong way to 'follow the sun,' especially if you're doing product development."

If we organize a team well, we can instead "follow the sun." For example, at the end of a workday, a team in Hanoi can pass a task over to a colleague in the London office to review. The London colleague would then pass the reviewed task to the team in California to implement. By the time the team in Hanoi begins their next workday, the task has gone full circle back to them, ready for the next phase.

While this might seem like an ideal scenario, the truth is that the cycle is usually not so clean. If the team in Hanoi has questions that only the team in California can answer—a rather likely occurrence—they would have to wait a full day for feedback. Enough instances like that could really slow down the long-term schedule. The travel-planning provider AirTreks found that "important meetings were not happening" as a result of their time zone conflicts.[15]

To address this, some remote teams are now experimenting with instead organizing themselves from North to South: meaning they're in the same time zone, regardless of the actual distance between them. And so they're able to maintain a reliable project schedule as well as, consequently, reliable quality. In the end, companies can still save money by offshoring—they just do so without having to compromise schedule or quality.

Interviewing: How to Screen for Desirable Traits

> *"Remote work isn't a fit for everyone. One of the biggest keys to a successful remote team is accurately identifying talent who will excel in a remote environment."*
>
> —Kate Harvey, *content & search marketing manager, Chargify*[16]

So how do you "accurately identify" the best talent? Armed with a clear picture of exactly what you need, you craft an interview to help you assess as well as possible how the candidate would fare on the job—down to replicating the remote communication that team members employ every day.

For example, as manager/owner Derek Scruggs shares:

> **There are a lot of little things to look for when hiring remote workers. Let's say you're trying to schedule a time to meet. Are they mindful of the time zone? Do they show up on time? Are they comfortable with video? These things are indicators of whether or not they're used to working remotely.**[17]

CEO Carrie McKeegan agrees:

> **In the beginning, I definitely took for granted a lot of the tech skills that our team has gathered from working remotely. Plus, we didn't know to probe that with candidates as much as we do now. Now, I interview using video, which helps me get a sense of a person's professionalism. I've interviewed people who don't realize there's inappropriate stuff in the background, or that there are kids screaming and running around behind them. These things make it clear to me that they don't know what it takes to work virtually.**[18]

The main point is that every new job can be a steep learning curve for new hires; you'll simply want to ensure they've got the "how to work remotely" part down already.

Similarly, since communication is so vital in any team, Zingword cofounder Robert Rogge recommends that the hiring process involve tests to ensure a candidate can communicate well at the level appropriate for the position. That means interviewing people using the full variety of different mediums (email, video, apps) that you commonly use at your company. You'll want to know from the get-go how fluidly they'll blend with your team's established lines of communication.

I do this myself when hiring someone. Before I talk to job applicants in person, I ask them to make a five-minute video answering a few questions. Those videos tell me more than half of what I need to know about how they'd fare on the job.

FEEDBACK FROM THE TRENCHES: ***"How Do You Conduct Interviews for Remote Jobs?"***

Eighty-five remote-friendly companies responded to Remote.co's question "How do you conduct interviews for remote jobs?"[19] In brief, via the same methods as for on-site positions: telephone, written answers, and real-time interviews. The only difference is the interviews are conducted by video rather than in person. To follow is a chart collecting the various replies.

"How do you conduct interviews for remote jobs?"

%*	REPLIES
84	REAL-TIME, TWO-WAY VIDEO CALL INTERVIEWS
31	WRITTEN QUESTIONS OR EXERCISES
28	MULTIPLE VIDEO INTERVIEWS
27	IN-PERSON INTERVIEW
25	TELEPHONE
14	PAID TRIAL PERIOD
14	VETTED BY HR/RECRUITMENT MANAGER
5	TEXT CHAT
4	TEAM TAKES NOTES IN SHARED DOC
2	CANDIDATE VIDEO RECORDS ANSWERS TO INTERVIEW QUESTIONS

*NOTE: SINCE A COMPANY MIGHT EMPLOY MORE THAN ONE LISTED METHOD, THE PERCENTAGES DON'T TOTAL 100.

Companies with established remote workers can enlist them to help develop questions to tease out how well a candidate would work remotely. For example, "What are your favorite tools?" (or even the more esoteric prompt, "Describe how you work out loud") could easily trip up those pretending to have more experience than they do. Similarly, the level of detail conveyed in the answers to "What are your favorite and least favorite things about working remotely?" could be very revealing. Also, questions like "What do you do to address loneliness?"—stated as though the topic is a given—could be very informative. The point is to draw out a level of detail that demonstrates both previous experience and personal feelings about the remote lifestyle. Plus, having a strong sense of what your best workers would answer to such questions could greatly help you identify excellent additions to your team. (Several such questions appear in the "Cheat Sheet: What to

Look For When Interviewing Remote Workers" in the Part III EXTRAS just following this chapter.)

> **The more you know about work style up front, the more successful the hire will be.**
>
> —Sheila Murphy, cofounder/partner, FlexProfessionals, LLC[20]

Hiring for Short-Term Gigs

The "Feedback from the Trenches: Fears About Hiring Remote Workers" sidebar earlier in this chapter highlights a common fear concerning hiring a "worker in the void." For example:

> **I think my biggest fears are when we lose touch with someone. Every once in a while, someone will just "disappear"—they don't answer emails, phone calls, or other contact. In those instances I'm left wondering, "Are they dead, or just flaky?"**
>
> —Ann MacDonald, director of content strategy, Love to Know[21]

One way to help determine what recruitment and hiring strategy would work best for you is to practice by hiring for short-term gigs. For example, you might:

- Interview via video, during which you'd discuss your expectations.
- For those candidates you take on, send a written confirmation on what was agreed to: the work to be done, by when, and how it is to be submitted. Most important: specify what level of communication you're looking for, both in terms of response time to inquiries as well as status updates and the like.
- Provide whatever documents, links, guidelines, contacts, or other information needed to complete the job.
- A few days before the first deadline, check in to see how the project is faring. (The benefit of this step is twofold: you alleviate your fears

by proactively requesting the assurance you seek, and you convey that you're on top of your game—and expect your freelancers to be on top of theirs.)

- Give constructive feedback.

If your industry doesn't immediately lend itself to obvious short-term work, try coming up with a few finite tasks to hire for, such as writing a newsletter, designing a small marketing campaign, transcribing a recording, conducting research, or facilitating a meeting.

Onboarding: Set Them Up to Succeed

"Having a well-planned onboarding process is crucial. The process should be visible and transparent to everyone."

—Jeremy Stanton, *SVP of engineering, Amino Payments*[22]

The value of having a deliberate hiring strategy extends to the onboarding process as well. Following an established plan during the ramping-up phase eliminates as much risk and uncertainty as possible, while also enabling a smooth and productive transition. Most important, an effective onboarding process will both clarify what you expect of new hires and help them integrate into the organization.

Now, some might consider that a no-brainer, but in fact many companies don't have an onboarding plan. As Jeremy Stanton puts it: "Onboarding is where a lot of companies drop the ball. They figure, 'We interviewed and now, we hope this person works out.' And then there's no follow-up."[23] This is not a recipe for success.

For example, years ago I got hired at a company in the Netherlands. (Though this concerns an on-site position, it's applicable nonetheless.) On the first day, the entirety of my instruction amounted to showing me to my computer station—which lacked both a chair and a monitor. No one gave me any direction; I was left to figure out the rest for myself. Now, this was not a welcome that inspired me to immediately tackle what I was hired for—

so imagine how even less inspiring a similar treatment would be in a remote scenario.

Jessie Shternshus, owner and founder at Improv Effect, takes the long view for every new hire: "When onboarding new people, think about the value proposition you offered to get this person to come work for you. How can you make that come to life the second the gig starts? Or even before it starts?"[24] How indeed.

A deliberate onboarding strategy gets your newest members integrated into the team and contributing as soon as possible. To do that we want to:

- offer a thoughtful and generous welcome;
- ensure they have the chance to get to know the team, who should extend that welcome;
- provide them with what they need to learn about the company; and
- set expectations.

First, as self-employed creative collaboration agent Yves Hanoulle puts it: "Make people feel WELCOME. You hired them because you thought they were a good fit for the job. Invest the energy to introduce them to their colleagues and show them where everything is. A surprising number of companies don't do this."[25] The most salient angle on this advice concerns first impressions. Most new hires won't know entirely what to expect, and so their first impressions could be lasting. Help them feel good about the job; make them want to be a part of your mission.

Next, INTRODUCE them to their new team members, who should also extend the welcome. Agile coach Ralph van Roosmalen, who simultaneously manages teams in three countries, recommends assigning buddies to new employees to help them get oriented. Web-development company Automattic does this as well; they "pair people with a mentor in [the same] time zone when they first join, so they have a designated person to chat with if they have questions about how we operate, or if they just want to chat."[26] Similarly, each new scientist at NASA is assigned a member of support staff so they know who to turn to. Web-application consulting team Bitovi goes even further: "We've learned that the ideal time to onboard a new hire is right before a company-wide event, so they can meet the entire team in person in the first month or two. We constantly get feedback that the company events are the clincher to making someone new instantly feel like part of the team."[27]

Next, INFORM them: provide them with the materials they'll need to learn about your culture and processes, perhaps compiled into a welcome document. Note, though, that such should be crafted as part of the welcome; generic information found on the company website won't feel personalized—and won't inspire immediate contribution.

And finally, most new hires aren't likely to jump in full force; they'll often wait for your cue. So be sure to SPECIFY precisely what is expected of them, and when, and to whom they can turn for additional guidance. A worker who feels stranded—like I did in that Netherlands office park—won't start off with sure footing.

For example, I am the remote team manager at Happy Melly, a global professional happiness association. We give new employees a task list to work through in their first two weeks, including such items as setting up virtual coffee sessions with team members, getting access to the Google Drive folder, and learning how to send invoices. By providing clear expectations—as well as the means via which to fulfill them—you set up the new hire to succeed. And since clear expectations are essentially measurable goals, they also help readily identify whether the recruits have both the aptitude and the attitude desired for that position—which helps determine sooner rather than later if they're a good fit or not.

An additional angle concerns having the onboarding process be a team effort. For this the Happy Melly team uses a Trello board (see figure to follow) to which anyone on the team can contribute. Trainees are added to the Trello board—and they, together with the team, ensure the onboarding process is completed. A team effort is important because a new employee isn't just an additional worker; when somebody joins a team, that team basically becomes a new team. The members' collected skills and personalities make up a new combination, one that everyone needs to adjust to.

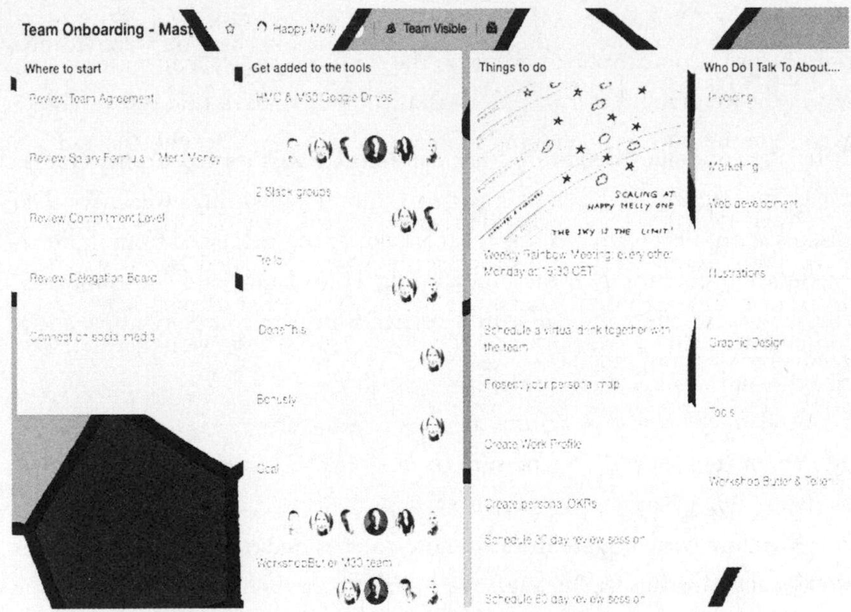

Sample Happy Melly Trello board for onboarding new hires (Happy Melly)

Offboarding

As it happens, the other side of hiring—when someone leaves the team—calls for much of the same process in reverse. This is because a team minus one becomes a new team, which will also require some adjustment. And just like having a plan for onboarding, it's wise to have a plan for offboarding as well. For these occasions Happy Melly follows their Team Farewell Process, which is enacted both just before and after a member leaves.

Before the departure, the team organizes the handover of responsibilities, plans a goodbye party, and arranges a gift. There is also an exit interview, which in Happy Melly style is a Farewell Chat. In a recorded video conversation, a few team members ask questions along the following lines:

- "What did you like most/least about working with us?"
- "What processes did you like most/least?"

- "What aspects of our work culture could be expanded or improved upon?"
- "What will you be gaining in your new situation that you weren't finding here?"

After the colleague's departure, that Farewell Chat is posted to our Google Drive, and the rest of the team is assigned to watch it within a week. We then discuss at our next team meeting what lessons are to be learned from it. Finally, the team goes through the Onboarding Trello board and "un-onboards" the person, in effect removing him or her from the company apps, social media profiles, and the like.

We close with a quote from Remote.co, this one from their Companies Q&A page, which asks: "What is the hardest part about managing a remote workforce?" Fog Creek Software's Allie Schwartz, VP of people & operations, responded: "Managing a remote work force isn't terribly hard as long as your rapport with your remote employees is strong. Doing the initial work during onboarding . . . to build trust amongst employees and managers goes a long way toward making remote management simple."[28]

Remote Reminders

HIRING

- Craft a deliberate hiring strategy that specifies both your priorities and the resources required to fulfill those priorities.
- Remember that ideal hires are often proactive communicators who are sufficiently tech-savvy and passionate about the work.

INTERVIEWING

- Go into the interview with a clear sense of everything you need the candidate to excel at.
- Interview applicants using the variety of different mediums (email, video, apps) that you commonly use at your company.

ONBOARDING

- A well-planned, transparent onboarding process can help new hires integrate, which gets them contributing as soon as possible.
- That process calls for offering a thoughtful, generous welcome, clearly communicating expectations, and ensuring new hires have the opportunity to both get to know the team and learn about the company.
- Since each team member makes a unique contribution to the team, both arrivals and departures call for group participation in adjusting to the change.

PART III *Extras*

HIRING CHEAT SHEET

What to Look For When Interviewing Remote Workers

PLUS SAMPLE QUESTIONS FOR ASSESSING CANDIDATES

TECH-SAVVYNESS

You'll want candidates to have:

- a great internet connection with no dropping out;
- a high-quality microphone—you can hear them well;
- good speakers—they can hear you well;
- an appropriate space for video calls; and
- facility with the equipment and protocols concerning online apps, video conferencing, and instant messaging.

EXCELLENT COMMUNICATION SKILLS

- Look for admirable responses to all application-relevant communication, both verbal (phone and video) and written (cover letter, emails, texts, IM)—as well as to any assignments, as appropriate.

GOOD WORK HABITS

You'll want to assess their:

- ORGANIZATIONAL SKILLS—for which you could prompt: "Describe your workspace." "How do you normally start your workday? What determines your first task or activity?"

- TASK-MANAGEMENT SKILLS—for which you could ask: "What task- or project-management tools have you used? Which do you prefer and why?"
- PRIORITIZING/TIME-MANAGEMENT STRATEGIES. For this you might present a jumbled list of daily or weekly tasks and ask in what order the candidate would tackle them and why.

PROBLEM-SOLVING/TROUBLESHOOTING SKILLS

- I personally like describing a tricky scenario and asking candidates how they'd go about solving it. Or I might assign a quandary to solve after the interview, requesting they get back to me describing their process. Similarly, the *Entrepreneur on Fire* podcast asks all its guests, "If you woke up tomorrow morning, and you still possessed all the experience and knowledge you currently have—but your business had completely disappeared, forcing you to start somewhere, anywhere, from scratch—what would you do?"[1] This question provides a sense of how each entrepreneur guest thinks; a comparable question targeted to your industry could produce some illuminating answers.
- Ask candidates to complete a very small project. For example, a programmer could write a short program; a marketer could create a newsletter; a virtual assistant could organize and assign tasks in a project list. How well they fare on this assignment would give you a glimpse of how well they'd fare for you across the board.

PREVIOUS EXPERIENCE WORKING REMOTELY

Some possible questions include:

- "What do you like most and least about working remotely?"
- "What do you do to address loneliness?"
- "What's meaningful to you about working remotely?" (For some this question can flush out a situational motivation—like "spending my commute time with my family"—that would underlie a candidate's dedication to making the position work. For others, this or a similar question could identify if the candidate has worked remotely long enough to have somewhat philosophical thoughts on the subject.)

INDEPENDENCE: PROACTIVE/SELF-MOTIVATED

Some considerations include:

- Work history: Upward movement within or across companies? Rehired by former bosses?
- Outside interests? Long-term pursuits? Personal development?
- Preferred tricks to staying motivated.
- Examples of resiliency in response to setbacks or hardship.

GOOD TEAM PLAYER/INTERPERSONAL GOOD FIT

You'll want the candidate to:

- be pleasant to interact with;
- demonstrate a collaborative, supportive nature; and
- demonstrate productive receptivity to feedback.

Possible questions include:

- "Describe the last misunderstanding you had with a coworker and how you handled it."
- "What do people like most about working with you? What annoys people about working with you?"

TEAM-FOCUSED WORK ETHICS

Possible questions include:

- "Are you willing to make work visible to others?" "Describe how you work out loud." "Are you amenable to other approaches?"
- "What do you think email is best for? What other tools do you use to communicate different work-related information?"

And, finally, note if the candidate

- responds quickly in all aspects concerning the application and interview process.

REMOTE-ONLY MANIFESTO

The following is excerpted from GitLab's Remote-Only Manifesto at https://remoteonly.org.[1]

REMOTE-ONLY WORK PROMOTES:

- HIRING AND WORKING FROM ALL OVER THE WORLD
  instead of from a central location.
- FLEXIBLE WORKING HOURS
  over set working hours.
- WRITING DOWN AND RECORDING KNOWLEDGE
  over verbal explanations.
- WRITTEN-DOWN PROCESSES
  over on-the-job training.
- PUBLIC SHARING OF INFORMATION
  over need-to-know access.
- OPENING EVERY DOCUMENT TO CHANGE BY ANYONE
  over top-down control of documents.
- ASYNCHRONOUS COMMUNICATION
  over synchronous communication.
- THE RESULTS OF WORK
  over the hours put in.
- FORMAL COMMUNICATION CHANNELS
  over informal communication channels.

While there is sometimes value in the "instead of" items, we have come to value the remote-only items more.

WHAT REMOTE-ONLY IS NOT

- As the name says, it is more than remote-friendly; it is remote-only. There is no main office or headquarters with multiple people.
- It does not mean working independently of each other. Remote-only workers work together and communicate intensely—they just do so remotely.
- Neither is it a substitute for human interaction. Coworkers still need to collaborate, have conversations, and feel part of a team.
- It is not an example of offshoring. There is no shore to hire off from. It is simply hiring from around the world.
- It is not a management paradigm. It is a normal hierarchical organization—just one that focuses on output instead of input.

HOW REMOTE-ONLY CHANGES THE ORGANIZATION

- Knowledge is written down instead of conveyed verbally.
- As a result there are shorter and fewer meetings.
- Since knowledge is documented, most communication is asynchronous rather than real-time, and more often official than informal.
- More documented knowledge allows for fewer interruptions and less on-the-job training.
- There is more transparency within and outside the organization.
- Everything is public by default.

DISADVANTAGES FOR THE ORGANIZATION

- It scares some investors. It scares some partners. It scares some customers.
- It scares some potential employees, mostly senior non-technical hires.
- Onboarding may be harder; for some the first month can feel lonely.

ADVANTAGES FOR THE WORLD

- Reduced environmental impact from no commuting.
- Reduced environmental impact from less office space.
- Reduced inequality from bringing better-paying jobs to lower-cost regions.

"To me, [it's not about] 'managing,' because if you try to manage and control people, you'll inevitably fail to build a strong remote team. . . . [It's about empowering] people to manage themselves, and also give them a sense of unity and connection to the team as a whole. When people are feeling positive and excited, things tend to take care of themselves."

—JON LAY, *founder, Hanno*[1]

PART IV

SUCCESSFUL REMOTE TEAMS 201

Managing Remote Workers and Teams

"A lot of managers are asked to manage remote teams with a sink-or-swim mentality. We need to train managers how to work with *remote teams. How will you collaborate? How will you build trust? You have to become more of a leader and less of a manager. There's a big difference between those two things. Instead of micromanaging, you have to set up your team for success."*

—PHIL MONTERO, *systems engineer, The Garam Group, LLC*[2]

Not surprisingly, the remote team manager's to-do list is rather extensive. Namely: ensure team members have (access to) all the knowledge, tools, training, processes, and cohesion they need to fulfill their agreed-to roles and obligations. As it happens, it's difficult to separate such a complex agenda into distinct sections organized by topic. Instead, the material is organized into the two stages of the development process.

The next two chapters cover what's called for in the planning stage:

- CHAPTER 7: Commit to providing strong, empathic, flexible leadership from a mind set of both trust in team members and belief that remote teams can succeed. Ensure team members have (access to) high-quality tools and equipment.

- CHAPTER 8: Facilitate that success, which calls for alignment throughout. First up, explore what solutions might be best for your particular personnel, objectives, and circumstances.

The last two chapters cover what's called for in the acting stage:

- CHAPTER 9: Engage the team in collectively deciding what tools, processes, and protocols to use; then document in a team agreement the expectations and etiquette of the work culture.
- CHAPTER 10: Bring it all together by running effective meetings, expressing thanks and celebrating success, and strengthening your relationship with each team member. Finally, experiment with small, reversible steps.

As is the case throughout this book, each chapter closes with a list of Remote Reminders that sum up the chapter's contents. In the Part IV EXTRAS, you'll find additional materials to help you put it all into practice, including a template for crafting a remote team agreement and tips for online meetings—plus a Manager's Action Plan that brings together the separate action items from these chapters. (This action plan is devised to guide both those already committed to remote working as well as those still deciding if it's a viable route to pursue—especially since the process of becoming remote-first will strengthen every team, even if you remain 100 percent colocated.)

If you're ready to get going, feel free to skip ahead to chapter 9. (The extra-ready could even jump to the Manager's Action Plan—and then later circle back to particular chapters as appropriate.) Or, if you prefer the slower, more thoughtful route, proceed with chapter 7.

Let's get started.

CHAPTER 7

Commit and Lead, Trust and Succeed

"Essentially, what managers should do is inspire people to use the tools at their disposal to take ownership and responsibility for their work."

—LUIS SUAREZ, *digital transformation and data analytics adviser, panagenda*[1]

As "an entrepreneur managing virtual teams, I need to be empathetic, emotionally intelligent, sensitive to what others need, and willing and able to provide whatever tools are necessary for success." In addition, "I must . . . be self-aware—in tune with my skills, capabilities, strengths, and weaknesses."

—MEGHAN M. BIRO, *"Telecommuting Is the Future of Work,"* Forbes[2]

As stated elsewhere in this book, successful remote working results from a finely tuned, consciously chosen combination of skill set, mind set, and tool set. But note that what remote teams need most from their managers concerns mind set. For a remote team to succeed, its manager must both believe that remote teams can succeed and trust that each member will come through as expected. (Again, "remote team" refers to a team with even just one remote worker. This is because the most effective remote teams function as though all its members were remote—even if only one member works off-site.)

For anyone reading this who hasn't fully embraced either that belief or that trust, then know two things: you're in good company; and many, many teams and organizations, whose achievements you'd be proud to match, can wholeheartedly attest that remote teams can be eminently successful. Indeed, such speaks to the entire purpose of this book: to convey the full landscape of the virtual working world—including the various concerns and pitfalls one might encounter—and to provide the map for getting you where you want to go, with solutions for whatever obstacles you find along the way. In the end, it's really up to you. Trust that it's possible by making it possible.

So how can we do that? With fresh perspective, mutual agreement, and creative implementation of technology and tools.

THE BELIEF ANGLE

For example, consider a primary concern: the question of how remote workers could be as productive and reliable as those operating on-site. (Set aside for the moment the concern about distraction or laziness; we'll come to that soon enough. This is just about sheer capacity for productivity.) To do that, let's look at some of the ways working on-site facilitates productivity and reliability—and then consider how such might be replicated online.

When you think about it, that on-site benefit really comes down to just a few points. One, access to coworkers facilitates efficiency in both individual tasks and in the collaboration required for group objectives. Two, proximity within a worksite facilitates quick and easy sharing of vital information. And three, the visibility of working together in the same location cultivates a sense of personal accountability: namely, seeing others follow through on their commitment to the shared mission encourages everyone else to demonstrate their dedication in turn.

These vital benefits can all be effectively replicated online. One, questions can still be asked, via phone or the typed word; files can still be shared. When you add to the mix workers' individual commitment to being accessible during all work hours, physical distance is no longer a factor. Two, online meetings can be as effective as in-person ones—in some cases more so, depending on the size of the group and the task at hand, be that updating and reporting or planning and brainstorming. All that's called for is implementing the necessary technology—in conjunction with establishing protocols around communication and documentation. As for the accountability angle, the solution is to find different ways of conveying that team-friendly "I'm working" message. Some of that gets established in the back-and-forth communication of a productive day's work. The remainder comes from a team agreeing to demonstrate their commitment by making their work visible to others. (We'll revisit this when we discuss the trust angle.) It's all very doable, and it can be done well. As coach and entrepreneur AgileBill Krebs notes: we just need to "take the time to learn new ways of working. It's only strange until we get used to it."[3]

I believe teams can work together online as effectively as they do in person. My interviews with remote team members and leaders have elucidated the many ways motivated virtual teams are mastering this ever-improving means of working. Of course, different approaches work for different setups and situations. The common denominator for everyone, though, is ensuring that it's easy to communicate with each other—as easy as leaning over to talk to the person at the next desk. This calls for high-quality internet and equipment. The simple fact is: the easier it is for teams to connect, the more they will do it.

THE BELIEF SOLUTION: *Ensure They Have the Tools They Need*

Step one is ensuring that workers have the tools they need to fulfill their obligations. But note that views differ concerning exactly what a company should provide and what workers should cover themselves. For example, many fully distributed teams supply employees with just software and apps; they expect employees to supply their own equipment. Other companies might also contribute computers, headsets, smartphones, and the like. The point isn't to say all employers should provide the tools discussed here; it's to say: all partially distributed employers should maintain high-quality technology and tools on-site—and would be wise to ensure that all remote team members have comparable equipment and software, regardless of exactly who purchases what.

The Basic Tech Tool Set

> *"Bandwidth is like oxygen. It should always be in plentiful supply. It is one of the critical pillars for remote working."*
>
> —MAARTEN KOOPMANS, *owner, physicist, team lead, and software developer, Vrijhed.net*[4]

In many companies, the tools employed are limited to what the IT department has approved. If you're suspiciously eyeing that old spider phone on your conference room table, you're right to do so. Technology has come a long way in just the last decade.

To work well together online, everyone needs: an effective computer, fast internet, a headset, a webcam, and a reliable video conferencing tool. To follow, let's expand on a few points.

INVEST IN GREAT INTERNET AND ACCESSORIES. This one is pretty straightforward. If our connection is unstable, or we're using low-quality equipment, communicating with colleagues becomes frustrating and annoying. We want crystal clear, high-bandwidth communication on our remote teams. In order to have that, we need great internet, and high-quality accessory tools.

MINIMIZE BACKGROUND NOISE. Even if we have a fast internet connection, background noise can distract everyone in the call. And as much as you don't want to hear a rowdy crowd at a remote worker's local café, note that the background chatter of an open office space is equally detracting. So make sure on-site employees have access to quiet spaces, both for individual calls and for larger video meetings.

EMBRACE VIDEO—AND DO IT RIGHT. Because non-verbal communication is a big part of our interactions, it's important to turn on the webcams. According to a 2017 global Polycom Inc. survey, 92 percent of 24,000-plus respondents believe that video collaboration technology helps improve relationships and fosters better teamwork.[5] Simply put, using video improves our communication, our productivity, and our team building—exponentially.

When you use video, there's a positive feedback cycle where you're more engaged because you're seeing my facial gestures, my movement, my energy, my passion. I'm communicating with you as you were designed to be communicated with.

—Nick Timmons, director of sales, Personify Inc.[6]

Those who have reservations about video probably haven't used it extensively enough. Because the fact of the matter is that once you've used it it's hard to go back. And yes, it takes some preparation. But it takes preparation to dress up and come to the office too. People like to hide. We're lazy and we like to hide behind slides or audio. But if we give in to that laziness in refusing video, we risk damaging long-term effectiveness and connectedness.

—Sumant Kowshik, VP product, Personify Inc.[7]

One caveat is that to utilize video well we have to pay attention to the details of lighting and background. It's all too easy in video calls to be backlit, or to have our faces in the shadows—and science has shown that when video lighting is poor, the conversation is less engaging. Citing *The Journal of Neuroscience*, the Zoom blog states: "In video conferencing, you are appearing in front of a camera, just like being on film. Before anything else you do, the lighting in your scenery has already chosen how your meeting will perform."[8] In brief: the more we can see each other, the better.

Another concern is background. If your background is messy, or busy with people walking back and forth, it can be a distraction. Chapter 3 notes the importance of remote workers having a professional setup for video. We need to do the same in the workplace as well.

There are a few last points to consider. We need to ensure employees are trained in how to use these tools effectively, and that they take the time to get savvy with them. Software changes the way we work; we need time to play with it to learn its ins and outs. Systems engineer Phil Montero calls this "sandbox time," and recommends the play be on non-work-related tasks.

NASA's Ricky Guest concurs: "We are constantly looking at new ways of helping our teams communicate remotely. But when we find something, we don't just give them software or hardware and say, 'Go do your thing.' We help support and integrate these things into their everyday working life."[9] Jackson River CEO Alice Hendricks adds: "It's important to keep an eye on more than the methods or tools of communication. You need to actively steward the tempo, cadence, and quality of that communication" as well.[10]

Also, keep in mind that there is rarely one tool that will supply all your team's needs. Most teams use a handful of tools, especially as they grow and change. Plus, new tools are being developed all the time. It's in our best interest to keep on top of what will best help us achieve our objectives.

> **We don't stick to just one technology. We're always on the lookout for the latest and the newest to see how it suits our teams.**
>
> —Ricky Guest, senior audio/video specialist, Solar System Exploration Research Virtual Institute (NASA)[11]

> **Don't wait for the technology. Start today and experiment. Grow the tools into the team.**
>
> —Lucius Bobikiewicz, trainer for distributed Agile teams, SpreadScrum.com[12]

A final point concerns tech support. As CEO Ryan Baker notes: "Being your own tech support is a pain in the proverbial. . . . [So] we've made good relationships with the 'dial a tech' services in our areas."[13]

We'll discuss various technology options in the next chapter.

THE TRUST ANGLE

Next, regarding the concern about trusting remote employees to fulfill their obligations: various methods of monitoring software have been developed to help ease employers' fears of workers slacking on the job. But as mentioned in the "Some Thoughts on Monitoring Software" sidebar in chapter 2, the general consensus is that such practices do much more harm than good. What's needed instead is a change in mind set from time-based working to results-based working. As previously noted, results-oriented working calls for evaluating output rather than hours.

Part of that amended mind set involves adding the remote worker's motivation to the equation. If someone really wants the option to work from home a few days a week, one of the most common reasons people seek job flexibility, then it behooves that person to make the experience as seamless as possible for fellow coworkers—especially so the opportunity isn't revoked.

The good news is that employers don't need to offer sheer faith that remote workers will come through with what they commit to. You can allow them to earn your trust by demonstrating their reliability. This is where the results-oriented philosophy comes into play. As systems engineer Phil Montero puts it: "We build trust by having clear objectives, accountability, and deliverables."[14]

THE TRUST SOLUTION: *Let Them Demonstrate Reliability*

It just so happens that the practice of "working out loud" can double as a trusting agent as well. ***Working out loud*** is the act of making your work observable to others so as to keep remote team members apprised of each other's progress. To repeat a quote from chapter 4:

> **I could be working hard all day—but you won't know that unless I share it with you. But if my document is posted to an online space and you're seeing the updates, and you're seeing things get accomplished on a shared to-do list, then there's no question that I'm working, or what I'm working on.**
>
> —Phil Montero, systems engineer, The Garam Group LLC[15]

On remote teams there are many different ways to work out loud, including practices such as email updates and daily stand-ups, and using tools such as intranets and online apps. Some workers keep their instant messaging status updated so their colleagues always know what they're working on. Many teams record their meetings for team members who couldn't attend. Whatever the method, the idea of working out loud is to replicate online the benefit of on-site proximity.

> **Everyone on our team is very good about checking in and checking out using our group instant message system. You'll see messages throughout the day: "I'll be out for three hours." "I've got to take the car for maintenance." "I'll be back on tonight to make up the time." And nobody worries about checking it because we can see what's happening.**
>
> **On our Agile team, we make commitments on a daily basis. We decide the work for the week and individual team members commit to tasks to complete that work. We meet during our daily stand-ups and update each other on how we're doing and if we need any help. It's about making small trust deposits to the rest of the team.**
>
> —MARK KILBY, Agile coach, Sonatype[16]

Peter Hilton is a consultant at Signavio, a vendor of business process management software. At Signavio they work out loud using a communal task board (Jira), team-collaboration software (Confluence), and Slack. Peter considers working out loud so effective he finds no need for regularly scheduled status meetings with his clients. If clients ever want to know what's happening on a particular task, they simply log in to Jira to find out. That way they reserve their meeting time for more important concerns.

And Luis Suarez, a digital transformation and data analytics adviser, works out loud using social networks. He recommends:

> **Stop using email. Instead, use social networks to work out loud and be more transparent to your colleagues. We need to adopt the mentality of "the more I share, the more powerful I become." The interesting thing about working out loud through social networks is that you become more open, more transparent, and you give people more opportunities to trust you. *Working out loud isn't just for the sake of being social; it's being social for the sake of getting the job done.* When we become more transparent about what we do at work, we reduce the chance of friction. Leaders need to understand that social networks are not just another broadcast communication channel. They are a conversation. And conversation is a two-way street. Always! No excuses. That's why it's called *con*versation.**[17]

We'll say more about different ways of working out loud in both the *Bonding* section of chapter 8 and "Technology & Tools" in the RESOURCES section.

> *"Developing a high level of trust and collaboration with people who are half-around the world [is] a challenge, but it's possible—and as the various digital tools improve, so does our ability to collaborate."*
>
> —FELIX DUBINSKY, *cofounder, SimpleTexting*[18]

Remote Reminders

- For a remote team to succeed, its manager must both believe that remote teams can succeed and trust that each member will come through as expected.
- Make communicating easy. The easier it is for teams to connect, the more they will do it.
- Ensure everyone has high-quality internet, equipment, and training. Everyone should be savvy with the designated tools.
- Embrace video to facilitate high-bandwidth communication—and use it effectively. Minimize background noise and distracting visuals; maximize good lighting.
- Make sure you have backup tools should the first fail.
- Continuously try new things. Experiment with new processes and tools to see what might suit you.
- Give remote workers the opportunity to earn your trust by demonstrating their reliability.
- In return, do the same for them: work out loud; make your work observable to others.

CHAPTER 8

Facilitate Their Success with Leadership, Alignment, and a Full Arsenal

"You can form a great team, but that team needs leadership and alignment if they're going to do great work."

—Lance Walley, *CEO, Chargify*

What does "leadership and alignment" mean exactly? Lance Walley elaborates on his point as it relates to his company, Chargify.

> **Long ago, we had a list of software development tasks that needed to get done. The tasks had no priority. The development team members could pick whatever they wanted. We thought this offered freedom and choice, but it did not work. The team wanted a team lead or product manager to decide priorities, so they could focus on doing instead of deciding.**
>
> **More recently, we started working on alignment throughout the company. It's harder than it sounds, but it makes a lot of sense: decide who our core customer is and what our company values are, and then make decisions around those ideas. And make sure everyone is aligned around these values and decisions.**
>
> **A great team, aligned around the same goals, does great work.**[1]

What Lance describes in the above quote basically spells out the road ahead. And, indeed, it's harder than it sounds. But fortunately we can be thoughtful and systematic in our approach—and then proceed by experimenting with small, reversible steps.

We return to the discussion of how to replicate in the virtual realm the benefits of the on-site realm. As it happens, many of the solutions available to remote teams can address more than one essential aspect of successful teamwork. In the sidebar to follow, those essential aspects are presented as a group of "truisms" first, along with a nutshell of possible solutions. Following that we'll consider in greater depth the various options for replicating those benefits online.

Bringing On-Site Benefits Online

Some Benefits of Working On-Site

EFFICIENCY AND ACCESSIBILITY. A successful team benefits from the efficiency of working in the same location, where the answer to a question or a copy of a report is just a few steps away.

PRODUCTIVITY AND COLLABORATION. That proximity aids the team's productivity, since coworkers can update, report, plan, and brainstorm as a group—thus enabling essential collaboration.

TRUST AND BONDING. A successful team benefits from the sense of personal accountability of working in the same location. The trust that such reliability develops strengthens the team as a whole. That trust helps the team members to bond with each other.

PREVENTING AND ADDRESSING CONFLICT. A successful team benefits from in-person communication because facial expressions and body language convey positive tone and intention—which add to the team's sense of connection. That buffering helps team members maintain effective interpersonal relationships.

Some Solutions for Replicating These Benefits Online

JUST TOOLS

- Group chat
- Task-management software
- Video conferencing and telepresence
- Virtual office software
- Video and online games

PRACTICES

- ONGOING: constant communication; working together online, which can include working out loud; opportunities to socialize; a forum for raising concerns and getting feedback; established means of expressing appreciation
- REGULARLY SCHEDULED: status updates and productivity meetings; one-on-one time with team members; unstructured social time
- AS NEEDED: discussion (perhaps moderated) and regular feedback to address conflict

Efficiency and Accessibility

A successful team benefits from the efficiency of working in the same location, where the answer to a question or a copy of a report is just steps away.

COMMUNICATE ONLINE—REGULARLY

> *"People think they want to be colocated. What they really want is high-bandwidth communication."*
>
> —AgileBill Krebs, *coach and founder, Agile Dimensions, LLC*[2]

Every on-site workplace has established protocols regarding what is expected of whom—some of which gets relayed just in how the boss greets a new hire, or whether the finance director welcomes a knock on her office door. To be successful working online, where we lack those in-the-moment cues, we need to be more deliberate in establishing protocols of how we will work *together.* As CEO Howard B. Esbin points out: "Because we can't see each other, and because we work from unique locations, there are plenty of opportunities for misunderstandings. *When we are clear about what normal behavior is on our team, we communicate more efficiently.*"[3] And since communication plays such a vital role in the collaborative process, to communicate efficiently is to work more productively.

As noted throughout this book, modern technology for enabling high-bandwidth communication is fast, efficient, and affordable—and getting better and cheaper every day. What's needed is a team agreement about which tools to use for which types of communication, as well as how those tools should be used—especially concerning expected response times.

As to which tools: to be entirely honest, the lineup changes so often that it's impossible to offer much here on which apps are currently available for consideration. But we can cover types of communication tools, and point you in a few directions. For example:

> **Since the "water cooler" talk isn't possible, we provide a wide variety of channels and tools for staff to communicate: email, HipChat [now Slack], and Google Hangouts [now Google Meet]; we also have a staff forum and a social media style site for informal discussions. We have an internal blog for large announcements and official company business and announcements.**
>
> —Tom Sepper, COO, World Wide Web Hosting[4]

The additional solutions that follow describe quite a few of these tools. You'll also find a concise listing of the various categories to choose from in "Technology & Tools" in the RESOURCES section. More updated information can be found at the Collaboration Superpowers webpage "Tools for Remote Teams" (https://collaborationsuperpowers.com/tools).

As for how the selected tools should be used, we cover team agreements in chapter 9.

Access

Another factor of on-site proximity is having quick and easy access to the tools and information needed to do one's job efficiently. As for the online version of that on-site benefit, fortunately the digital age renders physical filing cabinets no longer essential—if not obsolete—given the wide availability of tools that enable the centralization of information, from intranet or private wikis to Google Drive or task-management apps. And while restricted access for certain information is standard procedure, note that for some that approach is somewhat backward. Home services company ezhome shares: "The ability to access information regardless of perceived need is crucial. For us, everything (Google Docs, Slack channels, etc.) is accessible to anyone at ezhome by default, and is only made private if it is truly confidential." This from operations manager Liz Peterson, whose point also speaks to the benefit of trusting the remote workforce.[5]

Productivity and Collaboration

A successful team gains from the productivity of working in the same location, where all can update each other and plan and brainstorm as a group.

COLLABORATE ONLINE—REGULARLY

This solution is just an extension of the previous one: the modern capacity for efficient communication can facilitate efficient collaboration as well. Remote team members can meet as often as they would on-site—they just meet online instead. And since online meetings are easily recorded, team members unable to attend can still stay in the loop.

Online Communal Task Board/Task-Management Software

On-site coworkers often know all that needs to be done—and who is doing what—simply as a consequence of being colocated. To ensure an equal level of team-wide awareness, successful remote teams employ online task- or project-management software to document exactly what needs to be done and who is doing what. For example, billing software company Chargify uses Trello in their marketing department, while their development team utilizes Sprintly for iteration planning and tracking. Student marketplace StudySoup also uses Trello; they share the following in answering the Remote.co question "What challenges have you encountered building a remote team?": "At first we tried to have a casual meeting structure. This was extremely stressful and kept different team members in the dark about what others were working on. Since then we've implemented Trello and a consistent stand-up/meeting structure to avoid this."[6] This leads us to the next solution.

Stand-Ups and Retrospectives

Two of the more standard online practices for meetings originated amongst on-site software development teams.

STAND-UPS are regular (often daily) status-report meetings where all share what they did the day before, what they're doing that day, and if there's anything they're struggling with. (The on-site meetings were named "stand-ups" because they were conducted standing up—since they're meant to be so brief there was no reason to sit down—and/or because team members might also be standing around their physical task board.) Many remote teams conduct stand-ups as well, with or without a virtual task board.

RETROSPECTIVES are also regular meetings, often held every one to two weeks. But while stand-ups are about checking in to see what specific tasks people are working on, Retrospectives are about checking in on how the team is doing as a whole. They are facilitated feedback sessions for sharing progress, raising issues, and discussing solutions—often addressing four questions:

- What is going well?
- What could have gone better?
- What have we learned?
- What still puzzles us?

The simple, structured efficacy of Retrospectives have made them an essential practice in the virtual sphere as well, with different approaches and lengths for different setups and contexts. Plus, since they're regularly scheduled sessions designed for giving and receiving feedback, they greatly facilitate both productivity and alignment. (We'll return to Retrospectives later in the chapter, in the *Put Feedback Loops in Place* section.)

Online Brainstorming and Decision-Making Software

> *"There is always fear that collaboration is based on face-to-face contact, but it turns out it is not. People can work on things together asynchronously and be just as effective."*
>
> —James Law, *HR director, Envato*[7]

Cris Hazzard, partner of "full-service" digital creative agency Sanborn, shares: "We're fans of the whiteboard; there's a magic that happens when a few people are in a room together in a brainstorming session. We've done reasonably well at achieving that remotely by using video conferencing, screen sharing, and tools like InVision. It works best when the participants do a bit of prep work and have items ready to share—which of course benefits the entire process."[8] Tortuga CEO Fred Perrotta offers: "We use Asana and Instagantt to plan big projects like product development, product launches, and website redesigns. Having one tool 'of record' lets us all share the same view and see the same plan, regardless of where we are."[9] Ericsson, the multinational networking and telecommunications company in Stockholm, Sweden, took this concept to new heights when they built their own platform, IdeaBoxes, for collecting and implementing ideas from every level of their organization.[10]

On Medium.com, software engineer Noelle Daley shares the lessons she learned from researching how her temporarily distributed team could better weather the separation. Of particular concern was the fact that their "largely in-person culture didn't quite hold up as well for getting context on tasks and catching up on decisions." After consulting with established distributed engineering teams, she offers the following recommendation.

Document and discuss decisions on Google Docs, or somewhere everyone can easily access and refer back to. Describe the problem and proposed solution and have everyone on the team provide input by adding comments. Keep all of these decisions and project artifacts like diagrams and drawings in a Google Drive folder. This provides a history of decision-making, which is helpful for returning to a project after a while and for onboarding new teammates. Bonus: as one interviewee pointed out, collaborating on decisions asynchronously online makes space for diverse viewpoints. It "allows for multiple personality types to chime in . . . [and] gives people a couple days to think about their ideas and voice them, unlike in meetings where only the loudest voice is heard."[11]

As we'll see in chapter 9, creating space for diverse viewpoints—and personality types—is especially valuable when teams include different cultures.

Trust

A successful team benefits from the sense of personal accountability of working in the same location—of knowing that others will come through with their commitments. The trust that such reliability develops strengthens the team as a whole.

DEMONSTRATE RELIABILITY: WORKING OUT LOUD

"Ultimately, trust comes down to results."

—TEAGUE SODERMAN, *communications lead at NASA Solar System Exploration Research Virtual Institute*[12]

As noted in chapter 7, working out loud amounts to being transparent in your work habits. That means your fellow team members—and team leader—know when you're working, what you're working on, and what you've completed. Coworkers can't help but benefit from knowing you can be relied on to come through for the team.

Some possible means of working out loud include:

- Sending an email update of what you're working on
- Participating in a daily stand-up
- Posting a daily update in a group app such as Slack (described below)
- Keeping your IM status updated
- Updating files and having discussions via the company's intranet
- Participating in group chat (such as with Slack), usually regarding specific items
- Updating code in a central repository (GitHub)
- Updating the "updates" section of group apps, as applicable (such as with I Done This or the Progress View feature in Asana)
- Updating a task entry on a communal task manager (Asana, Trello)
- Participating in a virtual office app (Sococo, Walkabout Workplace)

We discuss many of the tools for these practices lower down, as well as in "Technology & Tools" in the RESOURCES section. Here we'll elaborate on one tip: POSTING A DAILY UPDATE. In the video "Slack Tips Tuesday: How to Not Look Like a Slacker on Slack," X-Team's Ryan Chartrand talks about their company's practice of "journaling." All team members maintain individual journals in which they report their day's accomplishments, even if that's just progress on a long-term task. Ryan recommends representing that progress with screen shots as much as possible, whether that be a video still or the business cards picked up at a conference. As he puts it: "People respect you more when they know how you contribute, and they question your value when they don't know how you contribute." An additional advantage is that team members can respond to the daily post with kudos or suggestions to further the progress. (In yet another plus, such record-keeping boosts your record as well—both in terms of your next performance review and in terms of your own sense of accomplishments. Since it's easy to forget how much work we put into our work, it can be invaluable to be reminded of the many pains we took along the way.)

Note that though X-Team's practice is done in Slack, one could use other platforms instead. (We describe Slack in the group chat section of the next solution.) For theirs, each team member's journal is its own channel, separate from whatever other posts that worker might contribute in other channels. That way other members—especially managers—can track any one worker's regular progress over time.[13]

Team members at Automattic, the web development company best known for the popular publishing and blogging platform WordPress.com, use the WordPress P2 theme to help them keep tabs on what everyone is doing. As blogger Tish Briseno describes: "You can make a P2 post about anything (an upcoming change, an idea, an update to your schedule, sharing a bug report, etc.), and then anyone in the company can comment on that P2. . . . By sharing your workflow, your schedule, something new you learned that you couldn't find documentation for, you're allowing everyone to learn alongside you."[14]

An additional point: it can be challenging for some to learn new company-initiated tools or processes without coaching or training. If team members don't express their difficulty, others may think they're slacking. And so it's important that workers feel free to communicate any concern—which could be done as part of working out loud.[15]

DEMONSTRATE RELIABILITY: TRACKING PRODUCTIVITY

Another option to consider is actually tracking productivity. Note that many teams don't do this; most companies focus on results, not time spent. But a lot of companies do use ***OKRs***—a term that stands for Objectives and Key Results. According to an article on Heflo.com: "The goal of an OKR is to precisely define how to achieve objectives through concrete, specific, and measurable actions." The benefit of this clarity is twofold: workers "focus on the activities and results that they need to achieve," and "nobody is lost doing something that isn't needed."[16] (Note too that having all employees clearly understanding how their roles fit into the larger operation contributes to everyone being aligned with the larger mission.) Whether to establish an OKR and, if so, which to use, could be discussed in the course of crafting a team agreement.

BUILD TRUST BY ACKNOWLEDGING GOOD WORK

An interesting flip side to this consideration utilizes another essential element of team building: appreciation. When we take the time to express appreciation for our coworkers' efforts, we do more than just strengthen our relationships with them; we also solidify our *own* awareness of their contribution. I'll elaborate on this point with an example from my own experience.

Trust via Appreciation: Merit Money

At Happy Melly, we use a "peer-to-peer bonus system" called Merit Money. Here's how this reward scheme works. Every month, each team member is given one hundred points. Over the course of the month, we distribute points amongst the team—including the managers—along with reasons why. The amounts people give and their reasons for giving are transparent to everyone. For example, as CEO Jurgen Appelo wrote in his *Forbes* article about it: "Last month on my team, Jennifer gave fifteen credits to Lisette 'for being the backbone of the organization.'" [Thank you, thank you.] "Lisette gave twenty-five points to Sergey 'for all the feedback and support.' Sergey gave ten credits to Chad for his 'terrific illustrations.' And Chad gave twenty credits to Hannu for his 'friendliness and clarity of communication.'"[17] At the end of each month Tahira, our finance queen, puts together our profit and loss statement; if there is profit, she sets aside a percentage for the monthly bonus—to be distributed amongst the team based on the number of points each individual received during the month.

I confess that at first I wasn't too keen on the Merit Money system. I didn't feel comfortable giving feedback to those whose skills I couldn't properly evaluate, like Sergey's code or Tahira's bookkeeping. But then I realized I shouldn't base my evaluation on those skills; my job was to base my contributions on what it's like to work with Sergey and Tahira. Are they reliable? Are they responsive? Are they nice to work with? (Yes, yes, and yes.) As former (and much-missed) Happy Melly colleague Louise Brace puts it: "Merit Money is a great way to make sure each of us knows how accountable we are, and what others perceive of our contribution. It assures that we all work on our communication skills, and it ensures that everyone knows what everyone else is doing."[18]

What I personally like about Merit Money is that each team member receives regular feedback from everyone else on the team. I find it both motivating and illuminating to learn what my colleagues appreciate about me—and I love that there's a standard forum where I can express my appreciation for them. This continuous, 360-degree feedback helps our team appreciate and learn from each other.

To return to the subject of trust and reliability: I've noticed that if I put off distributing my points until the end of the month, it's hard for me to remember what things people were doing at the beginning of the month. So while I know that my coworkers were working, I've lost a distinct sense of exactly how and how much—as well as how relevant their contributions were to me. But thanks to Merit Money, especially the transparency of it, I am vividly aware of just how vital each team member is to our group effort—which just makes me want to come through for them all the more.

Bonding

A successful team benefits from the social aspects of working together in the same location, since strengthened social ties strengthen the team as a whole.

> **After a few months of not spending time with your colleagues, you lose the human interaction. Life gets filled with other things. And the problem with remote communication is that you're usually talking about work. It's important to have the chitchat to see what's going on in your life; otherwise you're just a machine getting work done.**
>
> —ShriKant Vashishtha, cofounder and Agile coach, Malonus Consulting[19]

It turns out that the "team" part of working on a team is important. Working together on-site presents serendipitous moments where sharing an elevator can turn into grabbing coffee together. Seeing each other on a daily basis builds trust and increases camaraderie. But when we're remote, we have to work extra hard to feel we're part of a team. So, though we can digitally connect with people all over the world at the click of a button, we have to find new ways of emotionally connecting as well.

So how do we create closeness even though we're far apart? How do we reach through the screens? That's all coming up next.

The challenge for us is not the technology—it's for the human side to keep up with the technology. Our habits don't change fast enough.

—AgileBill Krebs, coach and founder, Agile Dimensions, LLC[20]

A lot of tools will help you collaborate, but they won't necessarily help you get to know each other personally. We've gone high-tech, but we also need to go high-touch and develop empathy for each other.

—Howard B. Esbin, CEO, Playprelude.com[21]

WORK TOGETHER ONLINE

We've discussed the concept of working out loud: advertising one's current activity and reachability. Working together online is a less-structured approach to working out loud. For some teams, it's as casual and low-effort as simply turning on the webcams just to feel more connected. But there are also tools for simulating a working environment, or even simulating the physical on-site office. To follow are just some of the diverse options to choose from, from the most accessible to the most far out. In the end, it doesn't really matter which tools you choose; what matters is that everyone on a team is comfortable with the technology, and everyone agrees on how it will be used.

Webcam and Video Conferencing

Just turning on the webcam undeniably adds to the remote-working experience—and not necessarily for a video call, as ShriKant Vashishtha describes:

We installed webcams for our teams so we could see who was coming and going at each of the offices. We got used to greeting each other when someone arrived, went out for lunch, or went home at the end of the day. We even started creating common gestures with each other. Being able to see each other built up a real sense of team.[22]

A few remote teams at Spotify do much the same—as conveyed by software engineer Thodoris Tsiridis:

> **While we work we keep a Hangout open where everyone connects via video with their microphones on mute. This is analogous to working in the same room: everyone can see each other, and when people have a question, they simply un-mute themselves and ask the others. This allows the team to talk as if they were physically in the same office together.**[23]

Agile coach Mark Kilby shares a bit more on why video can be so effective:

> **Sometimes the virtual experience can be more human because we're seeing so much of somebody's personal life in the background. That's important to share in virtual teams, and many of us actually like that blending of work and life. We want to know who's at the other end of that line. On my team, nobody gets upset if somebody's kid pops up in the background and says hi, or a family member walks past. In fact, it can help us build camaraderie.**[24]

Communal Task Board/Task Management

In some task-management tools (like Asana or Trello, for example), you can create a "workspace" that offers a bird's-eye view of an organization's various departments and projects (or even different locations). There are many such tools to choose from depending on your team's needs; for more, see "Technology & Tools" (*p. 301*) in the RESOURCES section. Of course, for some teams the company IT department has made a company-wide decision—and the tool has been decided for you. Regardless, most tools can serve their purposes admirably as long as the team agrees on how to use them.

Group Chat

Group chat is a platform for keeping tabs on the pulse of the work being done at any point in time, both past and present. This in-the-moment capability is like a virtual way of walking through the office and talking with colleagues, as well as a means of jumping into the conversation. It also enables group discussion, whether about work projects or weekend plans. In addition, it enables sharing files and documents, which are visible to everyone cleared for that project or channel. This rapid, lightweight approach can facilitate better communication than email can, and its company-wide visibility makes it a potent team builder.

As for its after-the-fact capability, each channel offers essentially a script of who did or said what and when, so anyone can review the conversation long after it happened. The collected knowledge of the workspace is also eminently searchable for later access—unlike email messages confined to the in-box. As noted in chapter 4, digital transformation and data analytics adviser Luis Suarez is a big fan of this searchability: "Typically, when you leave a company, the first thing that human resources does is delete your mailbox with the gigs and gigs and gigs of data and connections and knowledge that you've accumulated over the years. But with a social network, if you leave, your legacy is still there. People can go to the internal platform and look up your content, find the conversations, and see and interact with the networks you built. From an individual perspective, that's your legacy living beyond the point of your being there. And from an enterprise perspective, all of that precious knowledge is available to everyone else."[25]

Group chat tools can also be great virtual water coolers. For example, some teams have created a "getting to know you" channel to encourage the sort of sharing that builds camaraderie. And River Agency COO Tom Howlett appreciates that group chat helps to level the personality playing field, "enabling more of us to say what we want to say."[26]

Ironically, one downside to group chat tools is how easy they are—which can lead to work items getting buried in banter. But that's a consideration that can be addressed when you collectively determine in a team agreement how the tools are to be used. For example, one protocol could be to reserve less work-related posts for the non-work channels.

Virtual Office

A virtual office is exactly what it sounds like: an office you go to . . . online. One of the more widely used virtual office platforms is Sococo (sOcial cOmmunications cOmpany). When you log in, you see a floor plan and avatars that represent your fellow logged-in colleagues. You can move yourself from room to room, but you can only hear and speak to those who are in the same room with you—just like at an office. To follow, Sococo's Mandy Ross describes their own Sococo setup:

> **Our virtual office actually looks like an office. Every morning we launch Sococo and see a floor plan, a top-down view of the office. We all have our own offices, and there are also conference rooms. Usually when I log in I see Carrie, so I go and say hi to her. And the CEO, whose office is right next to mine, will come in a little later to talk to me.**
>
> **So that's where I go to work every morning.**

—Mandy Ross, director of community and distributed Agile coach, Sococo[27]

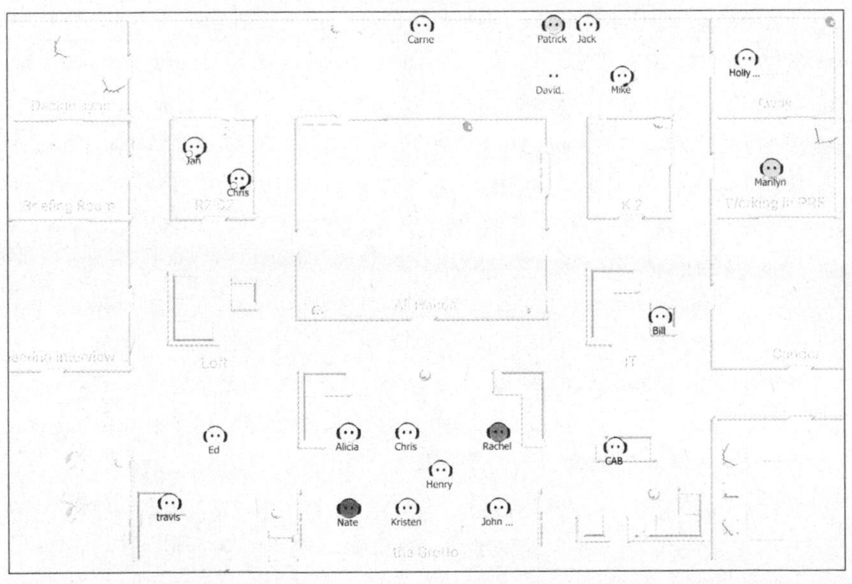

A screenshot of the Sococo team's virtual office (Sococo)

Just being able to see where everyone is in the virtual office makes colleagues feel more accessible and gives the team a surprising sense of togetherness. Sococo's Carrie Kuempel loves the platform in part because, as she puts it: "You're a virtual door knock away from giving others the answer they need to go full speed ahead with what they're doing. You're not sending an email. You're not scheduling a meeting. The fact that I can pop in and get an answer and move ahead is great. Accessibility and visibility are important for us because we're building something together and we need each other. Sococo is the lifeline to my teammates."[28] The platform lends itself to other uses as well: online workshops, conferences, even the virtual equivalent of a coworking space.

Telepresence

With telepresence, you can project your "presence" into an alternate location—much as you do with video—but with the added bonus of mobility. For example, the Revolve Robotics Kubi allows you to "beam in" (like with Skype) to any tablet device and move yourself from side to side and up and down. With this capability you can control what you see. Let's say you're using Kubi to participate in an on-site meeting. You'd be able to look at the whiteboard, and then turn to look at your colleagues. In addition, the movement of the Kubi offers you—the remote team member—a more human presence from the perspective of those physically in the room. You are literally more "present" with them than you'd be with just video. And, the technology is easier to use than you'd think.

Other telepresence robots are drivable: the user can beam into what is basically a tablet on wheels and drive through a remote location using just computer keyboard arrow keys. While this might sound futuristic, in fact these devices are widely used today. With telepresence, homebound children can still actively attend classes, bedbound patients can consult specialists in foreign locales, art lovers can explore a museum from afar, and both remote speakers and participants can attend distant conferences. Telepresence is remarkably effective at bringing people together, regardless of the distance between them.

Virtual Reality

Virtual worlds have been in existence for decades, and widely used in small circles: for classes and conferences—like with telepresence—and also with military simulations. Virtual Reality (VR) technology can be difficult for the average person to navigate, but as the technology develops, I believe VR will play an increasing role in how we work together. Why? Because interactive sensory experiences bring us closer to replicating the human experience.

FACILITATE SOCIAL TIME

Since casual, personal time spent together is so effective at bonding, it's important that team members also interact socially—separate from their work activities. This view is widely shared.

> **Organizations can have this myopia that just because you're an expert in your field and I'm an expert in mine, even if we've never met, it's assumed we'll just get on with the project. But research shows that, unless you have some kind of vehicle for team members to get to know each other, you're going to get just the opposite.**
>
> —Howard B. Esbin, CEO, Playprelude.com[29]

> **Proactively engage with your team as much as you possibly can. Make sure that people are connecting. Make sure there are social things happening. It can't just be about work all the time. In a physical office, people naturally socialize. In a virtual office, they need encouragement to socialize.**
>
> —Mandy Ross, director of community, Sococo[30]

> **It's important that companies create spaces like coffee breaks where people can virtually stop working and just chat with their coworkers. It helps keep everyone motivated and breaks the loneliness. It also gives us a chance to learn about each other's projects, to learn more about the people we're working with.**
>
> —Anna Danes, CEO, Ricaris[31]

> **Because our remote interactions can be so focused, we often don't make the time to just hang out together. If we want to create more serendipitous moments on our remote teams we (ironically) have to schedule it. One of the things I discovered was the importance of having both structured and unstructured time.**
>
> —JEREMY STANTON, SVP of engineering, Amino Payments[32]

To follow is an array of suggestions for how to facilitate that unstructured social time, often using video conferencing software.

- Brie Reynolds's remote team at FlexJobs has groups on Yammer where they have book clubs, cooking groups, and pet photo shares.
- Mark Kilby's team at Sonatype has adopted the practice of building social time into every meeting by inviting people to show up a few minutes early or stay late. This gives everyone a chance to be social without delaying the agenda.
- The Happy Melly team runs a weekly half-hour social session whose only rule is "no shop talk." It's called Kitten Talk—because in the beginning team members lured others online with pictures of kittens.
- FlexJobs's Brie Reynolds shares: "Every couple of weeks on a Friday night after work, everybody gets together with a drink and we host virtual trivia. It's similar to just going to a bar with your friends on trivia night. It's a fun way to virtually hang out with your coworkers."[33]
- Similarly, Sococo's Carrie McKeegan offers: "We do something called High-Five Fridays and Get-to-Know-You Wednesdays. They're silly things that just somehow work."[34]

Many teams enjoy playing games together, either video or card games, or more elaborate games:

- Dr.Clue.com hosts virtual treasure hunts wherein a combination of video conferencing tools and puzzles helps teams solve riddles together.

- PlayPrelude.com is a trust-building activity for virtual teams.
- The Management 3.0 team runs a Personal Maps session where the team members "mind map" themselves and then share with each other. It's surprisingly fun—sort of an internal "show and tell." (For more, see https://management30.com/practice/personal-maps.)

SPEND TIME TOGETHER IN PERSON

For all these effective means of bonding teams digitally, it must be said that nothing can equal actual face time. And so it's widely recommended that managers facilitate team members' getting together in person whenever possible—whether that means scheduling a bus ride, a train trip, or a plane ticket.

> **We encourage exchanges between offices. So an employee in Barcelona can go to San Diego and then an employee in San Diego can go to Barcelona. It does two great things at once. One, it allows team members to meet face to face. And two, it offers an awesome opportunity to travel to another city. Both of these things help us recruit better employees and make our current employees happier.**
>
> —Robert Rogge, cofounder and CEO, Zingword; cofounder and advisor, Managing Virtual Teams[35]

> **A webcam can replace a lot, but being able to see each other and have a drink at a local pub helps build the team so much more. That in-person time really pays off in the end.**
>
> —Ralph van Roosmalen, Agile coach and Management 3.0 facilitator[36]

Taking this concept to the next level, booking software company Timely considers "spending time together in the flesh so crucial" that they've "semi-centralized in a few cities."[37]

Addressing Conflict

Part of why a successful team benefits from in-person communication is that facial expressions and body language convey tone and intention—which of course are ideally always positive. Without that buffering, interpersonal relationships can erode, and minor annoyances can become extended conflicts.

From simple differences in opinion to larger misunderstandings, conflicts within virtual teams are inevitable. So we'll always want to have in place means of addressing conflicts once they arise—which we'll go over lower down. But first, there are also ways to prevent disturbances from occurring in the first place. We can:

- avoid task redundancy by using a communal task board/software to indicate who is working on what;
- avoid miscommunication and task redundancy by working out loud;
- communicate often, via video whenever possible;
- practice positive communication approaches;
- put feedback loops in place; and
- collectively document a team agreement that details how the team *wants* to work together.

To follow we elaborate on a few of these items.

INCREASE POSITIVE COMMUNICATION

> *"On remote teams we need to find opportunities to talk to each other. Sometimes it's difficult because of time zones and sometimes we're busy. That's very understandable. But if we don't have those conversations regularly, we start to lose that connection."*
>
> —Pilar Orti, *director, Virtual not Distant*[38]

The predominant advice for preventing interpersonal conflict is to communicate often. But note that the quality of those exchanges is even more important than the quantity. When we're remote, we need to ensure we're kind and constructive in how we communicate with each other. This calls for a few ground rules.

For starters, since it's easy to read negativity into written communication even when none is intended, it's wise to always be friendly, even overtly friendly. Try to ensure there's nothing in your phrasing that your recipients could interpret as annoyance or frustration on your part. The flip side of that is to always assume positive intent. In other words, even if your correspondents aren't overtly friendly, try to assume no ill will is intended, and that no annoyance or frustration should be read into their words. And third, resist the urge to express charged emotion. Expanding on this point: some of us are prone to express exactly what we feel as soon as we feel it. But of course, as much as that might feel good in the moment, such words can cause permanent damage to our relationships. It's always wiser to keep what we really want to say to ourselves—and instead respond as constructively as possible. (We'll cover these items again lower down.)

PUT FEEDBACK LOOPS IN PLACE

On a remote team, we need to proactively build and maintain positive connections. For that it's important to loop back with our teammates on a regular basis: to check how things are progressing, as well as to offer our feedback or support.

Now, for some the term "feedback" doesn't conjure a sense of "positive connection." Some people have a fear of receiving feedback. For others the fear is in giving it—especially when it's peer-to-peer. Feedback can be difficult when there is tension around professional roles and status, especially concerning differences in age and educational background. Those who believe expressing themselves could do more harm than good are likely to just swallow their grievances or try to ignore them. The trouble is, small disturbances often don't just go away; they can build over time—which can be detrimental to team alignment.

Whatever reluctance team members may have, there's no avoiding it: to achieve group-wide goals, teams needs to continually strengthen their relationships, which calls for the regular giving and receiving of feedback.

Note that this isn't about annual or biannual performance reviews, as virtual team consultant Pilar Orti clarifies: "When I think about feedback in an organization, I always picture it as coming from the upper layers in the organizational chart. When I think of feedback on virtual teams, I think of the physiology type of feedback where organs, muscles, neurons, and hormones are constantly talking to each other and affecting what happens next. On virtual teams, we all have to be involved."[39]

So how do we go about this? Different organizations have come up with different approaches to providing that full-voiced feedback. One consideration is mode of communication: text, email, phone call, video chat, or team-wide video conversation. Another consideration is format. As for the latter, it helps to establish in advance what formats you'd use regularly and what you'd use for the difficult conversations—which hopefully won't happen too often.

Standard Project Feedback

Chapter 4 shares how discouraging it can be when a team member comments negatively on a project when it's too late to act on the suggestions. To prevent the conflict such incidents can produce—and to ensure your projects get well-timed feedback to begin with—it's recommended that teams have an established protocol for both requesting and giving feedback. One effective approach is to specifically request different levels of feedback at different phases in a project. For more, see "The 30/60/90 Feedback Framework" sidebar (*p. 100*) in chapter 4.

Regularly Take Your Team's Temperature

As for the more standard team-wide fare, for many teams the aforementioned Retrospective offers the opportunity to give and receive feedback. Again, Retrospectives are regularly scheduled, facilitated feedback sessions for sharing progress, raising issues, and discussing solutions—often addressing four questions:

- What is going well?
- What could have gone better?

- What have we learned?
- What still puzzles us?

For example, in the Four L's Retrospective, team members share what they liked, learned, lacked, and longed for; a variation on this is the Mad, Sad, Glad Retrospective. The Stop, Start, Continue Retrospective is effective for gauging the direction a team wants to head in. In a Sailboat Retrospective, a team discusses what baggage slows them down—as well as what wind propels them forward.[40]

Retrospectives are most effective when a facilitator is on hand to guide the conversation and ensure that every voice is heard. Entrepreneur David Horowitz elaborates on this point:

> **The open mic concept for Retrospectives simply doesn't work, because usually some participants will dominate the conversation. And the other 95 percent just sit quietly, twiddling their thumbs or checking their phones. In a distributed setting, those troubles are just doubled, because it's easy to hide behind the technology. Retrospectives should be facilitated so as to include the entire team in the conversation.**
>
> —DAVID HOROWITZ, cofounder and CEO, Retrium[41]

As it happens, David cofounded Retrium to develop software for facilitating engaging online Retrospectives. The software replicates online the visual functionality—such as flip charts and sticky notes—of colocated Retrospectives, thus enabling effective collaboration in the virtual sphere. (For more, see the *Retrospectives* portion [*p. 316*] of "Technology & Tools.")

There are other approaches to regular feedback as well. At the outsourcing company Bridge Global IT Staffing, both clients and employees are asked every week how satisfied they were on a scale of 0 to 10. Some companies use WE THINQ, a tool that allows anyone to give feedback, post a comment, or ask a question. It's more than just a digital version of the old filled-out-form-stuffed-in-a-box approach—which some consider to be an exercise in futility. With WE THINQ, each submission is visible to everyone else, who can then add thoughts and feedback—allowing for an organization-wide conversation. This is the same concept as the previously mentioned IdeaBoxes. IdeaBoxes is browser-based software, not unlike a social network, where users can follow and submit ideas. Each idea gets categorized into a "box" and tagged so that it's easily findable. Since users can flag the ideas they like, the system enables like-minded people to continue the conversation.

Another way of getting team feedback is by taking the team's "temperature" using some sort of survey. There are numerous online tools for doing this, from sophisticated evaluations to simple clicks on smiley or frowny faces. (For more, see the *Feedback* section [*p. 316*] of "Technology *&* Tools.")

The digital music service Spotify uses what they call a Squad Health Check Model. Every quarter or so they host regular workshops where teams ("squads") evaluate themselves in eleven categories, such as product quality, teamwork, support, and fun. They then create a visual overview that summarizes all the teams' data so they can prioritize next steps. (See figure to follow.) Visualizing data helps turn cyphers into stories.

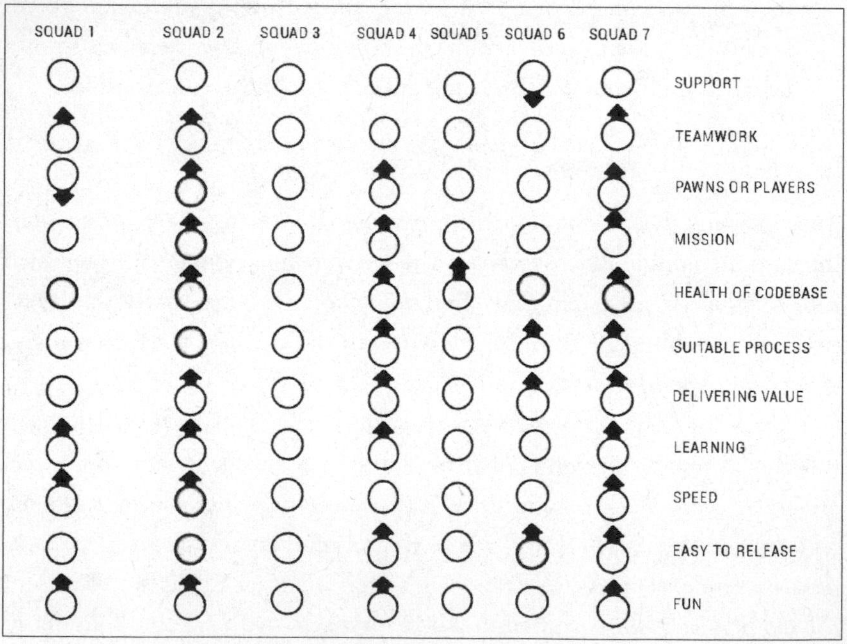

A Spotify tribe's Health Check Output. This graphic represents the self-assessment of seven teams ("squads"). The color of a circle signifies one of three states: good, some problems, or really bad. An arrow on the circle indicates a trend: up = "generally improving"; down = "getting worse." (Spotify)

Regardless of the tools you use, note the following guidelines:

- Keep it simple. Make the process easy, even fun.
- Present the data in a visual format to aid comprehension of the results.
- Take your team's temperature regularly—more than biannually. Just how regularly—weekly, monthly, or quarterly—depends on the team and the need, which can change over time.
- Do something with the data. There are two angles to this one. The first is just practical: there's no point in taking the team's temperature unless you're willing to act on the information gleaned from the process. But even more important is team morale: to repeatedly solicit this level of feedback and then to shelve it both wastes employees' time and tests their patience.

Spotify also recommends:

- Be clear about your motives for introducing the model. It should be about improvement, not judgment.
- Make sure there is no incentive to game the model. There should be no reason for a team to want to "look good."
- Involve teams in how the model is applied.

An additional detail is Spotify's recommendation to "gather data primarily through face-to-face communication, not online surveys." Their process involves one-hour workshops during which the team collectively discusses their votes—which engages the members and thus facilitates later follow-through of whatever action steps result. Of course, that option might not be workable for all teams. Nonetheless, it's recommended that the process be as engaging as possible.[42]

ADDRESS CONFLICT CONSTRUCTIVELY

Now for the stickier wickets. Team members can be very instrumental in addressing minor disturbances before they develop into conflict. That practice starts with ensuring we communicate positively and constructively. We can maintain positive communication by:

- being friendly, even overtly friendly;
- always assuming positive intent;
- resisting the urge to express charged emotion; and
- striving to keep interactions as constructive as possible.

We can help to keep more-heated interactions constructive by:

- avoiding critical language;
- keeping phrasing objective and fact-based;
- acknowledging one's own contribution to the situation; and
- addressing only one issue at a time.

Of course, sometimes more substantial intervention is called for. To follow are two structured approaches for resolving conflict and easing tension.

Feedback Wrap

At Happy Melly, where I am the remote team manager, we use Jurgen Appelo's Feedback Wrap whenever a team member feels even slightly annoyed or disappointed, which tends to happen every week or so. We start by setting context and describing the environment we find ourselves in. Then we list our observations—limiting ourselves to facts only. Then we express how we feel. We end with a suggestion on how to move forward. The entire objective is to be considerate and constructive, keeping the chance for hurt feelings to a minimum.

This approach was designed to be done in writing. However, note that written feedback can be precarious when the content is negative or emotionally charged—even if the phrasing is intentionally kind and constructive. If an issue seems too much for the written word, phone calls are much more effective. And if emotions are running strong, it's best to have a face-to-face conversation—in person if at all possible. If the conversation is especially hard, consider bringing in a moderator to help facilitate. Having someone moderate can help keep emotions in check, ensure everyone's voice is heard, and work toward a productive outcome.

Virtual Pillow Fight

We once used the moderator approach on the Happy Melly team in what was essentially a virtual pillow fight. Several members of the team had friction with one of the members but never said anything about it. As time passed and resentments grew, it finally came out—on the messaging platform Slack. Since that route wasn't productive, we got together on a video call to hash it out; to keep the conversation fair, we assigned a neutral team member to moderate it. In that conversation we clarified misunderstandings and misinterpreted behavior. We didn't solve everything then and there, but we did decrease the tension significantly. And we each left the meeting with one action item we would personally take to improve working together in the future.

Both the Feedback Wrap and the Virtual Pillow Fight are variations on Susan Scott's seven-point guide, outlined in the sidebar to follow.

Susan Scott's Seven-Point Approach to Difficult Conversations

In her book *Fierce Conversations: Achieving Success at Work and in Life One Conversation at a Time*, Susan Scott identifies the seven items to address at the start of a charged interpersonal discussion:

- Name the issue.
- Select a specific example that illustrates the behavior or situation you want to change.
- Describe your emotions about this issue.
- Clarify what's at stake.
- Identify your contribution to this problem.
- Indicate your wish to resolve the issue.
- Invite [others] to respond.[43]

To wrap up this portion, if we want to cultivate a sense of togetherness on our remote teams, we have to be deliberate and proactive about doing it. We need to decide how we can best stay aligned and up to date with what we're doing. We need to engage with our colleagues personally when we can, and to build some play into our agendas. And, if we have the luxury, we need to spend time together in person.

IN CONCLUSION: FORGE A STRONG, ALIGNED TEAM

> *"For me the challenge is knowing when to step in and when to let go. In my experience, people work better when they are armed with goals and the tools they need to achieve them, they know you have their back, and they are given the space to do what's been asked of them."*
>
> —Kristin Kanger, *VP of talent management, Working Solutions*[44]

The above covers an expanse of terrain. Hopefully along the way you found much that is applicable for your unique situation. Having now explored possible solutions for your personnel, objectives, and circumstances, it's time to engage your team in collectively deciding what tools, processes, and protocols to use. From there you can document in a team agreement the expectations and etiquette of your work culture.

Remote Reminders

REPLICATING ON-SITE BENEFITS ONLINE

- It's entirely possible for remote teams to be as effective as on-site teams; it's just a matter of finding what tools and practices will best enable that optimal productivity.
- Ensure quick and easy access to the tools and information needed to do one's job efficiently.
- Communicate and collaborate regularly—online. Consider scheduling regular daily and weekly or bimonthly check-in meetings. Record meetings for those who can't attend.
- Employ online task or project-management software to document exactly what needs to be done and who is doing what.
- Demonstrate reliability by working out loud; some teams also track productivity.
- Build trust by acknowledging good work.

TEAM BUILDING

- Be intentional about creating an atmosphere of togetherness.
- Turn on the webcam when possible, since visual connection helps to bond the team.
- Facilitate team bonding by encouraging team members to interact socially separate from their work activities. This often calls for scheduling unstructured time such as virtual lunches or game nights—even extra time before and after meetings.
- Arrange for teams to meet in person regularly—ideally quarterly or more often.
- Though conflicts will always emerge in teams, we can take steps to prevent them. For example, communal task board/software and working

out loud help avoid miscommunication and task redundancy; positive communication approaches help keep the atmosphere pleasant and constructive.

- Have feedback loops in place to facilitate fluid communication.
- When conflict does occur, address it constructively.

CHAPTER 9

Tune Your Team with a Team Agreement

"Have a clear process for what you're trying to achieve. What does the workflow look like? How are decisions going to get made? How are results going to get reported?"

—Robert Rogge, *cofounder and CEO, Zingword; cofounder and advisor, Managing Virtual Teams*[1]

"Teams tend to just start and get going. If you step back and do some brainstorming with your team on how you're going to work together and how you're going to communicate, it saves you a lot of trouble."

—Hugo Messer, *distributed Agile expert and founder, Bridge Global and Ekipa*[2]

Simply put, for remote teams to be successful, they need to establish protocols of how they will work *together*.

Consider the scenario of an orchestra performing a symphony. All the musicians may play their parts beautifully, but without a previously established agreement regarding the variables of dynamics (volume) and tempo (pace)—and especially whether the instruments are in tune with each other—a cacophony could erupt come curtain time. Just as the orchestra needs to determine in advance what details will produce the best sound, a remote team needs to determine in advance what will produce the best results.

We can "tune" our team by collectively crafting a team agreement. A ***team agreement*** delineates all team protocols, including what kinds of information will be shared, how members will communicate with each other, even how to know who is doing what. Essentially, team agreements provide a foundational glue that helps to bind teams together. This is true in part because creating a basic set of guidelines decreases the possibility of misinterpretation and disconnect within the team. How? By giving team members a platform for discussing assumptions. To repeat CEO Howard B. Esbin's point from chapter 8: "Because we can't see each other, and because we work from unique locations, there are plenty of opportunities for misunderstandings. When we are clear about what normal behavior is on our team, we communicate more efficiently."[3]

For example, consider the detail of just when work will be done. As part of their team agreement, Sococo employees decided to be predictable with their schedules, as such benefited their productivity. The team at Happy Melly instead chose to work whenever they want to, since concurrent work hours have minimal bearing for them. Many companies follow a middle path, where some parts of the week are blocked out for mutual time, while for the remainder workers are free to determine their own schedules.

Another common concern is alignment. As investment management partner Derek Scruggs shares: "We are very conscious of our communication and company culture because there's no real water cooler to inspire impromptu discussions. We use chat tools and have daily online stand-up meetings to discuss the day-to-day things. And we have a Retrospective every other week where we get together and talk about what's going on as a team."[4]

We'll cover how to create a team agreement later on. For now, let's consider all that the agreement needs to address. First up: communication.

Communication

Communication is the most potent means of fueling—or hampering—a team's productivity.

Company Culture, Defined

In their *Harvard Business Review* article "Culture Takes Over When the CEO Leaves the Room," Frances Frei and Anne Morriss offer a definition of company culture:

> **Culture guides discretionary behavior, and it picks up where the employee handbook leaves off. Culture tells us how to respond to an unprecedented service request. It tells us whether to risk telling our bosses about our new ideas, and whether to surface or hide problems. Employees make hundreds of decisions on their own every day, and culture is our guide. Culture tells us what to do when the CEO isn't in the room, which is of course most of the time.**[5]

Since on a virtual team the CEO isn't in the room—for the most part—*any* of the time, we have to find other ways to ensure we're adhering to our company's preferred culture. As just one example, the Happy Melly team has a #Values channel on Slack where we talk about any hard decisions we had to make and why we made them. The channel is an invaluable resource, since it can help a team member facing a similar dilemma determine what response would best align with the team's established values.

> **Sometimes serendipity may make up for the fact that you have bad processes, such as when you by chance see that someone's working on something you already completed. Or you overhear something and catch a mistake. When you're remote, you don't have that serendipity to catch what's falling through the cracks—so instituting processes around communication is really key.**
>
> —Ade Olonoh, chairman, Formstack; and cofounder, Jell[6]

> **If you ask why your software project got derailed when you worked with a remote team, the answer is always "communication."**
>
> —HUGO MESSER, distributed Agile expert and founder, Bridge Global and Ekipa[7]

Successful communication requires consistent, intentional effort. Not one team—colocated or remote—has told me their communication was flawless. Since each team has a unique way of communicating, and a particular combination of personality types, the objective is to find what tools and protocols will work best.

We do that by:

- establishing when we will use which tools and why;
- ensuring everyone has those tools, both hardware and software;
- establishing our preferred etiquette for all interactions; and
- agreeing to communicate from a mind set of positive intent.

For example, let's look again at Derek Scruggs's comment noted earlier: "We use chat tools and have daily online stand-up meetings to discuss the day-to-day things. And we have a Retrospective every other week where we get together and talk about what's going on as a team." So, one element of implementing team agreements is to establish what tools (chat tools) and practices (both daily and semi-monthly check-ins) will keep the team aligned.

COMMUNICATION TOOLS: WHICH, WHEN, AND WHY

To follow are the top-recommended tips for effective communication.

USE VIDEO REGULARLY—ESPECIALLY FOR MEETINGS. While some might think using video often is overkill for some types of communication, most team members I've spoken to have found regular use of video to be key to effective workflow. Video is also great for sending more complicated information; given that humans are so predominantly visual, a video message can be much more effective than email.

ALWAYS HAVE MULTIPLE COMMUNICATION CHANNELS. In terms of software glitches, of course, this is a no-brainer. But more so, the benefit is that different channels work better for different situations.

> **We use video and audio, but also chat because if our video and audio go down, we need to coordinate on how to get back together. You've got to be tech-savvy enough that you can use the different technologies and have your Plan B for when those technologies fail.**
>
> —MARK KILBY, Agile coach, Sonatype[8]

> **Stick to the facts online and save the complicated emotional stuff for a higher-bandwidth channel like video or face-to-face.**
>
> —PETER HILTON, consultant, Signavio[9]

> **In order to be virtual but not distant, real conversations are a must. We need to be able to agree and disagree quickly and be spontaneous. That's one of the drawbacks of email. Though a lot more thought goes into them, you still lose that spontaneity. And spontaneity is part of healthy communication.**
>
> —PILAR ORTI, director, Virtual not Distant[10]

MAKE IT EASY TO MOVE FROM ASYNCHRONOUS MODES (email or text) TO LIVE ONES (phone or video). "Non-expressive" modes of communication—such as email and text, which offer neither body language nor tone of voice—can be problematic if a conversation includes any confusion or emotion. So, many recommend switching from a more static mode to a more personal one as soon as the need arises.

> **A one-to-one IM chat can get tiresome. One of us will usually hit the voice button and turn it into a voice conversation. Those transitions need to be smooth and seamless on remote teams. Things need to happen fast—as quickly as walking up to somebody in an office, hopefully quicker.**
>
> —TOM HOWLETT, COO, River Agency[11]

We could work completely differently and independently and then hook up when we needed to. We used asynchronous communication most of the time and then went to synchronous communication as needed. When the communication by email was not flowing well, we booked a Skype call. Usually a short chat would solve everything.

—Luis Gonçalves, management consultant and founder, Evolution4All, on cowriting a book remotely[12]

AGREE ON THE TOOLS YOU'RE GOING TO USE—AND BE DISCIPLINED ABOUT USING THEM. Often on remote teams people will just start using whatever tools they like the best: some like email and some like IM, while others may prefer Slack. But communication works best when a team agrees on a tool—and the etiquette around that tool—and then sticks to that agreement. In his *Harvard Business Review* article "Communication Tips for Global Virtual Teams," Paul Berry notes how his team members, who span more than twenty different countries, stay aligned by using email as their primary mode. The reason this approach is effective for them is because each member commits to checking email as the "absolute highest priority."[13]

Once we've established when we will use which types of tools and why, we need to select the specific tools to use. For example, partner Cris Hazzard of digital creative agency Sanborn notes: "For us, a combination of Slack, Trello, Google Apps for Work, and Zoom does the trick. We're constantly trying new tools and integrating them when it makes sense."[14] And for the fully distributed accounting firm Why Blu, Scott Hoppe shares: "We use Asana, Slack, and G Suite. We use Slack for all the quick communications, the under-five-minute stuff. Anything that needs multiple inputs, anything over that five minutes, goes into Asana. Internally, we do not email each other, but we do use email with our clients."[15] (If you haven't yet read the previous chapter, note that we discuss different tools at length there. Also check out the RESOURCES section's "Technology & Tools," which starts off by naming the tool suites most commonly used by scores of companies [*p. 301*]. In the meantime, the following sidebar offers one company's collection of tools.)

SitePen's Tool Suite

Project management director Nita Tune shares the suite of tools that keeps fully distributed web developer SitePen on track:

PROJECT MANAGEMENT AND CUSTOMER INTERFACING: We currently use Redmine for tracking tasks in three different pipelines: internal, client-facing, or customer support. We've had Redmine quite a while, and have customized it to suit our needs. We are always evaluating other tools, and are actually in the midst of that process now. The one thing that will never change at SitePen is we require customer communications to be clearly documented in one of these systems so everyone can see it. We don't track email threads. If it's important, it goes into Redmine.

DOCUMENTS: We use G Suite: Email, Calendar, and, most important, Google Docs/Sheets, etc. Team collaboration on written documentation in a remote company is crucial.

CODE: We use GitHub for our customer projects, internal development features, and open-source initiatives (Dojo 2). Some of us also use ZenHub to get an eagle-eye view of multiple GitHub repositories for management.

CHAT: We use Slack for daily communication. We have a number of Slack channels, ranging from customer work to movie spoilers. And we have nearly 3,000 custom emojis—a lot of them useful for single-click answers, others just because they're funny.

VOICE CALLS/VIDEO/SCREEN SHARING: We stick with Slack for team chats. For customer calls, we use GoToMeeting. Both are really easy to spin up, so we can talk any time.[16]

Then, once those tools have been chosen, we need to make sure we're savvy in using them. And since some teams opt to try out a tool for a few weeks or months before making a final decision, for some the selection phase and the savvy phase go hand in hand.

Also keep in mind that we all can have different, random preferences. Some people like tools for seemingly weird reasons, and sometimes the "perfect" tool on a team just doesn't work for them. I once built a help manual using a wiki. It was a work of art; everything was hyperlinked to everything else, and it could be updated by anyone at any time. But no one used it—they preferred separate Google Docs. The upshot: if the team won't use the perfect tool, it's not the perfect tool.

COMMUNICATION ETIQUETTE: HOW

"Remote communication is a two-step tango."

—AgileBill Krebs, *founder, Agile Dimensions, LLC*[17]

Next up: establishing our preferred etiquette for all interactions, the *how* of the team agreement. This is when the chance for individuals to air their preferences will prove particularly helpful, since the personal style of one could be grating to another.

For example, I once worked with a woman who used email like an IM tool. Instead of sending just one email, she would send a flood of thoughts, one after another. At first it was slightly annoying but still manageable, especially since excess emails can easily be deleted. But over time I found I wanted to communicate with her less. And on remote teams, if physical distance is already a barrier, the addition of emotional distance can be downright destructive. Since small niggles can build into bigger frustrations, the setting of communication ground rules can keep the communication channels fully open and the team running smoothly.

As for quantity of messages, consultant Peter Hilton offers: "My rule of thumb is: don't send faster than you can receive, and then don't send faster than the other person is sending."[18]

Customer support specialist Laura Rooke has a different pet peeve about IM: "I treat my instant messages the same as I would a conversation. You wouldn't call across to somebody in the office and say, 'I have a question for you,' and then turn and walk away. So don't send someone a question via instant message and then not answer back. That's like a drive-by hello."[19]

Given the fact that incoming communication can often be a disruption, for many the most important factors of etiquette concern timing, the urgency of the content, and the effort required to respond. In Laura Rooke's example above, the "drive-by hello" was annoying because the very purpose of instant messaging is its spontaneous nature—which comes with the assumption that the intrusion is coming fast and its duration will be brief, its completion clear to both parties. (In chapter 4 we noted how one coworker's careful, slow typing made IM agonizing for his correspondents, who felt obliged to stare at that blinking screen awaiting whatever would eventually spill forth.)

As another example, I know of someone who collaborated with two outside freelancers whose work regularly required getting answers to questions. One freelancer saved up several questions and then called to ask them all in one shot; the other simply picked up the phone the second she had a question. (This was back when email was still being developed and was not yet widely used.) The one-shot freelancer enjoyed a good relationship with her contact; less so the other, since the annoyance of the constant phone calls eventually eroded that work relationship.

Though I personally prefer the one-message approach—and now I'm talking about email, not the telephone—I've corresponded extensively with someone who hated multi-issue emails. She got two-hundred-plus emails a day, most of them "one-item quickies," as she called them. When her meetings for the day were done and she turned to tackle her email, she'd want to quickly forge through them. So for her, receiving a message that called for more than she could produce in the moment both bloated her in-box and weighed down her nagging to-do list.

As an aside, note that an additional advantage to one-item quickies is that their subject lines are more likely to match their content. Hassan Osman at Cisco Systems recommends changing the subject line of email threads as the conversation changes so that the information can be more easily tracked down in the future. This searchability—as well as the option to group different topics in different channels—is one of the reasons many use Slack as one of their communication tools. (The Slack etiquette sidebar lower down details both different channels and threading conversations.)

As you can imagine, asking teammates to offer their preferences in an agreement conversation is invaluable, in part because any story behind a preferred work pattern gives the team a chance to learn more about each other. And note, the team agreement can also include which "standard" professional protocols your team might not want to follow. For example, the *Embrace Video—and Do It Right* section (*p. 166*) of chapter 7 specifies the professional approach to using video, especially for remote workers at home. Ideally, a video call from a home office will be no less professional than one from a work office. But as Agile coach Mark Kilby shares in chapter 8: "On my team, nobody gets upset if somebody's kid pops up in the background and says hi, or a family member walks past. In fact, it can help us build camaraderie."[20]

The following sidebar offers an example of one team's established communication etiquette, in this case Happy Melly's etiquette for Slack.

Sample Team Agreement Etiquette for Slack

Slack is a cloud-based team-messaging/team-collaboration tool. The following is the chosen Slack etiquette mutually decided upon by the team at Happy Melly, the global professional happiness association of which I am the remote team manager.

- You're responsible for managing your own downtime and notifications.
- @Tag people when you want them to see something.
- Segment topics into different channels.
- Use threading in conversations when possible.
- When in doubt, always post a message where everyone can read it.
- When referring to a Slack channel or name, always #link to it.
- Ask people to do a task in Slack. If it's a big task or a task with a deadline of >1 week, also create a Trello card for it, and include the link to that card in the Slack mention.

- Re: conflict issues: in general, start with a one-on-one conversation. If you choose to take it public, the #pillow-fight channel is the place designated for uncomfortable conversations.
- When posting messages, be specific with your needs and give context. Use full sentences. Link to the information you're discussing (Trello cards, Google Docs, etc.) to make it easy for everyone to access. Again, threading helps keep conversations organized by topic.
- When you ping people, give them all the context they'll need in order to get back to you when they can. Include links, docs, deadline, desired response time—anything that can move the conversation forward asynchronously.
- If you make a mistake in a message, edit your message rather than writing a new, corrected one. Remember to use threads to clarify.
- To help reduce text (or cut down on noise), consider responding with an emoticon if that makes sense—especially thumbs-up/thumbs-down votes and the like.[21]

COMMUNICATION MIND SET

Though we noted this in the previous chapter, it merits another mention. The last element to tuning your team is to agree to communicate from a mind set of positive intent. The simple truth is that misunderstandings happen when we don't have the full picture, and those misunderstandings can derail a team's alignment—not to mention its productivity. Since small frustrations tend to build up over time, it's a top priority to address misunderstandings as soon as possible so as to regain that alignment. In brief, don't let things fester. If something is irking a team member, it's important that he or she feels able to express it. But in that expression, it's essential to assume positive intent—as well as to use phrasing that's constructive rather than critical or accusatory. We cover this important issue again in relation to cross-cultural communication. But before we venture into different cultures, let's consider the game rules called for when team members simply work in different time zones.

Time Zone Concerns

> *"The issue of time zones is still fundamental. Somebody has to go to bed late or wake up early."*
>
> —Howard B. Esbin, *CEO, Playprelude.com*[22]

Those of us in regions that adjust the clocks for Daylight Savings know how easy it is to show up an hour early or an hour late on that first Monday after the change. So if you work with people in a different time zone from yours, it's practically guaranteed you'll have a time zone scheduling snafu at some point. Fortunately, such incidents can be kept to a minimum with the help of expanded awareness and a few tips noted below.

SCHEDULE IN ONE TIME ZONE. Choose one time zone as the time zone used with any scheduling. For example, if your team has members in Brussels, London, and New York, with the majority in London, then schedule any cross-team interactions by London's Coordinated Universal Time—UTC (previously known as Greenwich Mean Time or GMT). This standard will avoid confusion and scheduling errors.

USE A SHARED CALENDAR. Using a shared calendar is another way to minimize confusion and scheduling errors—again based on a single time zone. Also, if your team spans more than one country or culture, it can be helpful to include holidays in that calendar.

ORGANIZE YOUR TEAM EFFICIENTLY. If there are any tasks that require completion before handing over to a next phase, try scheduling them from East to West so as to avoid lag time. Similarly, any tasks that require synchronous collaboration are best assigned to workers in the same time zone, regardless of how far apart they are; this is also known as assigning "North to South." (We elaborate on this approach lower down.)

EXPAND YOUR TIME ZONE AWARENESS. Though you will be scheduling based on the chosen time zone, nonetheless get in the habit of checking what time it is for your distant colleagues. Many teams use a time zone app to help them coordinate their real-time interactions. This proves enormously helpful for teams like Happy Melly, whose eight core members span from Regina, Canada, to Visakhapatnam, India—which is a difference of nearly twelve hours. Such modern-day tools are a great improvement on the old-school rendering (shown below) of the widest time difference among the Happy Melly team. For more, see the TIME ZONES category (*p. 314*) in the *Nitty-Gritty/Logistics* section of "Technology & Tools."

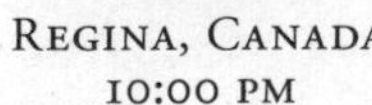

Regina, Canada 10:00 PM | London, U.K. 5:00 AM | Juba, South Sudan 7:00 AM | Visak, India 9:30 AM

DOUBLE-CHECK THE TIME. Get in the habit of double-checking your meeting times—also with the aid of the time zone apps mentioned above.

EXPRESS YOUR TIME ZONE AWARENESS. I regularly speak with a colleague in a time zone that's nine hours earlier than mine. I always start our calls saying: "Good morning, good evening!" so as to demonstrate my awareness of where *she* is in *her* day. I also include her location on Yahoo's weather app on my phone; that way I can get a sense of what the weather is like in her region at the same time that I check what time it is for her. Somehow just knowing if it's cloudy, drizzly, or sunny for her helps me feel more connected.

PRIORITIZE YOUR OVERLAP TIME. Schedule collaborative activities for any time in which *all* team members are working regular workday hours.

COMPOSE CONTENT-RICH COMMUNICATIONS. Nothing slows down time-zone lag time more than assignments that lack key information. Instead, make a point of providing all the context the recipient will need in order to complete the task, such as links, docs, the deadline, or a preferred response time—anything that can move the conversation forward asynchronously. For some teams (and for some types of communication) it might be wise to develop a template or checklist to ensure all the important info gets relayed in the initial request.

KNOW EVERYONE'S PREFERENCES. In his article "Visualizing Time Zone Challenges for Distributed Teams" on the Mingle blog, Patrick Sarnacke draws from his own experience regarding the lunch-time preferences—or even requirements—of his colleagues.

> **In the U.S., we're pretty used to grabbing fast food and eating at our desks. In other countries, lunch isn't that simple. In Brazil, lunch is the most important meal of the day, so it causes serious morale issues if we consistently schedule over it. In our office park in Chengdu, China, the cafeterias *plan* not to have leftovers. That means that if you don't eat by 12:30 PM you definitely won't get your first choice, and if you don't eat by 1:00 PM, they'll be out of food.**[23]

MAKE IT FAIR. For the times when you must schedule outside team members' work hours, be sure to share the pain of accommodating early morning or late night conversations and meetings.

TIME ZONES AND WIDELY DISTRIBUTED TEAMS

An additional consideration comes into play when the time zone differences span more than just a few hours—and when teams in one region rely on input and assignments from another. As mentioned in chapter 6, one solution is to hire workers who are in the same time zone, or at least workers who share a considerable overlap of working hours.

Established teams can also maintain smooth productivity via simple planning. Blossom VP Sebastian Göttschkes pads his schedule to cushion potential delays.[24] To address issues that require group input, ScrapingHub director Pablo Hoffman will schedule a call within everyone's working hours to "force" a decision.[25] And on Happy Melly's fully distributed team, Ralph van Roosmalen initiated a great approach for making efficient decisions: the "proposal document." This is a team-accessible Google Doc that includes: the decision to be made, its pros and cons, all variables—including if there's any pending information to be added, and a section requesting feedback. By this means everyone's voice gets a chance to be heard—asynchronously.

In one last point, RebelMouse CEO Paul-Andrea Berry-Breanna offers: "You can also prevent communication frustration by making sure everyone has multiple tasks in their queues. That way, if something gets stuck in a communication bottleneck, remote employees can move on to the second or third task on their list while they wait for a response. . . . This keeps everyone moving full speed ahead—no matter where they are in the world."[26]

Now, let's add cultural differences into the mix.

Cross-Cultural/Multilingual Game Rules and Etiquette

> *"There's this concept that a culture is a different country. But you'll notice that there's a big difference between somebody who grew up in the middle of New York City and somebody who grew up in the Amish countryside. That's not a different country—that's a different location. Culture is generational. It's different life experiences. It's personality. In a way, everything is multicultural. And if we start looking at it that way, we open up a curiosity to better understand how are we different."*
>
> —VANESSA SHAW, *workplace innovator, Human Side of Tech*[27]

The process of getting everyone on the same page is all the more important when team members cross not just time zone boundaries but also country borders—and especially when a different culture accompanies a different language. In the quotation just above, Vanessa Shaw speaks of opening ourselves to better understanding how we are different. It's in that sort of acknowledging—in respecting and appreciating our differences—that we can work together better.

That process begins by expanding our worldview.

Our cultural background affects how we respond to others. When we work in the same location with people from other cultures, we have the chance to better understand our differences by picking up on others' social cues, especially those expressing comfort or discomfort. But when we're not in the same room with our coworkers we lose important context—even when communicating with video. And diminished context can lead to misunderstandings. The particular trouble with misunderstandings arising from different cultures is the fact that we don't know what we don't know.

We can succeed in working with anyone, from anywhere, when we take the time to learn as much as we can about each other. Do what you can to learn about your remote colleagues' traditions and customs—including, ideally, the motivation and reasoning behind those customs.

Consider the following. In some cultures, being direct is considered impolite. Or someone might equate accepting a compliment, even gracefully, as being conceited. Some see asking for feedback as a form of weakness. Some would be reluctant to pronounce an opinion before learning the views of those higher on the totem pole. Others refrain from making a decision before getting input from the entire group. As Agile coach Ralph van Roosmalen puts it: "We all have our own user manual."[28]

Many of my interviewees warned of the dangers of making assumptions about a remote coworker's actions—or lack thereof. For example, let's say you're having a video call with a coworker who keeps averting her gaze. It would be easy to assume that she is shy, or even rude. But as it happens, in some cultures it's inappropriate to make eye contact. So you could easily form an erroneous opinion about that person—which could hinder your chances of mutually developing a strong working relationship.

Fortunately, there are ways to develop good remote relationships.

> **Each individual has his or her own traits, obviously. But there are patterns in how people in different regions behave, and in particular, communicate about things. So you just have to be aware that this difference exists, and then train yourself to be slower to react.**
>
> —Fernando Garrido Vaz, independent product manager[29]

Some people overestimate the influence of culture. In the end, it's just people working together. In my opinion, it doesn't matter what culture you work with. You just need to get used to it. If you get a new colleague in your office, you need to get used to that too. We just need to adapt.

—Hugo Messer, distributed Agile expert and founder, Bridge Global and Ekipa[30]

First up: mind set.

RESPECT AND APPRECIATION

Agile expert Hugo Messer puts it succinctly: "Accept that there will be cultural differences, and organize around them."[31] To follow we'll cover many ways to organize around those differences. But before we get too clinical, we'd be wise to deepen that awareness to one of respect and appreciation.

While it's true that managers hire some far-located workers with cost savings in mind, those workers were nonetheless carefully selected for what they bring to the table. What those from other cultures bring should not be considered within the caveat of an unavoidable "minus," as in, "they're great—except for the language barrier . . ." This is because in many cases the pluses of diverse teams far outnumber any supposed minuses. (For more, see the sidebar to follow.)

Scott Page's "Ketchup Principle"

As he describes in his 2007 book *The Difference: How the Power of Diversity Creates Better Groups, Firms, Schools, and Societies*, researcher Scott E. Page, professor of complex systems at the University of Michigan, uses a commonplace scenario to illustrate the value of crafting diverse teams. The discussion arises from the simple question: "Where do you keep your ketchup?" As it happens, in some regions, many people keep their ketchup in the refrigerator, whereas in other regions ketchup is stored in the cupboard.

He shared this next portion in a 2016 podcast on Gimlet Media's show *Reply All*: "Suppose you run out of ketchup. If you're out of ketchup and you're a ketchup-in-the-fridge person, what are you gonna use? You might use mayonnaise, you might use mustard, because those are the things . . . [usually] next to ketchup. If, alternatively, you're a ketchup-in-the-cupboard person and you run out of ketchup, what's next to the ketchup in the cupboard? Malt vinegar."[32]

His point: when faced with a dilemma, a team made up of only ketchup-in-the-fridge people is more prone to seek solutions in a narrow field. But a team that also includes ketchup-in-the-cupboard people will draw upon a wider field. Working together, they produce more innovative solutions.

Essentially, if you work with people from other cultures, respecting their differences and appreciating their particular contributions will enhance the benefit you all bring to the table—including your own.

StarterSquad cofounder Tiziano Perrucci encapsulates his experience with three lessons: "The first is to listen. If you're not able to listen, you're not going to get far in understanding others. The second thing I learned through a lot of pain: don't make assumptions; instead, ask questions. Most of us are usually happy to answer questions about ourselves. And the third thing: don't take things personally."[33] Note that, though Tiziano names it second, the advice to not make assumptions was the one most cited among my interviews—along with the important follow up: "Ask questions; be curious." And when your colleagues answer your questions, listen carefully to what they share.

The advice to not take things personally links with another offering: give your colleagues the benefit of the doubt. The aforementioned Paul Berry emphasizes the importance of a positive mind set from a few different angles. He recommends being "intentionally positive"—especially in emails. This is because what could seem to be perfectly benign to the writer can all too easily be perceived negatively by the recipient. Similarly, he urges his team to offer suggestions, not critiques. When recipients feel the positive aspects of their contributions are being appreciated, they're more likely to listen openly to suggested changes. He adds: "In general, I've found when I have something positive to say, I send it immediately. When I have something negative to say, I sometimes give myself some time to mull it over—and I'm usually glad I did."[34]

Another angle of respect and appreciation involves simply making the effort to learn about the other cultures represented on the team. Better yet, try to learn at least the most basic phrases in others' languages, especially greetings. For more, see the *On Working with Other Cultures* portion (*p. 325*) of BOOKS & GUIDES in "For Further Reading, Listening, and Consultation" in the RESOURCES section.

MULTILINGUAL COMMUNICATION

The all-important topic of communication has its own concerns in the multilingual sphere. Just as teams might choose a common time zone, multilingual teams will often choose a common language. While this is likely the only viable means of aligning the team, it still leaves some members speaking and writing in a non-native language. That means all but those fluent in the chosen language start out with a disadvantage.

That disadvantage is often most prevalent with the written word, since many find it easier to speak in a foreign language than to write in it. But then again, for some the difficulty is in parsing a strong accent. Either way, opportunities for misunderstanding abound.

The best way to address this concern, ironically, is to have an open, honest, team-wide conversation. This way you can assess exactly what language disadvantages exist within the group, as well as learn each member's preferred workaround. For example, this is why Conteneo designed their Weave decision support platform to provide a built-in chat interface along with decision-making frameworks. As CEO Luke Hohmann explains: "When teams with mixed languages need to reach a decision, they need to have the time to reflect on their choices. The integrated chat capabilities of Weave provide exactly this capability, enabling the group to make decisions that motivate action."

Now, that conversation might seem easy enough, but note that people from some cultures might be reluctant to air their personal views. In his article "Managing Cultural and Language Divides Within Your Remote Team," Deven Bhagwandin explains how "employees from Japan, who typically speak perfect English and can communicate with ease," often don't express their thoughts "because it is traditionally not within their culture or rights to express their own opinions in the workplace." And so Deven recommends leading by example by "encouraging open communications from day one, especially with the internationals on your team."[35] One way to effectively identify any reluctance: have team members complete an anonymous questionnaire that asks, in part, how likely they'd be to ask questions and offer opinions. And then lead by example, emphasizing that those questions and opinions are welcome—because they're conducive to team building and productivity.

For this reason and others, the various multilingual concerns can be summed up in two recommendations. One: do your best to avoid using idioms, jargon, and slang words. And two: overcommunicate.

But note, as Silvina Martínez from the consulting company Managing Virtual Teams points out: "Overcommunication doesn't mean that you're constantly talking to your team or sending a thousand emails per day. It just means that you're making an extra effort to explain what you need to share."[36] Essentially, the best way to ensure that all members have the information they need is to convey it more than once and in more than one mode—perhaps even in more than one language. Just as it's prudent to follow up a phone call with an email confirming what was discussed, take every opportunity to clarify your meaning, especially for those reluctant to express that they're confused. Similarly, Brie Reynolds recommends speaking up if you don't understand something. Model a culture of open honesty.

The concept of conveying information in more than one mode applies to visuals as well. In a *Fast Company* article, John Rampton suggests using signs, cue cards, and other visual aids whenever possible, especially for conveying instructions and assignments.[37] As phrased on Sococo's People-Centric Communications blog, "Whatever you're trying to communicate, it's vital that you spend some time thinking about how you can use visuals to help get your meaning across."[38] (To get you started, check out the following sidebar.)

Say It with Pictures

To follow are some suggestions for how you can augment your communication with visuals.

- EMOTICONS: In group chat conversations, some text responses can be conveyed with an emoticon of, say, a heart, or a smiley face, or a thumbs-up. (Another benefit to these is that emoticons are often seen as friendly—and, as we noted in chapter 8, it's good practice to always be friendly—even overtly friendly.)
- KUDO CARDS: Kudobox.co allows you to send a visual thank you via Twitter.
- VIDEO: Send a video message instead of an email.
- VIRTUAL MEETING CARDS: In online meetings, it can be uncomfortable to interrupt the conversation when we need to express something. But with virtual meeting cards, we can hold up a card to share that "you're on mute" or "you're breaking up" or even that we'll "be right back." I'm such a fan of this concept that I produced a beautiful set of twenty-four different Collaboration Supercards that I sell on my website (https://collaborationsuperpowers.com/supercards).
- ONLINE DOC OR SPREADSHEET: Here's an example where the virtual solution is more effective than the colocated one. With a team editing an online doc or spreadsheet together, everyone has an equally close view of the content at hand, and can jot notes, ask questions, and make changes for all to see. Distributed Agile team trainer Lucius Bobikiewicz excels at using spreadsheets for powerful online collaboration. As he relates: "We use simple online spreadsheets to visualize our thoughts and keep notes during meetings. Everyone can edit in parallel, which is sometimes even better than using the flip chart in an in-person meeting."[39]
- VIRTUAL WHITEBOARD OR MIND MAP: Similar to the benefit of the previous entry, a virtual whiteboard or mind map also helps to focus both attention and conversation.

- ACTUAL WHITEBOARD: But don't be afraid to go lo-fi! Pointing the video camera at a whiteboard and writing or drawing can be a very effective way to help information stick for your viewers. Academic life coach Gretchen Wegner uses a mini whiteboard to create visuals while she teaches. Just make sure you have good lighting.
- VISUALIZATIONS: As an experiment on the Happy Melly team, we asked everyone to draw their version of the company's business model and share it with the others, which we did by sharing our screens. The fact that no one's drawing even closely resembled another immediately told us we had a problem—much more effectively than words could have done.
- PRELUDE: Prelude is a trust-building tool for virtual teams. It involves using interactive whiteboards to mutually create a drawing that incorporates visual representations of everyone's personalities, strengths, talents, and assets (www.playprelude.com).

Now that we've considered our options, let's move on to actually crafting a working agreement.

Creating a Team Agreement

There are a number of ways to create team agreements. The Team Canvas is modeled after the one-page Business Model Canvas (http://theteamcanvas.com). The Delegation Board is a Management 3.0 practice for delegating decision-making in an organization (https://management30.com/practice/delegation-board)—though note this could be done in addition to team agreement. I personally recommend the ICC Workflow (Information, Communication, and Collaboration), designed by Garam Group engineer Phil Montero. With this approach, team members brainstorm the best solutions for the team's particular needs regarding information, communication, and collaboration. (See the sidebar to follow, as well as the "Remote Team Agreement" [*p. 256*] in the Part IV EXTRAS.)

Sample Considerations for an ICC Workflow Team Agreement

"Document your culture, not just for yourself, but also so your team can help you maintain it."

—Jeremy Stanton, *SVP of engineering, Amino Payments*[40]

INFORMATION

What kind of information do you need to share? What kind of information do you need shared with you? Shall we use a centralized file system? Shall we use a centralized task system? Shall we use shared calendars? Do you need access to a shared database? How do you prefer to track time? Do you have any concerns about security? (Note that for established teams the "shall we" questions could be rephrased along the lines of "Do you have any problems with our established task system?")

COMMUNICATION

Note which of the following you will use to communicate with each other: *email, text, instant messaging, phone, video calls, video chat, virtual office, in person*. What should be our expected response times for each? Would you prefer any of these means to be what we primarily use for particular tasks/situations? Should we establish core hours when everyone will be accessible? [For teams that span more than one time zone] Which time zone should be the one we use when scheduling?

COLLABORATION

SCHEDULING: Should we establish core hours when we will collaborate? (Note that hours for collaboration are usually shorter time frames than hours for when all are *accessible*.) [For teams that span more than one time zone] Which time zone should be the one we use when scheduling? What should be our primary means of visualizing our different locations/zones?

TASK MANAGEMENT/DESIGNATION AND WORKING OUT LOUD: How shall we assign tasks? Do you have any concerns about unintentional task redundancy? If so, how should we make sure that doesn't happen? What tools should we use to know what everyone else is doing? (For more, see Technology & Tools" [*p. 301*] in the RESOURCES section.)

PRODUCTIVITY/RESULTS: What should our measurable goals be? How and how often will we assess where we are with those goals? Should we implement some kind of OKR (Objectives and Key Results) system? (For example, as a means of addressing worker burnout, Kenyan nonprofit technology company Ushahidi implemented an OKR system to allow workers to set their own goals.)

TIME TRACKING: How should we track our time? (Submit our hours individually? Use a manager-accessible digital tracking tool?)

INTERPERSONAL CONCERNS

What approach should we use to give each other feedback? Should we adopt a formal protocol such as the "30/60/90 Feedback Framework"? How should we address interpersonal concerns and misunderstandings? How can we regularly express appreciation of each other?

Note: in the Work Together Anywhere workshop we walk participants through the process of creating a team agreement. For more, see page 333 or visit https://collaborationsuperpowers.com/anywhereworkshop.

As noted earlier, the ICC Workflow is just one method of creating an agreement. But regardless of which method you choose, the point is to discuss the assumptions everyone has concerning all regular aspects of working together. Only after airing everyone's views and considering the pros and cons of different approaches can you determine the team's consensus for each item. The beauty is that a practice or protocol that each member has agreed to is far more likely to be followed than one that is merely assigned and expected. Team alignment begins with team agreement.

Ideally a team agreement is a living document. Since the way people work will naturally evolve over time, it's recommended to review the agreement regularly, especially if there's a change in the team's lineup.

Remote Reminders

STEPS OF TUNING A TEAM

- Establish when you will use which tools and why.
- Ensure everyone has those tools, both hardware and software.
- Establish your preferred etiquette for all interactions; for many the most important factors of etiquette concern timing, the urgency of the content, and the effort required to respond.
- Agree to communicate from a mind set of positive intent.

TIPS FOR EFFECTIVE COMMUNICATION

- Use video regularly—especially for meetings.
- Always have multiple communication channels.
- Make it easy to move from asynchronous modes (email or text) to live ones (phone or video).
- Choose a primary mode of communication for important matters —and commit to it.

TIPS FOR WORKING ACROSS TIME ZONES

- Talk in one time zone and use a shared calendar.
- Organize your team efficiently.
- Expand (and express) your time zone awareness; get in the habit of double-checking.
- Prioritize your overlap time.
- Know everyone's preferences.
- Make it fair.

TIPS FOR WORKING ACROSS CULTURES AND LANGUAGES

Respect and Appreciation

- Respect that there will be differences among team members.
- Don't make assumptions; instead, ask questions—be curious.
- Listen carefully to what your colleagues have to say.
- Be intentionally positive; offer suggestions, not critiques.
- Strive to not take things personally.
- Take the time to learn about other members' cultures.
- Try to learn at least the most basic phrases in other members' languages, especially greetings.

Communication

- Have an open, honest, team-wide conversation to assess any language disadvantages and learn each member's preferred workaround.
- Convey all important information more than once and in more than one mode; for example, put in writing what you also say verbally.
- Take all opportunities to clarify your meaning, especially for those reluctant to express confusion.
- Similarly, speak up if you don't understand something; model a culture of open honesty.
- Avoid idioms, jargon, and slang words.
- Offer translations or hire an interpreter, as appropriate.

Tools

- Augment your communication with visuals whenever possible.
- Keep communication channels as fluid as possible with high-quality, well-maintained technology and tools.

CHAPTER 10

Bring It All Together

"While the degree to which companies embrace flexibility has matured, the ability to strengthen competencies of managers who lead distributed teams has not. Learning and development continues to be a key aspect to helping managers lead high performance distributed teams."

—Emily Klein, *"The World of Work in 2018: How the Workplace Will Evolve," Flexwork Global*[1]

In collectively crafting a team agreement (as covered in the previous chapter), the team also commits to abiding by its details—which solidifies team alignment. The manager can help maintain that alignment by ensuring that all team members have (access to) the knowledge, tools, training, processes, and cohesion they need to fulfill their agreed-to roles and obligations. This calls for three practices in particular. One, running effective meetings. Two, boosting morale—by expressing appreciation and celebrating success. And three, continually strengthening your relationship with each team member.

That much covers the last of the "what" on the manager's to-do list. We'll wrap that up with a few words on how to proceed in any new phase—including growing.

Let's get to it.

Run Effective Meetings

Of course, meetings are essential for sharing information and moving projects forward. Unfortunately, online meetings are notorious for being awful. From technical challenges to unengaged participants, there are all too many snags that can get in the way of trouble-free communication. Fortunately, my interviews produced a host of tips on how to run problem-free meetings in which everyone contributes. The most fundamental of these we've already discussed: invest in fast and stable internet, minimize background noise, and use great equipment—preferably video.

As for more-detailed advice, this book offers two sets of "Tips for Online Meetings"—one for facilitators and one for participants. To follow is the facilitator's list, after which we'll elaborate on a few points. (The Part IV EXTRAS section repeats the facilitator's list [*p. 260*] for easy access, followed by the participant's list.)

IN ADVANCE

TECHNICAL/GENERAL CONCERNS

- Use video when possible.
- Use high-quality equipment, including noise-canceling headsets.
- Have a tech/tools back-up plan in case your tech fails. (More on this to follow.)
- Assign someone to deal with tech challenges.
- Request that participants choose quiet locations.
- For video, request that participants have good lighting.
- Record your meetings for those who can't attend.

INTERPERSONAL/FACILITATOR CONCERNS

- Select a facilitator to run the meeting and keep to a timed schedule.
- Prepare an agenda with guidelines regarding time allotment.
- Ensure the agenda is accessible to all.
- Establish meeting etiquette. (More on this to follow.)
- Welcome participants to arrive early or stay late for personal time.
- Reserve time for an end-of-meeting "***parking lot***": when you attend to

miscellaneous "parked" questions after the primary agenda has been covered.

- Plan how you will keep track of parking lot items during the meeting.
- Determine how participants can indicate they wish to speak. (With video meetings, this could be to raise one's hand until acknowledged or to hold up a virtual meeting card [see next item]. With audio-only meetings, participants could use group chat or instant messaging to indicate that they want to jump into the conversation; or they could just interrupt.)
- Building on the previous item, consider using virtual meeting cards to enable non-intrusive communication. (More on this to follow.)
- Determine how you as facilitator will acknowledge a participant's wish to speak.
- Determine how participants can use ELMO (Enough—Let's Move On) if they want to reign in a wandering discussion. (More on ELMO to follow.)
- Whenever possible, use collaborative tools to help participants visualize the discussion. (More on this to follow.)
- For optimal engagement, don't include information that could be conveyed in writing. (Many recommend having a standard place for posting status updates—such as in Asana, Jira, or Slack.) Instead, reserve meeting time for discussion.
- Keep presentations to a minimum.
- Give participants a five to ten minute break for every hour of meeting.

As-Needed Considerations

PARTLY DISTRIBUTED TEAMS (*Some Colocated, Others Remote*)

- Agile coach Mark Kilby recommends using a buddy system, matching each remote worker with an on-site buddy to help with any troubleshooting.[2]
- If two people start speaking at the same time, and one is on-site and the other remote, favor the remote participant.

LANGUAGE-BARRIER CONCERNS

- Have a ***back channel*** to allow for real-time online conversation alongside the meeting—to share additional information and help facilitate comprehension of non-native-language participants. (For more, see the *Group Chat* portion [*p. 305*] of "Technology & Tools" in the RESOURCES section.)
- Use video as much as possible so participants can read lips.
- Use visuals instead of text whenever possible.

TIME ZONE ISSUES

- Choose one time zone as the time zone used with any scheduling. (For example, if your team has members in Brussels, London, and New York, with the majority in London, then schedule any cross-team interactions in Coordinated Universal Time—UTC.) This standard will avoid confusion and scheduling errors.
- Using a shared calendar is another way to minimize confusion and scheduling errors.
- As much as possible, schedule collaborative activities for any time in which all team members are working regular workday hours.
- Take turns sharing the pain of meeting before or after regular work hours.

DURING THE MEETING

TECHNICAL/GENERAL CONCERNS

- Test technology, lighting, and connection *before* start time. (Many recommend giving yourself at least five minutes before the meeting starts.)
- Disable tones and announcements.
- Mute yourself when not speaking.

INTERPERSONAL/FACILITATOR CONCERNS

- Arrive early to build in personal time; take the opportunity to bond with any others who arrive early.
- Start with an icebreaker to facilitate engagement. (More on icebreakers to follow.)
- Convey meeting guidelines at the outset, especially: how to signal a wish to speak—and how you'll acknowledge that wish, the request to keep till the end any extraneous questions or discussion points, and how to implement ELMO if necessary. (More on ELMO to follow.)
- Make sure everyone gets a chance to speak; strive to keep everyone engaged in general.

As-Needed Considerations

- Cut short miscellaneous questions, postponing them for the end-of-meeting parking lot.
- Utilize ELMO (Enough—Let's Move On) if a participant starts to dominate the discussion.
- Request feedback from/ask questions of lesser-engaged participants.

BEFORE ADJOURNING

- Commence parking lot items.
- Announce/reiterate post-meeting action items, specifying who, what, and by when.
- Thank participants for attending and end on a high note. (More to follow.)

A FEW FINER POINTS

Now, let's elaborate on a few of these tips.

Establish Meeting Etiquette in Advance

Regarding video conferencing etiquette, two items of advice stand out. The first is to make eye contact with the speaker. After all, one of the points of using video is to visually demonstrate one's full engagement with the joint mission. But even for those who normally avoid eye contact, this can still be tricky with webcams, since looking in the eyes of the people on the screen doesn't result in actual eye contact, at least at their end. For this reason, many recommend looking into your camera's eye instead—though that approach robs *you* of the ideal eye-to-eye connection. Combining the two, Sally French at *The Wall Street Journal* recommends moving the "video-chat window near your computer's camera so you can both look at people's faces and into the camera at once."[3]

The second advice is widely shared: don't engage in non-meeting activities. That means "don't tap out a work email"—with or without your mute on—as much as it means "don't play solitaire." Offer your teammates your undivided attention, just as you want from them.

Start With an Icebreaker to Facilitate Engagement

We can launch our virtual meetings on a positive track with a short "icebreaker" question or prompt. Some of my favorites include:

- Is there a story behind your name?
- What's your favorite food/drink/movie/type of music?
- Take a picture of your shoes.
- Complete this sentence: "When I dance I look like ______."

Just a brief, warm beginning can be surprisingly effective in smoothing the way for an engaged session. In addition, if you employ particularly fun icebreakers like the dance sentence example above, you might find participants more likely to join on time just so they don't miss out. (If you have meetings often, you might want to become an aficionado in icebreaker suggestions.

For more, see the *Virtual Icebreakers* portion [*p. 310*] of "Technology & Tools" in the RESOURCES section.)

Another plus: engagement, especially of the fun persuasion, contributes to team building—which in the end is our penultimate objective. (That's *penultimate* as in "next to last." Achieving your particular goals is, of course, your ultimate objective.)

This screenshot of the Happy Melly team showing pictures of their shoes appeared in *The Wall Street Journal* (21 December 2016) under the heading: "What's Worse Than an Office Holiday Party? A Virtual Office Holiday Party."[4] (Lisette Sutherland)

Have a Back-Up Plan Should Your Tech Fail

It's unavoidable: even high-quality technology will fail at times. But when we plan for that inevitability, we can get back on track as soon as possible. A simple option is to stick to audio-only should the video fail. Some teams have a rule that if Skype doesn't work, they should try Google Meet instead. Many rely on IM for discussing how to proceed

How to Implement ELMO if Called For

"ELMO" is an acronym that stands for "Enough, Let's Move On." This is a polite, effective way to keep an on-site meeting on track at times when the topic goes off course or if someone starts dominating the discussion. Different organizations utilize this approach differently. Some have attendees call out "ELMO" if they're tired of the topic at hand—at which point the facilitator takes a vote on if the majority agree to move on or want to continue that particular angle. Some keep an actual Elmo toy in the center of the conference table as a reminder. In one organization the Elmo toy is accessible to just the facilitator; if she picks up Elmo, that's a warning to the "rambler" to get back on topic; should that not happen quickly enough, she'll actually throw Elmo at the chatterbox![5]

Of course, a physical Elmo won't do much good in an online meeting. It so happens that Collaboration Superpowers has created a deck of ELMO cards to use in video meetings. (For more, see the sidebar to follow.) These enable anyone to voice a desire to move on—just by holding up an ELMO card until it's acknowledged—without having to verbally interrupt the speaker. In any case, regardless of how the ELMO technique is used, it's important that the team has agreed on the preferred ELMO etiquette *before* the meeting starts.

Tools to Help Participants Visualize the Discussion

As noted in chapter 9, there are many ways to add visuals to a virtual meeting. You can point the webcam at a (properly lit) physical whiteboard or poster—or use utilize virtual whiteboards or mind maps. You can also have participants collaborate on an online doc or spreadsheet.

End on a High Note

Just as it's ideal to start a meeting on a personal note—spending some bonding time and then launching with an icebreaker—we can end a meeting on a high note as well. Consider officially adjourning the meeting with the sort of mutual cheering, clapping, or otherwise "hurrah"ing that a sports team might do when starting a game. While this might sound silly, the plain truth is that our brains are hardwired to respond positively to participating in some form of team cheering, even if it's just a visual fist bump or thumbs-up. Indeed, if we force our faces into a smile, the brain gets tricked into thinking,

Huh—I'm smiling. I must be happy!—and our moods brighten, even if just by a little.[6] Of course, a few moments of cheering might not get you invited to either the cool-kids' club or the stuffy gentleman's club, but it will certainly make your team at least a bit more amped to head off and get great work done.

Using Virtual Meeting Cards

The above-mentioned ELMO card is just one of two types of Collaboration Supercards. The second deck offers twenty-four different cards with messages such as: YOU'RE ON MUTE, SLOW DOWN, and YOU'RE FROZEN—all messages that participants can convey to each other without interrupting the speaker. (For more, visit https://collaborationsuperpowers.com/supercards.)

YOU'RE
ON

The "You're on Mute" card from the Collaboration Superpowers deck of Supercards (Alfred Boland)

Boost Team Morale and Camaraderie

Just as it's ideal to end our meetings on a high note, we'll want to close any segment of work with appreciation of some kind—especially since expressing appreciation for a job well done is a sure-fire way to boost morale.

EXPRESS APPRECIATION

> *"Thank-you notes, short sweet messages, and birthday acknowledgments are much more relevant and important when you are all remote."*
>
> —Soulaima Gourani, *CEO, Trade Conductor*[7]

In chapter 4 we introduced Personal Kanban inventor Jim Benson, who advocates focusing on just three tasks at a time in order to complete them well—which pleases ourselves as much as it pleases those we work for. This entire book has been about how to help workers to do the kind of great work they'd feel proud of. But don't rely on that self-pride; it's important that you regularly express your thanks for their contribution.

Unfortunately, we can often forget to say thank you. The bad news is, not acknowledging contributions isn't just a lost opportunity; that lack of appreciation hurts morale, producing a negative effect.

While this might sound more pertinent to a preschool center than to a work setting, let's put this in perspective. As previously noted, how engaged employees feel in their work is tied to how appreciated they feel about their work. Plus, in 2017 *Forbes* reported that "66 percent of employees would quit if they feel unappreciated."[8]

So it won't be enough to just try to remember to say thanks once in a while; it's important that you work up a number of ways to ensure that all feel valued for their contribution. In chapter 8 we describe Happy Melly's Merit Money, which is essentially a 360-degree appreciation system that everyone engages in year-round. (The app Bonusly utilizes the same approach.) There are also feedback apps intended to facilitate the sharing of good will. Bonusly, HeyTaco.chat, and YouEarnedIt are great peer-to-peer recognition tools. With Tinggly and SnappyGifts.co, you can reward employees with fun outings—like going wine tasting. And one I'm particularly fond of: using Kudobox.co you can send a "kudo card" with a personal message via Twitter—which provides the additional benefit of public acknowledgment. Again, don't let this easily overlooked practice fall by the wayside; facilitate regular, team-wide appreciation. (For more, see the *Appreciation* portion [*p. 315*] of "Technology & Tools" in the RESOURCES section.)

In addition, you'll want to be sure to personally thank each team member for his or her particular contribution. But note: this isn't about a (virtual) pat on the back and a "Thanks, great job!" This is about specifically identifying some aspect of an individual's work that speaks to her or his commitment and value—something that indicates your praise was inspired by the actual work. This isn't voice candy; this is genuine appraisal and approval. (For more, see the sidebar to follow.)

Praise Effort, Not Ability

During the course of her extensive research on mind set, Stanford University psychology professor Carol S. Dweck has concluded that two different kinds of praise produce two very different outcomes. Describing Dweck's findings, Vernon Gunnarson writes: "Praising effort rather than innate ability helps people develop a 'growth' mind set instead of a 'fixed' mind set. . . . People with a growth mind set believe that their skills and abilities can be developed through perseverance and hard work; whereas those with a fixed mind set think their abilities are determined mostly by their natural talent or intelligence."[9]

In other words, Professor Dweck views the praising of a person's innate talent or intelligence, while seemingly high praise indeed, as not particularly motivating. This is in part because the smart or talented individual wouldn't necessarily know what did the trick—and what to repeat next time. Whereas praise that commends a person's expended effort is actually gratifying to receive, especially as it indicates the contribution was given more than just cursory attention. This gratifying praise is also incredibly motivating—since the recipient knows exactly what is needed to earn more of it.

One last point: you can extend your support of your team members well beyond expressing appreciation. I'm not the only one who feels that the tried-and-true top-down annual performance review is archaic—not to mention uninspiring. Today there are much more innovative and useful ways of capturing performance and motivating improvement. For starters, Thanksbox.co offers a range of digital tools to maximize employee engagement, whether via Peer-to-Peer Recognition, Rewards & Recognition, or their IdeasBoard, which facilitates collecting feedback, setting challenges, and creating incentives.

To wrap up this section: implement regular, team-wide appreciation; consider rethinking the performance review; and express genuine thanks yourself—every day.

CELEBRATE SUCCESS

The same advice applies to the larger expressions of thanks: celebrating milestones. Apart from the times when you can celebrate in person, there are plenty of ways to toast success remotely in between. As mentioned before, many teams use video tools to host trivia nights and group games. Some companies get snack boxes delivered to remote employees, or give gym memberships or housecleaning services. Brie Reynolds's remote team at FlexJobs has groups on Yammer where they have book clubs, cooking groups, and pet photo shares. Our fully distributed Happy Melly team once hosted a virtual dance party as a break during a long meeting. (Though some simply bobbed up and down in their seats, others—ahem—boogied like no one was watching, complete with furs, hat, and sunglasses.)

What's tricky is how to celebrate success when a team is only partially distributed. All the experts I've spoken with have expressed the importance of ensuring that *everyone* enjoys the party. For example, Ralph van Roosmalen offers: "When we celebrate with our team in the Netherlands, we also celebrate with our team in Romania. The only difference is that we're 1,700 kilometers apart."[10] And in an interview with Remote.co, communications lead Allie VanNest shares the following about tech company Parse.ly, only half of whose staff works on-site:

> **The biggest challenge of our remote team has been building team camaraderie. When we have a company-wide success, like closing a big sale or hitting a quarterly goal, we naturally want to celebrate it. Making sure our remote employees are a part of this celebration is so important, especially because all of our product team works remotely, so they serve an integral role in every one of our successes. We try to work around this with our retreats, which give us a chance to celebrate and get some work done as well. Last week we had a big win on the marketing team and decided to go to the spa to celebrate, so we sent a gift certificate to our remote marketing team member and joked about having her join a Google Hangout while she got her nails done.[11]**

One last point: taking the time to celebrate and to acknowledge important milestones also gives us an opportunity to take a closer look at the work that was done, to take a step back and realize just how much we've achieved. To bring this full-circle, my entrepreneur husband, Florian Hoornaar, shares a view that's worked well in his company: "Celebrating success isn't just a way to let off steam after a lot of hard work. It's also a way to help motivate people to tackle the next chapter."

Strengthen Your Relationship with Each Team Member

Erin Davidson, recruiting coordinator for global services company Appirio, offers the following:

> **The toughest part about managing a remote workforce is making sure everyone feels connected to the team and culture of Appirio. We work very hard to have local team events, virtual events, and constant video meetings; however, it can still be difficult to ensure everyone feels connected. Since you don't see your team members in the office on a regular basis, you may not always know what is going on in their day to day, so it is crucial to find ways to stay in touch regularly.[12]**

Similarly, Chris Arnold, partner at web design and technology studio Authentic Form & Function, notes the importance of "consistently checking in with, and taking the pulse of, how the team is feeling over any given week."[13]

Of course, it's ideal to have a happy team, with each member feeling connected and valued. But the concern runs deeper than that. Claire O'Connell, the director of people & culture at open-source software company Canonical, specifies: "Without the luxury of seeing colleagues each day, it can, at times, take longer to identify issues. For this reason managers need to see engagement and communication as key priorities."[14] This advice mirrors that concerning how small misunderstandings, left to fester, can bloom into more problematic disconnect amongst team members—whether the "issues" she speaks of concern just one worker or an entire team.

Now, just how to go about strengthening your relationship with each team member will differ from company to company—even from team to team. The main point is to, one, identify how you will strengthen those relationships and, two, make sure you consistently work to do so. And since there are many ways to go about that particular task, consider trying out one approach for a few months to see how it works—and then assess how you might continue. This point leads right into our next topic.

Experiment with Small, Reversible Steps

> *"Try things in little chunks so that there's limited risk and an opportunity to change quickly if things don't work."*
>
> —Jeremy Stanton, *SVP of engineering, Amino Payments*[15]

Since remote working calls for constant monitoring of tangible progress, it makes sense that advice about implementing the remote option would take a cue from the process framework known as Scrum, a subset of the Agile project methodology. Agile is an approach to project management and workflow that originated in the software development realm. (Some describe it as being the opposite of the waterfall workflow approach.) It's an "iterative" approach, meaning that the work is broken into small, measurable milestones. With Scrum, those milestones (sometimes called "sprints") are usually one- to two-week segments that end in a distinct deliverable—even if that deliverable isn't a completed project. At the end of each sprint the team meets (usually in a Retrospective, as described in chapter 8) to discuss where they stand and how best to proceed.[16]

The iterative approach is ideal for numerous reasons. Two primary ones are that the client always feels that progress is being made, and that any problems are identified—and subsequently ironed out—as soon as they happen, preventing long delays and postponed completion dates. Essentially, the beauty of the Agile mind set is the expectation of regularly assessing just how well a process is working, which allows for tweaking, switching gears—or scrapping altogether, as necessary.

It's been mentioned how Remote.co asked questions of 135 remote-friendly companies. One is: "What has changed about how your remote team operates?"[17] Some of the answers illustrate the iterative process in action—mostly concerning productivity, as it happens. Student marketplace StudySoup offers: "Our planning process used to be off the cuff, and mostly done in the meeting with the whole team. We've moved to a planning process where my cofounder and I plan our priorities for the week, and then connect with individual departments about what they can accomplish that day."[18] And tech COO Nathaniel Manning recounts: "At the beginning everyone just 'worked hard' when we were a start-up. But as we got older, people burned out. . . . This was sad, as it hurt the morale of the team, and we didn't have systems for finding these folks before they needed help. We implemented an OKR system to try and allow people to set their own goals, and then use that to measure our productivity." (This from nonprofit technology company Ushahidi in Nairobi, Kenya; they make open-source software "to help people raise their voice, and to help those who serve them listen and respond better, particularly for crisis response, human rights reporting, and government transparency.")[19]

Another example of the Agile method in action resulted from the question "What is the hardest part about managing a remote workforce?"[20] Casey Cobb, partner and developer at web development and design agency Project Ricochet, shares:

> **The hardest thing for me is that the tools we use to communicate can contribute to and enable an organization-wide urgency addiction that makes it hard for people to prioritize, focus on their craft, and achieve a flow state in their work. Slack, for all its greatness, can cause people to jump from conversation to conversation—and it can very easily lead to burnout. At Ricochet, we spend a lot of time making sure people don't get sucked into false urgency. Each team member makes a plan at the start of the day, and we go over their ability to achieve their plan during our one-on-ones. If they are unable to actualize their plans each day, it often means they need coaching on either doing what they set out to do or discerning between true urgency and false urgency. But it can also mean that the organization needs to get better at its own planning—and needs to stop throwing urgent tasks at people, especially since that can so easily lead to burnout.**[21]

Again, the beauty of the iterative process is the ability to make short-term, low-risk, isolated experiments—and to benefit readily from the knowledge they produce.

A Few Words on Growing

> *"Don't believe what others will say . . . that there comes a point where remote 'doesn't scale.' We're still growing at 150."*
>
> —FRAZIER MILLER, *COO, Articulate Inc.*[22]

The process of reassessing efficacy applies as much to fledgling operations as it does to ones ready to soar higher. As for the latter, numerous experts have offered their suggestions on how to expand a remote operation. The upshot: ensure communication tools and practices keep up with growth, and reorganize company structure as appropriate, such as adding layers of management once the company passes a certain size (some cite fifty-plus as the magic number). And some recommend a combination of the two points:

reorganizing into teams, in part so as to have smaller meetings where everyone can contribute and benefit equally.

> **The tools and habits that work effectively at eighty people are radically different to what works at three hundred people. Your communication has to be far more regular and have more clarity—and requires much more forethought. And this is especially important when it comes to communicating organizational change. You have no choice but to evolve both the tools you use and your habits around them in order to scale well.**
>
> —Coby Chapple, product designer, GitHub Inc.[23]

> **As Trello has grown, we've had to implement various other communication tools. For example, we have a weekly "Company Overview" board, where we update projects regularly so everyone in the company can know what is going on.**
>
> —Stella Garber, VP of marketing, Trello[24]

> **As we've grown, we've incorporated technology more into our daily operations. With more people involved in each process, it's important to continually increase efficiencies. We have more structured communication—from our performance management process to quarterly "state of the union" type meetings—to ensure everyone is receiving the information they need.**
>
> —Kristin Kanger, VP of talent management, Working Solutions[25]

> **As we grow, we build out more processes and planning. Done wrong, this could equal bureaucracy. Done right, these systems help us function despite not being colocated.**
>
> —Fred Perrotta, CEO, Tortuga[26]

Some Closing Thoughts

We've covered a huge terrain in the past four chapters. Perhaps you've already begun implementing suggestions found here; perhaps you're still letting it sink in. In any case, we needn't rehash with sweeping summaries. Instead, to follow are simply a few tips and words of advice to succinctly close our discussion.

- Communicate well and often—face-to-face whenever possible.
- Be transparent—let your team know both the good and the bad.

Kristin Kanger, VP of talent management at Working Solutions, points out that "learning how to effectively communicate remotely takes practice. How much to share, how often, who to include, and how to ensure the intended message is received"—all these details take time to get right.[27] Be patient with yourself as you proceed.

- Get to know the people you're working with.
- Take time to take care of your team.

As it happens, the sheer fact that you need to connect with your team members highlights one of the ways you can make remote working better than colocated working. How so? Some can take for granted that working in the same space everyday creates its own bond—even if no genuine personal connection ever really blooms. But the efforts needed to forge bonds despite the distance calls for giving more of the self—which can foster a great deal more connection. The point is to keep at it.

- Be intentional with everything you do.
- Experiment and improve continuously.

Some summary advice is blunter than others. Alex Frison, co-owner and project manager of WordPress solutions provider Inpsyde GmbH, says it straight-up: "If you fail in managing remote workers, it is not the system causing the failure, it is you."[28] Others take a softer line. Martin Van

Ryswyk, EVP of engineering at data management software vendor DataStax, started out thinking that managing a remote workforce "would be harder than it actually is. In fact, the management problems are the same regardless of location."[29] As it happens, the middle line feels the most apropos, as conveyed by Paul Jun, content marketer for the help desk software company Help Scout:

> **There's arguably more overhead placed on the shoulders of leaders in a remote company. The hardest thing is to acknowledge the overhead and be really organized about it. Being transparent and keeping everyone connected is something leaders in your company have to be constantly on top of. Of course, the wonderful tradeoff is a very productive workforce if you get this stuff right.[30]**

Remote Reminders

RUN EFFECTIVE MEETINGS

- The best quality meetings result from fast and stable internet, minimal background noise, and great equipment—preferably video.
- Always give yourself extra time beforehand in case troubles arise—and have a back-up plan should your tech fail.
- Establish meeting etiquette to set expectations.
- Start with an icebreaker to facilitate engagement.
- Whenever possible, use collaborative tools to help participants visualize the discussion.
- Use ELMO as necessary to keep the conversation on track.
- Record your meetings for those who can't attend.
- Keep presentations to a minimum.
- End on a high note. Consider allowing participants to take some extra social time after (or before) the meeting.

BOOST MORALE

- Establish an environment of mutual appreciation such that expressing thanks is a natural aspect of the team's culture.
- Explore various ways to regularly express thanks for each individual's contribution. Praise effort rather than ability.
- Take time to celebrate success. If your team is partly distributed, or you have colocated teams in more than one hub, be sure to celebrate equally.
- Continually strengthen your relationships with your employees.
- Maintain an open line of communication with each team member. Check in often to ensure everyone has what he or she needs.
- Take the time to get to know your team members individually; make it clear that you genuinely value who they are and what they offer.

GROWTH

- Ensure communication tools and practices keep up with growth.
- Reorganize company structure as appropriate.

PART IV *Extras*

MANAGER'S ACTION PLAN

Note that only the lists requiring a particular order are numbered.

COMMIT TO PROVIDING STRONG, EMPATHIC, FLEXIBLE LEADERSHIP

1. Read Chapter 7: Commit and Lead, Trust and Succeed (*p. 163*).

» BELIEF

2. Consider if you believe your team can succeed—and why. If you already believe, skip to the TRUST section (starting with item #9).
3. If you don't yet (fully) believe, write out any reasons you do believe or don't believe, one sentence per reason. Try to be as specific as possible. *For example, positive answers could include, "They would need to be _____ to succeed, and they're definitely that." More skeptical answers might include, "I'm not sure they have enough good communication skills—I think rifts would occur before long." Or, "I just don't think it's possible to be productive working alone."*
4. For each reason you don't believe, write out what would have to happen for you to change your mind on just that point. (Let's call these possibilities.) *Examples include, "If there were a way I could keep tabs on how well they're interacting, and time passed and everything still seemed okay, then I might believe." Or, "I might believe they could be productive if I saw that all deadlines were being met."*
5. For each possibility, consider if there is something you could do to initiate or facilitate that possibility becoming reality. *For example, "I could*

(a) establish a team-wide communications hub that includes a forum for members to express dissatisfaction, and (b) encourage everyone to speak up if there's a problem." Or, "I could (a) break down longer assignments into short-term deliverables; and (b) implement a team-wide task board, which would indicate what deadlines had and hadn't been met."

6. Get the ball rolling on each possibility you can initiate or facilitate in some way.
7. Continue working through this checklist. As you read more about what options are out there, keep in mind what details might address all the possibilities that are still pending.
8. If over time you end up changing your mind about any points, write a new sentence to reflect your new belief. Maintain a list of the lasting beliefs in a place where you'll regularly see it.

» TRUST

9. Consider if you trust your team members to come through with what they individually commit to. If you already trust, skip to the next section: ENSURE TEAM MEMBERS HAVE THE BASIC TOOLS THEY NEED.
10. If you don't yet (fully) trust, write out at least one sentence per team member specifying why you do or don't trust that person to come through with all commitments. (See the BELIEF entries for suggestions.)
11. For each reason you don't trust, write out what would have to happen for you to come to trust.
12. Consider if there is something you could initiate or facilitate that would help develop that trust.
13. Get the ball rolling on any "trust possibility" you can initiate or facilitate in some way.
14. If over time you end up changing your mind about any points, write a new sentence to reflect your new trust. Maintain a list of the items and people you continue to trust in a place where you'll regularly see it.

ENSURE TEAM MEMBERS HAVE THE BASIC TOOLS THEY NEED

- phone
- computer (desktop or laptop)
- headset
- external monitors or keyboard (if necessary)
- webcam capability
- video-friendly setup/space/screen
- modem (DSL/Wi-Fi/Ethernet, etc.)
- access to company email (such as with Outlook or Mac Mail) via the company server
- access to phone numbers and email addresses
- access to the files they're currently working on
- access to a virtual private network (VPN), as applicable

For those in the office (if partly distributed):

- quiet/private space and technology for video calls
- guaranteed space for remote workers to use on the days they need to work on-site (sometimes called "hot" desks)
- guaranteed space (such as a meeting or conference room) for collaborative working as a group

ENSURE YOUR TEAM IS SAVVY WITH THOSE TOOLS

15. Provide training when appropriate.
16. Check in with everyone to learn who needs extra support.

EXPLORE REMOTE-FRIENDLY TOOLS AND PRACTICES

17. Read Chapter 8: Facilitate Their Success with Leadership, Alignment, and a Full Arsenal (*p. 172*). Take notes along the way, considering what tools and practices might be best for your particular personnel, objectives, and circumstances.

18. Review "Technology & Tools" (*p. 301*) in the RESOURCES section. Flag (and perhaps research further) any possibly viable candidates.

CONSIDER THE TEAM AGREEMENT

19. Read Chapter 9: Tune Your Team with a Team Agreement (*p. 203*); take notes along the way.
20. Review the Remote Team Agreement template (TA template, *p. 257*).
21. Tweak the TA template based on your research thus far, especially concerning ideal tools and practices. Include any descriptions or URLs that will help the team consider each option.
22. Distribute the template to the team, requesting they review it on their own. They should consider which tools and practices they'd like to *try out*, noting their preferences and preparing explanations for their choices.
23. Schedule a meeting to discuss the TA.

DISCUSS THE TEAM AGREEMENT

Ideally the TA template is visible to all, such as on a physical or virtual white board or even on a document printout. If time allows, the goal is to reach a mutual agreement at the end of the discussion.

24. During the TA discussion meeting, walk your team through the template, having them weigh in on their preferences. Remind them that the point is to consider what the team will try out (first); nothing is to be set in stone.
25. As applicable, adjust the template as the meeting progresses.
26. Request a final vote on the adjusted agreement.
27. Distribute the approved document or ensure it's accessible to all (such as in a Google Doc).

ACTUALIZE THE TEAM AGREEMENT

Schedule and assign all action steps called for in the finalized team agreement.

28. Ensure all team members have access to the selected tech and tools—and that they get savvy with them.
29. Provide training and/or extra support as appropriate.
30. Schedule a time to check in about completing the actualization process—meaning, getting all the elements in place. Thereafter, the team will put all items in the TA into practice.
31. Schedule a time to check in regarding how that TA practice is going.
32. Schedule a time to check in (perhaps three to six months after implementation) regarding the TA to reassess its efficacy. Tweak the TA as applicable.
33. Schedule regular, periodic TA check-ins. (Some teams revisit their TA every six months or every time there is a change in personnel, whichever comes first.)

RUN EFFECTIVE MEETINGS

34. Read the *Run Effective Meetings* section (*p. 229*) of Chapter 10: Bring It All Together.
35. Consider your tech/tools back-up plan in case your tech fails. This includes knowing to whom you can assign the role of dealing with on-the-spot tech challenges.
36. Consider which icebreakers would likely be effective for your team. List out as many as you can research within a reasonable amount of time so you have them handy for the weeks to come.
37. Consider how you could keep track of action items to recap later.
38. Consider how participants could indicate they wish to speak. (With video meetings, this could be to raise one's hand until acknowledged. With audio-only meetings, participants could use instant messaging to indicate they want to jump into the conversation.)
39. Consider how you can acknowledge a participant's wish to speak.

40. Consider ways you and/or participants could use ELMO to reign in a wandering discussion.
41. Consider what tools you could use to help participants visualize the discussion.

BOOST TEAM MORALE—BY EXPRESSING APPRECIATION AND CELEBRATING SUCCESS

42. Read the *Boost Team Morale and Camaraderie* section (*p. 238*) of Chapter 10: Bring It All Together.
43. Consider practices you could implement to ensure that everyone feels that you value their contribution—such as offering Tinggly experiences or sending a Kudobox.co "kudo card." Note that this would be in addition to whatever ways you participate in the peer-to-peer appreciation practiced by the team as a whole (and as decided on in the team agreement).

CONTINUALLY STRENGTHEN YOUR RELATIONSHIP WITH EACH TEAM MEMBER

44. Create a checklist of items to discuss with each team member—including expressing appreciation for their specific contributions and efforts. Discussion questions could include:
    - » *Do you feel comfortable with all the tools we've chosen to use?*
    - » *Do you feel you get enough support from me?*
    - » *Are you happy with the work you're doing?*
    - » *Is there anything you need to help you be more productive?*
    - » *Are there any impediments that I can help to address?*
    - » *Do you feel valued on the team?*
45. Schedule repeating, periodic conversations with each member.
46. Schedule any action items that result from each discussion.

REMOTE TEAM AGREEMENT

Instructions & Template

Team agreements work for teams of any number. But note that team agreement discussions conducted online work best with a maximum of twelve participants. Also, it's ideal if the team is already comfortable using tools such as video conferencing and chat.

Instructions

The process for creating a team agreement falls into a series of phases:

1. Consider what your needs are based on your team and situation.
2. Research what options there are to best suit your needs.
3. Finalize (or create afresh) the Team Agreement (TA) template that you will present to your team, including some specific options based on your research.
4. Distribute the template, requesting that team members review it and prepare to discuss their preferences.
5. Meet to discuss and finalize the agreement.

To follow are some prompts to get you started thinking about what your needs are. You'll find the remaining prompts in the template itself. (Note that a digital version of the template is available at https://collaborationsuperpowers.com/extras.)

- Do you need to share your calendar or schedule with your team? If yes, consider which online calendars would serve your purposes; or, note that many task-management apps include calendars within their functionality.
- Do you need to track productivity?
- Do you have security protocols in place?
- Do you need a secure connection when accessing your networks?
- Is there anything preventing your access to needed information?
- Does the team need access to an intranet, online file system, or database in order to complete their work? If yes, consider what kind of access, permissions, and security protocols they'll need to connect to the system.
- Are there any team members who need support working with tools or technology? If so, consider your training options and/or if this factor should influence which tools you suggest.

Template

> For established teams, rephrase any "shall we" questions along the lines of: "How happy are you with [tool/practice/system]?"

INFORMATION

- What kinds of information do you need to share?
- What kinds of information do you expect to be shared with you?
- Shall we try out a communal task board such as [*insert some options here*]? Or any others?

- Do you have preferences re: tools for sharing how you can be reached—such as [*insert some options here*]?
- Do you have preferences re: tools for knowing what everyone is working on—such as [*insert some options here*]?
- Do you have preferences re: stand-up/Retrospective software—such as [*insert some options here*]?
- Do you have preferences re: time-tracking tools such as [*insert some options here*]? Or any others?

COMMUNICATION

- In the following chart, please note:
  - » *the mediums you prefer to use for work purposes (add an "X" or note particular kinds of work);*
  - » *your preferred response times for each medium; and*
  - » *the mediums you prefer to use for social purposes.*

MEDIUM	PREFER FOR WORK PURPOSES	PREFERRED RESPONSE TIME	PREFER FOR SOCIAL PURPOSES
EMAIL			
GROUP CHAT			
IM			
IN PERSON		N/A	
PHONE			
TEXT			
VIDEO CALL		N/A	
VIRTUAL OFFICE		N/A	

- Do you have preferences re: group chat tools—such as [*insert some options here*]?
- Do you have preferences re: video conferencing tools—such as [*insert some options here*]?
- Do you have preferences re: virtual office tools—such as [*insert some options here*]?
- Shall we have an established forum for sharing and discussing ideas—such as [*insert some options here*]? Or just bring up ideas in our regular meetings?
- We'll want to have an established forum for expressing appreciation of each other. Some possibilities are Merit Money or Bonusly, and YouEarnedIt. Would you like to try out any of those—or do you have other suggestions?
- We'll want to have an established protocol for requesting feedback on our projects—such as [*insert some options here, perhaps including the 30/60/90 Feedback Framework*]. Would you like to try out any of those—or do you have other suggestions?
- We'll want to have an established forum for addressing conflict—such as with [*insert some options here, perhaps including the Feedback Wrap or the Virtual Pillow Fight*]. Would you like to try out any of those—or do you have other suggestions?

COLLABORATION

- [*If your team spans more than one time zone*] Which time zone should we use when scheduling activities?
- Should we set (some) core hours for collaboration purposes?
- Some tools that facilitate online collaboration include [*insert some options here*]. Would you like to use any of those—or do you have other suggestions?

TIPS FOR ONLINE MEETINGS

Facilitators

Note that a separate list of tips for participants follows this list.

IN ADVANCE

TECHNICAL/GENERAL CONCERNS

- Use video when possible.
- Use high-quality equipment, including noise-canceling headsets.
- Have a tech/tools back-up plan in case your tech fails.
- Assign someone to deal with tech challenges.
- Request that participants choose quiet locations.
- For video, request that participants have good lighting.
- Record your meetings for those who can't attend.

INTERPERSONAL/FACILITATOR CONCERNS

- Select a facilitator to run the meeting and keep to a timed schedule.
- Prepare an agenda with guidelines re: time allotment.
- Ensure the agenda is accessible to all.
- Establish meeting etiquette.
- Welcome participants to arrive early or stay late for personal time.

- Reserve time for an end-of-meeting "***parking lot***": when you attend to miscellaneous questions after the primary agenda has been covered.
- Plan how you will keep track of parking lot items during the meeting.
- Determine how participants can indicate they wish to speak. (With video meetings, this could be to raise one's hand until acknowledged or to hold up a virtual meeting card [see next item]. With audio-only meetings, participants could use group chat or instant messaging to indicate they want to jump into the conversation; or they could just interrupt.)
- Building on the previous item, consider using virtual meeting cards to enable non-intrusive communication.
- Determine how you as facilitator will acknowledge a participant's wish to speak.
- Determine how participants can use ELMO if they want to reign in a wandering discussion.
- Whenever possible, use collaborative tools to help participants visualize the discussion.
- For optimal engagement, don't include information that could be conveyed in writing. (Many recommend having a standard place for posting status updates—such as in Asana, Jira, or Slack.) Instead, reserve meeting time for discussion.
- Keep presentations to a minimum.
- Give participants a five to ten minute break for every hour of meeting.

As-Needed Considerations

PARTLY DISTRIBUTED TEAMS (*Some Colocated, Others Remote*)

- Use the buddy system.
- If two people start speaking at the same time, and one is on-site and the other remote, favor the remote participant.

LANGUAGE-BARRIER CONCERNS

- Have an established ***back channel*** (such as group chat or instant messaging) to allow for real-time online conversation alongside the meeting—to share additional information and help facilitate comprehension of non-native-language participants.
- Use video as much as possible so participants can read lips.
- Use visuals instead of text whenever possible.

TIME ZONE ISSUES

- Choose one time zone as the time zone used with any scheduling. (For example, if your team has members in Brussels, London, and New York, with the majority in London, then schedule any cross-team interactions by Coordinated Universal Time—UTC.) This standard will avoid confusion and scheduling errors.
- Using a shared calendar is another way to minimize confusion and scheduling errors.
- As much as possible, schedule collaborative activities for any time in which all team members are working regular workday hours.
- Take turns sharing the pain of meeting before or after regular work hours.

JUST BEFORE/DURING THE MEETING

TECHNICAL/GENERAL CONCERNS

- Test technology, lighting, and connection *before* start time. (Many recommend giving yourself at least five minutes before the meeting starts.)
- Disable tones and announcements.
- Mute yourself when not speaking.

INTERPERSONAL/FACILITATOR CONCERNS

- Arrive early to build in personal time; take the opportunity to bond with any others who arrive early.
- Start with an icebreaker to facilitate engagement.
- Convey meeting guidelines at the outset, especially: how to signal a wish to speak—and how you'll acknowledge that wish, the request to keep till the end any extraneous questions or discussion points, and how to implement ELMO if necessary.
- Make sure everyone gets a chance to speak; strive to keep everyone engaged in general.

As-Needed Considerations

- Cut short miscellaneous questions, postponing them for the end-of-meeting parking lot.
- Utilize ELMO (Enough—Let's Move On) if a participant starts to dominate the discussion.
- Request feedback from/ask questions of lesser-engaged participants.

BEFORE ADJOURNING

- Commence parking lot items.
- Announce/reiterate post-meeting action items, specifying who, what, and by when.
- Thank participants for attending and end on a high note.

TIPS FOR ONLINE MEETINGS

Participants

Note that a separate list of tips for facilitators precedes this list.

IN ADVANCE

GENERAL CONCERNS

- If you will be providing an update, for optimal engagement note the following two guidelines. One, reserve any items that don't require discussion for another medium such as email or group chat. Two, for the information you do present, avoid reading from a script. Instead, engage fellow participants with conversation. (To help with this, perhaps keep your notes in outline form rather than complete sentences.)
- If you will be presenting anything, use video if you can.

TECHNICAL CONCERNS

- Use high-quality equipment, including a noise-canceling headset.
- Have back-up tech/tools available in case of tech failure.
- If using video, ensure you have sufficient lighting. Also consider having a screen behind you to reduce visual distraction.
- Set up in a quiet space, keeping background noise to a minimum.
- Test your technology, lighting, and connection *before* start time.
- Disable tones and announcements.

LANGUAGE-BARRIER CONCERNS

- Tell the meeting facilitator if you would benefit from a back channel (group chat or instant messaging) for language comprehension.
- Request video-based meetings to enable lipreading.

DURING THE MEETING

- Mute yourself when not speaking.
- Make note of questions to ask during the "parking lot" period.
- Strive to engage in the meeting without dominating. Respect any requests to postpone further discussion until later.
- Make note of and commit to action items assigned to you.

CONCLUSION

Doing Great Things Together

The purpose of this book has been to help you—whether you're a team member or a team leader—know what it takes to work remotely, successfully, with others. But beyond the specifics of just what to do when and why, there is a larger, even higher message. Being a successful remote worker also makes you a more successful person, a better person. It calls for you to know yourself: to know what you need, what you're made of, what you're capable of.

Working well remotely calls for being more intentional, more conscious, more thorough. It calls for taking the time to take care of yourself, to be willing to try new things, to constantly work to improve, even to indulge in your passions.

Working well remotely calls for being more caring and helpful, more conscientious and aware of others. It calls on us to communicate more, to share more, to ask more, and to ask for more. To offer the benefit of the doubt, and to assume positive intent. To express appreciation. It calls on us to be curious—to learn about others. To respect others' processes, and to trust that others will do what they say they will.

Connection happens when we pay attention to each other. And magic happens when teams align and dreams become goals and goals become reality. When we focus on trust, agree on how to work together, and cultivate closeness, we can do great things together. We can collaborate with people we respect in pursuing what we love most.

Doing great things means being an attentive parent, creating a new form of transportation, or stopping aging. It means working where we are most productive and pursuing what we love most. It means building a company we're proud of, and collaborating with people we respect.

What I find so personally exciting about being able to work from anywhere is that those of us who want to change the world can easily find each other—and proactively make amazing things happen. Join us!

ACKNOWLEDGMENTS
&
Early Adopters

I OFFER heartfelt, glowing thanks to:

- Florian Hoornaar, for having this stupid idea to begin with—and for being so patient with me ever since.
- Rapunza, for helping me to both finish this book and become a better person.
- Alfred Boland, for being my favorite graphic designer of all time and making me look so cool.
- Pilar Orti, for being the best collaborative competitor a girl could ask for.
- Jurgen Appelo, for the years of mentorship, opportunities, and trust.
- The Happy Melly team and community, for the support, promotion, mentorship, and happiness experiments.
- The Virtual Team Talk community for the support, fun, and virtual coworking.
- Gretchen Wegner, for being the best virtual coworker I have yet to meet in person—and for inventing virtual pie.
- Laura Mazer, for your amazering and delightful promotional wordsmithing and guidance.
- Hannu Heljala, for managing and updating my website and for being a great colleague.
- Marja Hautala, for your ready creativity and for being so delightful to work with.
- The Collaboration Superpowers facilitators, for helping people work better remotely all over the world.
- Marcus Rosenthal, for introducing me to Kendra the Kubi.

- Sococo and their amazing support team, for providing the VTT community with a virtual coworking space.
- Maria Quesada, for creating beautiful, content-rich newsletters, and for being the best, most competent virtual assistant I've ever had.
- Nick Jaworski, for being an amazing podcast producer and making my interviews sound so pro.
- Abdul Muhit Matin, for transcribing my interviews.
- Betsy Goolsby, for reviewing the early manuscript.
- Louise Brace, for reviewing the early manuscript and for being a fun remote colleague.
- Abe Heward and Loyal Basset, for the platonic love and for not abandoning me.
- Maarten Koopmans, for being my Dutch welcoming committee, my first interviewee, and a supportive friend.
- Wouter van Aalst, for keeping me healthy, sane, and moving.
- Margit van Harten, for healing my heart.
- All who contributed to the cover design (Alfred, Imran, Rapunza, Marja), and Erin Seaward-Hiatt, for running with it and making it great. Thanks too to Erin for your patience and professionalism.
- And to Cheech, for the furry companionship and entertainment.

THANK YOU as well to all those who expressed an early interest in this book:

Robert Aston
David Baer
Thomas Bär
Bianca Barone
Henrik Berglund
Keith Bernard
Alexander Birke
Anne Birnbaum
Arina Bondar
Maxime Bonnet
Brendan Boyd
Milenko Bugueno
Orestes Carracedo
Andrea Chiou
Andy Cleff
Steven Crago
Alexandre Cuva
Richard Dallaway

Tuan Dang
Kathryn Dekas
Claire Donald
Kayt Edwards
David Eliasen
Sergey Erlikh
Helena Evans
Peter Farkas
Pierre Fauvel
Jesse Fewell
Thomas Francis
Daniel Fritzler
Robert Galen
Stephen Giles
Andre Gomes
Ellen Gottesdiener
Growing Agile
Yves Hanoulle
Fredrik Happ
Jeffry Hesse
Jerome Hoerig
Martin Hultman
Sabine Igler
Impavid Consulting Inc.
Denis Jallet
Michael Kaufman
Andrew Kidd
Jason Knight
Hannes Kropf
Patrik Liljecrantz
Thomas Link
Jason Little
Jan Lundberg
Pedro Medas
Graziela Merlina
Fabiano Morais
Cuan Mulligan
Shaun Newman
Harry Nieboer
Yavor Nikolov
Zornitsa Nikolova
Oluf Nissen
Francis Norton
Sheila Olds
Adekunle Olonoh
Pilar Orti
Hassan Osman
Barry Overeem
Tracey Perkins
Christian Pfister
Darlene Pike
Project Leadership Academy Inc.
Mark Rehberg
Eva Reiterer
Chris Ridgewell
Jennifer Riggins
Chontelle Sundborn
Richard Sutherland
Gregory Tutunjian
Pascal van Beek
Jeroen van Hertum
Bart Van Loon
Adriana Vela
John Westworth
Michel Wicky

RESOURCES

GLOSSARY

Agile methodologies: in general, an "iterative" (meaning that the work is broken into small, measurable milestones) approach to project management and workflow that originated in the software development realm.

asynchronous: describing communication (such as via email or text) that doesn't take place in real time (as would a telephone call or video conference).

asynchronous interview: an interview in which a candidate video-records answers to questions. (Also known as *one-way interview* or *pre-recorded interview.*)

Baby Boomer: the generation born between 1945 and 1964.

back channel: a real-time online conversation (usually via chat technology) held simultaneously with another activity (such as a video conference or event) so as to augment understanding, such as for foreign-language comprehension.

colocated: working at the same site.

Coordinated Universal Time (UTC—for Universal Time Coordinated): the primary standard by which the world regulates clocks and time. Previously known as Greenwich Mean Time (GMT).

coworking space: a facility that offers work stations or rooms for rent.

digital nomads: those who use the internet and portable technology (cellphones, laptops, cloud-based applications) in order to maintain a nomadic lifestyle. For example, Piero Toffanin works as an IT business consultant from the camper he shares with his wife, Danielle—wherever they happen to be. And, for three months every year, trainer, speaker, and consultant Andy Willis leaves his coastal town in New South Wales, Australia, to both work in and hike the French Alps.

ELMO: an acronym for "Enough—Let's Move On"; used in meetings to keep the agenda on track.

freelancers: individuals who engage in supplemental, temporary, or project- or contract-based work.

fully distributed: when all team members work remotely. (Compare with *partly distributed.*)

Generation X (Gen X): the generation born between 1965 and 1984.

Generation Y: see *millennial.*

Generation Z: the generation born after 2004.

hours-oriented work: work where the *primary* expectation concerns putting in hours, especially during a set period—as opposed to producing distinct results. (Compare with *results-oriented work.*)

hybrid [workspace] model: regularly using more than one workspace, often to best accommodate the task and/or the personnel involved.

ICT: Information and Communications Technologies. (See also *T/ICTM.*)

instant messaging (IM): a text message session between two participants, usually between computers (rather than texts, which are usually sent by phone). An IM session remains connected until ended by one of the parties.

intranet: a private network accessible to only those granted authorization.

iterative: describes the Agile project-management approach, indicating that the work is broken into small, measurable milestones.

Kanban ("kawn-bawn"): a method for visualizing workflow so as to balance demand against capacity. (Originated by Japanese lean production, adapted by software developers.)

millennial (or Gen Y): the generation born between 1985 and 2004.

MMS (Multimedia Messaging Service): a text message sent via a cellular phone service, often limited to 160 characters. Unlike SMS, MMS can include images, video, or audio.

non-teleworkers: those who do not telecommute at all in their role (according to the 2016 PGi Global Telework Survey[1]).

OKR (Objectives and Key Results): a document that defines company and team objectives and measurable key results to provide "a critical thinking framework and ongoing discipline that seeks to ensure employees work together, focusing their efforts to make measurable contributions."[2]

office optional: a term indicating that an employer equally welcomes both remote and on-site employees.

one-way interview: an interview for which a candidate video-records answers to questions. (Also known as *asynchronous interview* or *pre-recorded interview.*)

online work(ing) (web)site: a website that helps match remote workers with jobs.

parking lot: the concept of putting off till the end of a meeting non-agenda issues that come up during the meeting. Other terms for this include Issue Bin, Coffee Pot, Water Cooler, Limbo, Chestnuts, Popcorn, and Refrigerator.[3]

partly distributed: when some members of a team work on-site and others work off-site. (Compare with *fully distributed.*)

portable technology: technology that enables productivity outside a fixed space.

pre-recorded interview: an interview in which a candidate video-records answers to questions. (Also known as *asynchronous interview* or *one-way interview.*)

remote-first: strictly speaking, an approach of organizing workflow such that a remote worker can contribute as much as those on-site do. In practice it can also be considered a default contingency plan to allow for seamless productivity when one or more employees on occasion must work off-site due to inclement weather, traffic, illness—even citywide disruption.

remote-friendly: a company open to hiring remote workers.

remote-only: an organizational configuration and mind set wherein employees only work remotely. (See the "Remote-Only Manifesto" [*p. 158*] in the Part III EXTRAS.)

remote teams: groups of people who work together on a project.

results-oriented work: work where the *primary* expectation concerns producing results—as opposed to simply putting in hours, especially specific hours spent in a distinct location. (Compare with *hours-oriented work*.)

Retrospective (or *sprint review*): regular, facilitated session for sharing progress, raising issues, and discussing solutions, often held every one to two weeks. Different Retrospective approaches are used to suit different setups and contexts. (For more, see the *Retrospectives* portion [*p. 316*] of "Technology & Tools," as well as the "Retrospective Plans" wiki at http://retrospectivewiki.org/index.php?title=Retrospective_Plans.)

Scrum: a subset of the Agile project methodology. Described by some as being the opposite of the waterfall workflow approach, Agile is an "iterative" approach, meaning that work is broken into small, measurable milestones. With Scrum, these milestones (sometimes called "sprints") are usually one- to two-week segments that end in a distinct deliverable—even if that deliverable isn't a completed project. At the end of each sprint the team meets (usually in a Retrospective) to discuss where they stand and how best to proceed.

Silent Generation: the generation born between 1925 and 1944.

SMS (Short Message Service); also MMS (Multimedia Messaging Service): a text message sent via a cellular phone service, often limited to 160 characters.

solopreneur: a small business owner with no employees.

sprint review: see both *Retrospective* and *Scrum*.

stand-up: a short status update, often done daily, where all share (1) what they did the day before, (2) what they're doing that day, and (3) anything they're struggling with. (The term "stand-up" originates from the on-site realm; the status update was meant to be so brief there would be no reason to sit down.)

super-commuter: someone who commutes for ninety minutes or longer.

T/ICTM: Telework/ICT-mobile work: the use of Information and Communications Technologies (such as smartphones, tablets, laptops and desktop computers) for the purposes of working outside an employer's premises.[4]

team agreement: a mutually crafted document that details how a remote team has chosen to work together, especially regarding tools, procedures, practices, and etiquette.

UTC (Universal Time Coordinated—or Coordinated Universal Time): the primary standard by which the world regulates clocks and time. Previously known as GMT (Greenwich Mean Time).

video conferencing: an internet-based means by which to enable real-time, video communication between two or more locations, often without including such features as file sharing, screen sharing, etc. (Compare with *web conferencing.*)

virtual office: software that enables access to a digital "office" complete with floor plan and avatars representing colleagues. You can move yourself from room to room, but you can only hear and speak to those who are in the same room with you—just like at an office.

virtual private network (VPN): a network that enables a secure connection to another network over the internet.

voice conferencing: real-time, audio-only communication between two or more locations. (Compare with *video conferencing* and *web conferencing.*)

web conferencing: an internet-based means by which to enable real-time, audio/video communication between two or more locations, often used to conduct meetings, training, or presentations; often includes desktop sharing, application sharing, and/or file sharing. (Compare with *video conferencing.*)

webcast: a broadcasting of material via the internet. Can be live or recorded, and is usually noninteractive. (Compare with *webinar.*)

webinar: a usually interactive broadcasting of material via the internet, often for small groups for instructive or educational purposes. (Compare with *webcast.*)

wiki: a collaborative website, usually a repository of information, that can be edited by anyone. The term derives from the Hawaiian word for "quick." To quote the founder of the first wiki, Ward Cunningham: "The idea of a wiki may seem odd at first, but dive in, explore its links, and it will soon seem familiar. Wiki is a composition system; it's a discussion medium; it's a repository; it's a mail system; it's a tool for collaboration. We don't know quite what it is, but we do know it's a fun way to communicate asynchronously across the network."[5]

work(ing) out loud: a means of continually demonstrating one's dedication to the team effort, usually using remote tools to advertise what one is working on and how one can be reached.

working together online: using remote tools to simulate online the experience of working together on-site. (See also *virtual office.*)

INTERVIEWEES

GERARD BEAULIEU is cofounder and COO of Forsche Enterprises Ltd., known for its innovative skating trainer @tornadosedge.com. He is also the cofounder and CEO of Barefoot Innovations Ltd., which in April 2015 launched Virtual Ice Breakers, the product of experimenting with short games at the beginning of conference calls to foster team building (www .virtualicebreakers.com). His top tip for working remotely: ESTABLISH A HUMAN CONNECTION IN YOUR ONLINE MEETINGS. You can watch the interview, listen to the podcast, or read the transcript at https://collaboration superpowers.com/52-virtual-icebreakers-with-gerard-beaulieu.

DAVE BLUM runs Dr. Clue.com, a company that provides team-building adventures for colocated and remote teams. Treasure hunts are playful ways for people to experience collaborative teamwork and give insight into the building blocks of trust (http://drclue.com). His top tip for working remotely: EVERY DAY, THINK ABOUT SOMETHING YOU'RE GRATEFUL FOR. You can watch the interview, listen to the podcast, or read the transcript at https://www.collaborationsuperpowers.com/74-solve-the-puzzles-of-remote -teamwork-with-dr-clue.

LUCIUS BOBIKIEWICZ is a trainer for distributed Agile teams at Spread Scrum.com in Berlin, Germany. He has managed globally dispersed teams—with members from Indonesia, Israel, Russia, Ukraine, and the United Kingdom—using just online spreadsheets (http://spreadscrum.com). His top tip for managing remote teams: PROVIDE A WORKING ENVIRONMENT WHERE PEOPLE FEEL SAFE TO ASK QUESTIONS AND BE THEMSELVES. You can watch the interview, listen to the podcast, or read the transcript at https://www.collaborationsuperpowers.com/45-powerful-collaboration-with -simple-spreadsheets.

REINOUD BOLAND runs Waterland-Huisje in Eindhoven, the Netherlands. Waterland-Huisje is the Dutch exponent of the tiny-house movement. It is inspired by the traditional architecture of the Zaan region and named after

Waterland, the peat meadow area just above Amsterdam (http://waterland-huisje.nl). You can watch the interview, listen to the podcast, or read the transcript at https://www.collaborationsuperpowers.com/97-tiny-house-office-for-remote-workers.

BRANDON BROWN is an American who followed his heart to Hungary; to pay the bills, he works as a virtual assistant and finds interesting work from clients all over the world using Upwork. He calls himself the Swiss Army Knife kind of virtual assistant. His goal is to make his clients forget what they're stressed about (https://www.upwork.com/o/profiles/users/_~0170815817e346823a). His top tip for working remotely: TO HUMANIZE YOUR ONLINE INTERACTION, GET TO KNOW YOUR CLIENTS. You can watch the interview, listen to the podcast, or read the transcript at https://www.collaborationsuperpowers.com/124-work-with-a-virtual-assistant-like-brandon-brown.

YEGOR BUGAYENKO is the CEO of Zerocracy.com and the founder and former CTO of Teamed.io, which develops software in an "extremely" distributed mode. They have no central office, no meetings, no conference, calls, and no Skype chats; instead, they work through task-management systems. The more than one hundred Teamed.io freelancers can take on as much or as little work as they want, and are paid as tasks are completed (http://www.teamed.io). His top tip for working remotely: GIVE PEOPLE TECHNICALLY CHALLENGING TASKS AND PAY THEM WELL. You can watch the interview, listen to the podcast, or read the transcript at https://www.collaborationsuperpowers.com/extreme-results-oriented-working-yegor-bugayenko.

ANNA DANES is the CEO at Ricaris, a website outsourcing company (http://www.ricaris.com). She is also an advisor and consultant for Managing Virtual Teams, which provides management consulting for distributed teams (http://managing-virtual-teams.com). Her top tip for working remotely: IF A COMPANY WANTS TO BE SUCCESSFUL WITH REMOTE WORKING, THE HR TEAM HAS TO BE ON BOARD. You can watch the interview or read the transcript at https://collaborationsuperpowers.com/interview-managing-virtual-teams.

BRIAN DAY, lead for citizen science and community development at NASA's Solar System Exploration Research Virtual Institute (SSERVI), works with a team who built an app via which you can virtually tour the moon (https://sservi.nasa.gov/articles/moon-tours-explore-the-moon-with-a-new-app-from-nasa). He shares: "WE HAVE THE CAPABILITY OF BECOMING A SPACE-FARING CIVILIZATION. IT IS GOING TO HAPPEN IN OUR LIFETIME." (http://sservi.nasa.gov) You can watch the interview, listen to the podcast, or read the transcript at https://collaborationsuperpowers.com/6-take-a-virtual-tour-of-the-moon-nasa-sservi.

STEPHAN DOHRN is a managing partner at Radical Inclusion. The partners at R-I live and work on three continents: Europe, South America, and the United States. With their virtual office functioning in different time zones, they rely on collaborative work methods that walk their talk of "globally local" strategic management, project management, leadership, and facilitation (www.radical-inclusion.com). His top tip for working remotely: INVEST TIME IN LEARNING HOW TO USE YOUR TOOLS, SETTING UP USEFUL PROCESSES, AND GETTING TO KNOW EACH OTHER. You can watch the interview, listen to the podcast, or read the transcript at https://www.collaborationsuperpowers.com/66-what-it-takes-to-be-a-great-virtual-team-leader-with-stephan-dohrn.

HOWARD B. ESBIN, PHD, is a social entrepreneur. He developed the Prelude Suite, an experiential learning platform for virtual teams that fosters soft skills essential for psychological safety, trust, and effectiveness. Teams are guided through online interactive exercises using self-assessment, self-expression, cocreation, and storytelling (http://playprelude.com). His top tip for working remotely: CREATE A TEAM CHARTER TO ESTABLISH A FRAMEWORK FOR HONEST, SAFE COMMUNICATION. You can listen to the podcast or read the transcript at https://www.collaborationsuperpowers.com/episode-2-tuning-virtual-team-howard-esbin.

JESSE FEWELL is the founder and principal coach at Fewell Innovation in Washington, DC, U.S. A writer and trainer in innovation and Agile methods, he founded the PMI Agile Community of Practice, cocreated the PMI ACP Agile certification, and wrote a MiniBük (an "ultra-short," 3.5-by-5-inch printed book) called *Can You Hear Me Now? Working with Global, Distributed, Virtual Teams* (http://jessefewell.com). His top tip for working remotely: DON'T EXPECT TO GET THINGS RIGHT ON THE FIRST TRY. IT'S A PROCESS OF SMALL EXPERIMENTS AND ITERATIONS. Watch the interview, listen to the podcast, or read the transcript at https://www.collaborationsuperpowers.com/80-let-go-of-old-habits-with-jesse-fewell.

PER FRYKMAN is a reputation advisor at Your Professional Reputation in Stockholm, Sweden. He helps people discover their potential so they can find jobs they love. He enjoys working from anywhere (https://perfrykman.com). His top tip for managing your reputation: DECIDE TO DO SOMETHING, AND THEN HAVE RESPECT FOR THE TIME IT TAKES. You can watch the interview, listen to the podcast, or read the transcript at https://collaborationsuperpowers.com/22-managing-your-reputation-remotely-per-frykman.

IWEIN FULD is cofounder and lean business hacker of StarterSquad, a self-organized company of developers that build software for start-ups in Utrecht, the Netherlands (https://www.startersquad.com). His top tip for working remotely: WHEN YOU'RE FEELING STUCK, PAIR UP WITH SOMEONE ELSE. You can watch his two interviews, listen to the podcasts, or read the transcripts at https://www.collaborationsuperpowers.com/25-a-remote-team-perspective-with-startersquad and https://www.collaborationsuperpowers.com/build-a-company-of-entrepreneurs-iwein-fuld.

FERNANDO GARRIDO VAZ is a freelance product manager from Brazil with experience managing distributed teams, multiple nationalities, and different time zones. Fernando says: "It's interesting to have people with different backgrounds and slightly different views of things, thinking about the same problems. You are likely going to get more innovative and creative suggestions that you wouldn't get if your team was more homogeneous." (http://blog.garridovaz.com) His top tip for working remotely: FOCUS ON DOING GREAT WORK. You can watch the interview, listen to the podcast, or read the transcript at https://www.collaborationsuperpowers.com/89-build-reputation-in-the-freelance-economy-with-fernando-garrido-vaz.

LUIS GONÇALVES is a management consultant, author, speaker, and blogger. In 2016 he founded Evolution4All, a management consulting firm that helps executives of medium-size companies become more effective, efficient and more rewarded. Based in Munich, Germany, Luis cowrote—remotely—*Getting Value Out of Agile Retrospectives: A Toolbox of Retrospective Exercises* with Ben Linders, who is based in Tilburg, the Netherlands (http://lmsgoncalves.com). His top tip for working remotely: GET A SMALL PIECE OUT THERE. GET YOUR IDEA VALIDATED. GET PEOPLE TALKING ABOUT IT AND THEN CONTINUE AS YOU GO. You can watch the interview, listen to the podcast, or read the transcript at https://www.collaborationsuperpowers.com/interview-with-ben-linders-and-luis-goncalves.

RICKY GUEST is the senior audio/video specialist at Wyle@NASA Ames Research Center. He provides support for the three virtual institutes at NASA, SSERVI (Solar System Exploration Virtual Institute), NARI (NASA Aeronautics Research Institute), and NAI (NASA Astrobiology Institute). His top tip for working remotely: CONSTANTLY LOOK FOR OTHER SOLUTIONS AND OPPORTUNITIES THAT MIGHT BETTER FIT YOUR TEAMS OR EVENTS. Watch the interview, listen to the podcast, or read the transcript at https://collaborationsuperpowers.com/episode-3-collaboration-space-exploration-nasa-sservi.

YVES HANOULLE is a creative collaboration agent at PairCoaching.net in Gent, Belgium, and the author of *Who Is Agile? A Book of Personal Reflections on the Journeys of People Who Stumbled on Agile*. He built a home "walking office": an electronic sit-stand desk combined with a treadmill so that he can walk while working. It helps him focus (www.hanoulle.be). His top tip for working remotely: GIVE PEOPLE SPACE TO STEP UP AND TAKE RESPONSIBILITY. You can watch the interview, listen to the podcast, or read the transcript at https://collaborationsuperpowers.com/20-welcome-people-and-develop-trust-while-walking-yves-hanoulle.

TEO HÄRÉN, one of the most requested experts on creativity in Sweden, is the author of *Härabete*, a book about working wherever you are most productive. Remote work clicked for him when he was asked to do some tasks while on vacation. He found that he was inspired by his surroundings and produced some of his best work (http://teoharen.se). His top tip for working remotely: REALIZE THE POWER YOU HAVE TO CHOOSE HOW YOU DO YOUR WORK. You can watch the interview, listen to the podcast, or read the transcript at https://collaborationsuperpowers.com/29-work-where-you-are-most-productive-with-teo-hren.

DAVE HECKER, cofounder at SourceSeek, is a seasoned tech executive, speaker, and author with an exclusive focus on distributed team software delivery. Before working with any offshore team, Dave will spend time with them in person to assess whether it will be a good fit or not (http://www.sourceseek.com). His top tip for outsourcing: LEARN ABOUT THE REGION YOUR TEAM IS FROM. You can watch the interview, listen to the podcast, or read the transcript at https://www.collaborationsuperpowers.com/93-manage-expectations-on-distributed-teams-with-dave-hecker.

JEFFRY HESSE is an Agile coach at Sonatype in Alaska, U.S. He works with a distributed software development team of approximately forty people. He loves his work, mountain climbing, photography, and spending time with his grandmother. Because he can work from anywhere, Jeffry combines his passions by working while traveling (www.sonatype.org). His top tip for working remotely: PUSH THE BALL FORWARD EVERY DAY. You can watch the interview, listen to the podcast, or read the transcript at https://www.collaborationsuperpowers.com/39-how-to-be-a-self-organizing-remote-team.

PETER HILTON is a consultant at Signavio who works remotely from Rotterdam, the Netherlands. He works on teams that have to determine how they are going to work together. Sometimes that's remote and sometimes that's in the office together—it depends on the day (http://hilton.org.uk). His top tip for working remotely: TEST YOUR ASSUMPTIONS. Watch the interview, listen to the podcast, or read the transcript at https://collaborationsuperpowers.com/17-the-need-for-face-to-face-on-virtual-teams-peter-hilton.

LUKE HOHMANN is founder and CEO of Conteneo Inc. Conteneo improves group performance through scalable decision-making frameworks (http://conteneo.co). His top tip for working remotely: LOOK AT PROBLEMS FROM MULTIPLE ANGLES. You can watch the interview, listen to the podcast, or read the transcript at https://collaborationsuperpowers.com/creating-epic-wins-through-collaborative-games-luke-hohmann.

SCOTT HOPPE is the founder of Why Blu, a fully distributed accounting firm that files tax returns for businesses in the United States. He left the traditional "up or out" accounting world to start a company that valued happiness as well as profit (https://whyblu.com). His top tip for working remotely: EXPERIMENT, FAIL, AND LEARN. You can watch the interview, listen to the podcast, or read the transcript at https://www.collaborationsuperpowers.com/160-prioritize-happiness-and-profit-with-scott-hoppe.

DAVID HOROWITZ is the founder and CEO of Retrium, which provides software for facilitating remote Retrospectives. David considers continuous improvement the most critical aspect of a highly effective software team. Since Retrospectives are usually conducted in person using flip charts and sticky notes, he saw a need to replicate this functionality for remote teams—which led to Retrium (http://retrium.com.). His top tip for working remotely: SILLINESS, PLAYFULNESS, AND LACK OF STRUCTURE ARE ALSO IMPORTANT FOR A TEAM. Watch the interview, listen to the podcast, or read the transcript at https://collaborationsuperpowers.com/37-abolish-the-postmortem-with-david-horowitz.

TOM HOWLETT is COO at River Agency. Their mission is to "make great days at work for our clients, their employees, and their customers" through tailored employee engagement, sales and channel incentives, business insight solutions, and live events (https://www.riveragency.com). Tom is also an avid blogger (https://diaryofascrummaster.wordpress.com). His top tip for working remotely: MAKE COMMUNICATING WITH EACH OTHER EASY. You can watch the interview, listen to the podcast, or read the transcript at https://collaborationsuperpowers.com/27-build-trust-on-remote-teams-through-pair-collaboration.

MARC HUGHES is cofounder at ScrumDo, a tool that supports online Scrum and Scrumban (a combination of Agile and Lean Kanban on top of Scrum). They use ScrumDo to keep everyone aligned with company priorities and tasks (https://www.scrumdo.com). His top tip for working remotely: KNOW WHEN YOU WORK BEST AND SCHEDULE YOUR MOST IMPORTANT WORK DURING YOUR MOST PRODUCTIVE TIMES. You can watch the interview, listen to the podcast, or read the transcript at https://www.collaborationsuperpowers.com/64-align-your-remote-team-in-scrumdo-with-marc-hughes.

NICK JAWORSKI transitioned from being a music teacher to being a business owner through the use of online platforms like Upwork. His modus operandi: building authentic relationships with his clients. He believes that human touch enables a great remote connection (http://podcastmonster.com). His top tip for working remotely: TAKE TIME TO LOOK BACK AND APPRECIATE HOW MUCH YOU'VE ACCOMPLISHED. You can listen to the podcast or read the transcript at https://collaborationsuperpowers.com/128-use-the-human-touch-for-remote-connection.

COLLEEN JOHNSON is cofounder of ScatterSpoke, a tool for conducting remote Agile Retrospectives (https://www.scatterspoke.com). Her top tip for working remotely: HAVE SYSTEMS TO MANAGE THE WORK, NOT THE PEOPLE. You can watch the interview, listen to the podcast, or read the transcript at https://collaborationsuperpowers.com/68-manage-the-work-not-the-people-with-colleen-johnson.

MAGNUS KARLSSON is the director of new business development & innovation at Ericsson, a company that employs over 110,000 people worldwide and does business in more than 180 countries. His team developed a way for all employees to contribute ideas for improvement and innovation. Magnus says: "We wanted to encourage multiple disciplines to collaborate. We also wanted the ability for employees and contractors to be able to look at the same idea at the same time. Gradually, people started to see that keeping ideas to themselves is an old way of thinking. *Secret ideas don't go anywhere.*" (http://www.ericsson.com) You can read the interview summary at https://collaborationsuperpowers.com/ideaboxes-a-management-system-for-innovation-magnus-karlsson.

MARK KILBY is an Agile coach who for over two decades has cultivated more distributed, dispersed, and virtual teams than colocated teams. Currently, Mark serves as an Agile coach with Sonatype, a distributed Agile software development company focusing on automation of software supply chains. Previously, Mark led Agile transformations, from start-ups to Fortune 500 companies. In his spare time, Mark also cultivates communities, such as Agile Orlando, Agile Florida, VirtualTeamTalk.com, and the Agile Alliance Community Group Support initiative (http://markkilby.com). His top tip for working remotely: BE VISIBLE TO YOUR REMOTE COLLEAGUES. Watch the interview, listen to the podcast, or read the transcript at https://collaborationsuperpowers.com/9-coaching-distributed-agile-teams-mark-kilby.

MAARTEN KOOPMANS is a physicist, team leader, and a software architect. We worked together (remotely) from 2006 to 2009 helping to build an online project-management tool. He's done everything from technical architecture to project programming to implementation to producing to engineering. He is the first person I interviewed for this book (http://vrijheid.net). His top tip for working remotely: PROJECTS, LIKE ELEPHANTS ARE BIG. HOW DO YOU EAT AN ELEPHANT? ONE BITE AT A TIME. You can read a summary of the interview at https://collaborationsuperpowers.com/hire-right-people-remote-working-maarten-koopmans.

SUMANT KOWSHIK is VP of product at Personify Inc., where his teams created imaging and computer vision technology and video apps for depth (3-D) cameras on PCs, mobiles, and immersive platforms like VR/AR. His top tip for working remotely: TAKE CARE OF YOURSELF AND TAKE TIME OFF WHEN YOU NEED IT. You can watch the interview, listen to the podcast, or read the transcript at https://www.collaborationsuperpowers.com/31-embody-your-team-online-with-personify.

AGILEBILL KREBS is a coach and founder of Agile Dimensions, LLC. Back in 2009, he traveled to deliver trainings at different locales, but when his company ran into hard economic times, he had to find less-expensive alternatives. It was then he discovered a virtual conference for educators and virtual world best practices in education, which gave him the opportunity to interact with more PhDs than he had ever met in one place before—just virtually. The experience was so powerful that he got certified (virtually) by the University of Washington program in virtual worlds. Ever since he has dedicated himself to using virtual technology for teamwork, collaboration, and project management. As he puts it: "Take the time to learn new ways of working. It's only strange until we get used to it." (http://www.agiledimensions.com) Watch the interview, listen to the podcast, or read the transcript at https://www.collaborationsuperpowers.com/15-collaborating-in-virtual-worlds-agilebill-krebs.

CHRISTIAN KREUTZ is an author, speaker, strategic advisor, and expert in open and social innovation. He is the Director at Crisscrossed, the makers of WE THINQ, social software for change makers. Christian works with colleagues in London, the Far East, and the United States who all work from different places: home, innovation labs, and coworking spaces (https://www.wethinq.com). His top tip for working remotely: DARE TO EXPERIMENT WITH NEW IDEAS. You can watch the interview, listen to the podcast, or read the transcript at https://www.collaborationsuperpowers.com/76-create-horizontal-organizations-with-wethinq.

CARRIE KUEMPEL is the director of customer success at Sococo. She uses storytelling and social technologies in innovative ways to connect people, facilitate insights, and create brand advocates (https://sococo.com). Her top tip for working remotely: LEAD BY EXAMPLE. You can watch the interview, listen to the podcast, or read the transcript at https://www.collaborationsuperpowers.com/60-be-a-high-functioning-connected-team-in-a-sococo-virtual-office.

TOM LAMBOT is the lead engineer at rLoop, a team of four hundred remote volunteers from around the globe that built a functioning prototype Hyperpod for the SpaceX Hyperloop design competition (http://rloop.org). He is also an aerospace engineer at NASA Ames. He says: "The Hyperloop is a cool, twenty-first-century problem to work on. I really feel like I'm working on something out of the ordinary and futuristic." You can watch the interview, listen to the podcast, or read the transcript at https://www

.collaborationsuperpowers.com/83-a-self-organized-team-of-remote-redditors-competing-for-spacex-hyperloop.

BRENT LESSARD is cofounder and project manager at rLoop, a team of four hundred remote volunteers from around the globe that built a functioning prototype Hyperpod for the SpaceX Hyperloop design competition. He says: "We broke off into a dozen or so engineering-based teams and assigned leaders for each team, just to guide the workflow. And then everybody joined those teams based on their interest or their education. No one was restricted to participate within a single team. It simply organized organically, by necessity." (http://rloop.org) You can watch the interview, listen to the podcast, or read the transcript at https://www.collaborationsuperpowers.com/83-a-self-organized-team-of-remote-redditors-competing-for-spacex-hyperloop.

BEN LINDERS is a trainer, coach, and advisor based in Tilburg, the Netherlands. He cowrote, remotely, *Getting Value Out of Agile Retrospectives: A Toolbox of Retrospective Exercises* with Luis Gonçalves, who is based in Munich, Germany (https://www.benlinders.com). His top tip for working remotely: INVOLVE OTHERS FROM YOUR COMMUNITY IN THE PROCESS. THE MORE YOU SHARE, THE MORE YOU'RE IN CONTACT WITH OTHER PEOPLE. YOU CAN LEARN FROM THAT. You can watch the interview, listen to the podcast, or read the transcript at https://collaborationsuperpowers.com/interview-with-ben-linders-and-luis-goncalves.

MARIO LUCERO is an Agile coach and experienced Scrum Master based in Santiago, Chile; he works with remote teams in Argentina, Peru, and the United States. He stresses the importance of good equipment, communication, interaction, and generosity. He also believes it's the little things that can drive the biggest changes (https://cl.linkedin.com/in/luceromet). His top tip for working remotely: BE INTENTIONAL ABOUT CREATING AN ATMOSPHERE OF TOGETHERNESS. You can watch the interview, listen to the podcast, or read the transcript at https://collaborationsuperpowers.com/23-create-big-results-small-changes-mario-lucero.

SILVINA MARTÍNEZ is a project manager at Calico Spanish, an interactive Spanish curriculum for elementary students and homeschools (https://calicospanish.com). She is also a media marketing specialist at Managing Virutal Teams (http://managing-virtual-teams.com). Her top tip for working remotely: ADDING SOMETHING PERSONAL OR A CHEERFUL SENTENCE TO AN EMAIL CAN MAKE A LOT OF DIFFERENCE WHEN YOU'RE WORKING WITH A VIRTUAL TEAM. You can watch the interview or read the transcript at https://collaborationsuperpowers.com/interview-managing-virtual-teams.

CARRIE MCKEEGAN is the director of Greenback Expat Tax Services, a global, virtual business that prepares U.S. federal tax returns for American Expats living all over the world. Her fifty-odd U.S.-based team members work well in part because of how they've agreed to work together, especially regarding set working hours and communication (http://www.greenbacktaxservices.com). Her top tip for working remotely: HIRE THE BEST PEOPLE YOU CAN AS EARLY ON AS YOU CAN. You can watch the interview, listen to the podcast, or read the transcript at https://www.collaborationsuperpowers.com/62-build-a-global-virtual-business-with-carrie-mckeegan-of-greenback-expat-tax-services.

HUGO MESSER is a distributed Agile expert with more than ten years' expertise in acting as intermediary between companies in the Netherlands and employees in India and Ukraine. He is the founder of Bridge Global, an IT solutions provider; and Ekipa, an Agile training and coaching agency based in India and Indonesia. He has coauthored six books on "lessons learned in offshoring and nearshoring." The most recent, Book 6 of the Art of Managing Remote Teams series, is *How to Manage People in Your Remote Team* (http://www.bridge-global.com, www.ekipa.co, and www.ekipa.co.id). His top tip for working with offshore teams: ACCEPT THAT THERE WILL BE CULTURAL DIFFERENCES AND ORGANIZE AROUND THAT. Watch the interview, listen to the podcast, or read the transcript at https://www.collaborationsuperpowers.com/13-managing-remote-teams-hugo-messer.

PHIL MONTERO is a systems engineer at the Garam Group and a virtual office expert. His interest in telework started when he was a child watching his dad commute back and forth between New Jersey and New York. Even then he thought, "There's got to be a better way." Phil is passionate about enabling companies and the people he works with to work remotely and have more work-life balance. He also devised the "ICC workflow" approach to crafting team agreements, focusing on information, communication, and collaboration. His top tip for working remotely: INVEST IN TRAINING MANAGERS TO BECOME GOOD REMOTE TEAM LEADERS. You can watch the interview or read the transcript at https://collaborationsuperpowers.com/apply-right-technology-phil-montero.

ASHCON NEJAD is the technical systems specialist at the NASA Ames Research Center. He works on web and application development and the technical production of agency-wide virtual and in-person events. His top tip for working remotely: BE CREATIVE AND MOLD A TECHNOLOGY SYSTEM THAT WORKS FOR YOU. You can watch the interview, listen to the podcast, or read the transcript at https://www.collaborationsuperpowers.com/episode-3-collaboration-space-exploration-nasa-sservi.

CHRISTINA NG is software developer and director of product at Dynamic Signal. This technology company offers a mobile-first company communications platform. Just for fun, she also developed a work-from-home excuse generator: when a user submits an excuse, an online community votes on it—up or down. Watch the interview, listen to the podcast, or read the transcript at https://collaborationsuperpowers.com/51-validate-your-work-from-home-excuses-with-christina-ng.

ADE OLONOH is chairman and founder at Formstack, a company that made the decision to transition from being colocated to remote years ago. The company was growing, and they wanted to take advantage of being able to hire top talent outside of Indianapolis, Indiana, U.S. During the transition, they experimented with small iterations, and eventually found a remote working cadence that made sense for their teams. Now they have a headquarters office that people use as needed. He is also cofounder of Jell (https://jell.com). His top tip for working remotely: CONTINUOUSLY TRY NEW THINGS. EXPERIMENT WITH NEW TOOLS AND PROCESSES. You can watch the interview, listen to the podcast, or read the transcript at https://www.collaborationsuperpowers.com/78-focus-on-process-not-tools-with-ade-olonoh.

PILAR ORTI runs the Virtual not Distant consulting firm in the U.K. Her specialty is coaching teams through the transition of going remote (http://virtualnotdistant.com). Her top tip for working remotely: STOP MAKING ASSUMPTIONS AND START ASKING QUESTIONS. BE CURIOUS. You can watch the interview, listen to the podcast, or read the transcript at https://www.collaborationsuperpowers.com/4-humanizing-remote-work-pilar-orti.

HASSAN OSMAN is a PMO manager at Cisco Systems and the author of *Influencing Virtual Teams*, a book filled with practical and concrete tips and advice on managing virtual teams. He leads large and complex projects with virtual teams around the world, all from his home office. He also runs a blog and teaches an online course about virtual teams. He is, in his own words: "obsessed with life hacks and productivity." (www.thecouchmanager.com) His top tip for working remotely: BE GENEROUS WITH YOUR INFORMATION AND RESOURCES. You can watch the interview, listen to the podcast, or read the transcript at https://collaborationsuperpowers.com/5-managing-your-virtual-team-hassan-osman.

DIRK-JAN PADMOS is a hands-on HR interim manager/HR consultant with special expertise within the technical wholesale, ICT, and health care branches. He advises owner-managed businesses on how to structure and implement HR policies. Dirk-Jan says: "Management is not just a job, it's a real skill. And it's a skill that can be taught up to a point, but if you don't have the basic talent for it, you will never be a fantastic manager." (https://www.linkedin.com/in/dirkjanpadmos) His top tip for working remotely: GIVE BACK TO YOUR COMMUNITY. You can read a summary of the interview at https://www.collaborationsuperpowers.com/management-skill-job-dirk-jan-padmos.

YVONNE PENDLETON is the director of SSERVI. During her time as a research astrophysicist in the Space Science and Astrobiology Division (1979–2005), she published eighty scientific papers about the origin and evolution of organic material in the universe. She says: "By studying and learning how astronauts can work effectively in the field here on Earth, we can better prepare the astronauts that would later go to more remote distance places." You can watch the interview, listen to the podcast, or read the transcript at https://collaborationsuperpowers.com/episode-3-collaboration-space-exploration-nasa-sservi.

TIZIANO PERRUCCI is a back-end developer and Scala magician for StarterSquad, a self-organized company of developers that build software for start-ups in Utrecht, the Netherlands. He enjoys solving interesting and challenging problems (https://www.startersquad.com). His top tip for working remotely: TO UNDERSTAND OTHERS, START WITH LISTENING. You can watch the interview, listen to the podcast, or read the transcript at https://www.collaborationsuperpowers.com/25-a-remote-team-perspective-with-startersquad.

ERIN RAPACKI is founder & product strategy consultant at Machine Inbound Inc. At the time of our interview she was the marketing director for Suitable Technologies, makers of the Beam telepresence robot. The Beam allows people to beam into what is basically Skype on wheels, and then drive themselves around using the arrow keys on their keyboards. The company was founded in 2009 when a remote electrical engineer living in Indiana became frustrated that he wasn't a more prominent part of his team in California. Using spare robot parts, he built the first prototype. The team found it so useful that they decided to commercialize it and turn it into a product. As Erin puts it: "Telepresence is a technology worth experiencing." (https://www.linkedin.com/in/erapacki) You can watch the interview, listen to the podcast, or read the transcript at https://collaborationsuperpowers.com/47-be-in-two-places-at-once-with-beam-smart-presence.

JUDY REES, a former journalist and media executive based in London, U.K., is now known worldwide as a practical implementer of an inquiry methodology called Clean Language. She is also the coauthor of the best-selling book on the topic, *Clean Language: Revealing Metaphors and Opening Minds.* An Agile enthusiast, she works as an online facilitator, trainer, and coach. She recommends using metaphors to visualize personalities and challenges on remote teams (http://judyrees.co.uk). Watch the interview, listen to the podcast, or read the transcript at https://www.collaborationsuperpowers.com/33-discover-a-common-language-with-judy-rees.

BRIE REYNOLDS is the senior career specialist at FlexJobs, creators of Remote.co—a resource providing information and best practices on starting, training, and managing remote workers and teams. FlexJobs has about one hundred team members working from all over the United States. They use Sococo as their virtual office and Yammer as their virtual water cooler (http://flexjobs.com). Her top tip for working remotely: OFFER YOUR REMOTE EMPLOYEES CREATIVE BENEFITS, such as tech stipends, house-cleaning services, food delivery services, gym memberships, and the like. You can watch the interview, listen to the podcast, or read the transcript at https://www.collaborationsuperpowers.com/56-communicate-proactively-and-build-culture-with-brie-reynolds.

CHRIS RIDGEWELL is cofounder and director of Wisework, a specialist U.K.-based management consultancy company that helps organizations plan, implement, and manage their Agile/smart-working programs. This can include working from home, using office space more efficiently, mobile working, and converting old farm buildings into managed offices or coworking spaces. He's also the principal and owner at Charterhouse Consultants group, which implements change management programs in large companies and organizations around the world. He was also a founder member of the U.K. Telework Association (http://www.wisework.co.uk). His top tip for working remotely: TAKE A LOOK AT WEARABLE TECHNOLOGIES FOR SOME FUN PRODUCTIVITY TOOLS. You can watch the interview or read the transcript at https://www.collaborationsuperpowers.com/episode-1-implement-flexible-working-chris-ridgewell.

ROBERT ROGGE is cofounder and CEO for Zingword, a site that facilitates freelance translators getting translation jobs by offering them both space for a digital portfolio and free tools (http://zingword.com). He is also the cofounder and advisor for Managing Virtual Teams, which provides management consulting for distributed teams (http://www.managing-virtual-teams.com). His top tip for working remotely: TRAIN PEOPLE TO BE GOOD COMMUNICATORS. You can watch the interview or read the transcript at https://collaborationsuperpowers.com/interview-managing-virtual-teams.

LAURA ROOKE is a freelance customer support specialist in California, U.S. After many years as a computer programmer, she quit her job to raise her children. When her kids got older, she wanted to start working again—but this time from home. She started by getting involved on the Hewlett Packard online forums for people using iPaqs, a tool she loved using herself. She now does online technical support for a few different companies. She finds that she gets enough social interaction just from talking with her customers and from regular meetings with her teams (https://www.linkedin.com/in/laurarooke). Her top tip for remote working: GET TOGETHER IN PERSON PERIODICALLY AND HAVE VIRTUAL LUNCHES IN BETWEEN. You can watch the interview, listen to the podcast, or read the transcript at https://collaborationsuperpowers.com/14-remote-technical-support-laura-rooke.

MARCUS ROSENTHAL is the principal consultant at Innovative Impact Consulting. He is also cofounder and former CEO of Revolve Robotics—creator of the Kubi, a portable video teleconference device. Marcus emphasizes that WHEN REMOTE COMMUNICATION INCLUDES MOVEMENT, THERE IS A JUMP IN ENGAGEMENT OF ALL PARTICIPANTS. Not surprisingly, he recommends using video regularly. Watch the interview, listen to the podcast, or read the transcript at https://collaborationsuperpowers.com/18-teleport-with-the-kubi-teleconference-robot-revolve-robotics.

MANDY ROSS is the director of product marketing at AgileCraft, "the world's best-scaled Agile software management platform." She is the former director of marketing at Sococo, which provides virtual office software (https://www.sococo.com). Her top tips for working remotely: ESTABLISH TEAM NORMS. CALL THINGS OUT WHEN YOU SEE THEM HAPPENING. You can watch the interview, listen to the podcast, or read the transcript at https://www.collaborationsuperpowers.com/60-be-a-high-functioning-connected-team-in-a-sococo-virtual-office.

JOHANNA ROTHMAN is a management consultant for software managers and leaders. She is also the author of many books, most recently *Agile and Lean Program Management: Scaling Collaboration Across the Organization*. She started working with geographically distributed teams in 1988 (http://www.jrothman.com). Her tips for geographically distributed teams: SHARE THE BURDEN OF TIME ZONE DIFFERENCES. COMMUNICATE OFTEN. You can watch the interview, listen to the podcast, or read the transcript at https://www.collaborationsuperpowers.com/87-organize-your-distributed-team-with-johanna-rothman.

DEREK SCRUGGS is a partner at Blue Spruce Holdings, "real estate investing made simple." (https://bluespruceholdings.com) He was previously CTO of ContentBLVD. At the time of our interview, Derek was the vice president of Staunch Robots. Their company worked with remote teams in Colombia and the United States. When many U.S. companies were following the trend of outsourcing to India and Eastern Europe, Staunch Robots had the idea to outsource in South America, thus solving the time zone challenge. Derek mainly works from his home office and finds that having a regular routine helps him stay on track. His top tip for working remotely: USE TOOLS TO AUTOMATE PROCESSES WHENEVER POSSIBLE. You can watch the interview, listen to the podcast, or read the transcript at https://www.collaborationsuperpowers.com/26-using-tools-and-increasing-productivity-with-derek-scruggs.

VANESSA SHAW is a freelance learning designer and facilitator who builds leadership programs on creating human-centered workplace cultures. She emphasizes that culture is not just about being from another country. For example, you can be a mountain person, a city person, or a beach person. You can be a cat person or a dog person. We define ourselves by a wide variety of characteristics besides the country we live in or come from (http://www.humansideoftech.co). Her top tips for working with other cultures: BE AWARE THAT WE HAVE A REDUCTION IN CONTEXT WHEN WE GO REMOTE. UNDERSTAND THAT WE'RE ALL DIFFERENT AND BE CURIOUS. You can watch the interview, listen to the podcast, or read the transcript at https://www.collaborationsuperpowers.com/54-helping-you-tech-better-with-vanessa-shaw.

JESSIE SHTERNSHUS is founder at Improv Effect and coauthor of *CTRL Shift—50 Games for 50 ****ing Days Like Today*, a book with original improv games tailored to the kind of ****ing day you're having. She also uses improv (virtually and in person) to help software teams with onboarding, communication, and team building. She notes that improv is a great tool for learning about and accepting each other's uniqueness, thinking on the spot, and being self-aware. It can also help teams find similarities with each other and solve problems creatively. (www.improveffect.com) Her top tips for working remotely: LEARN HOW TO ACTIVELY LISTEN TO EACH OTHER. FIND THE THINGS THAT ARE UNIQUE ABOUT PEOPLE. You can watch the interview, listen to the podcast, or read the transcript at https://www.collaborationsuperpowers.com/85-make-shift-happen-with-jessie-shternshus.

MICHAEL SLIWINSKI is the founder of Nozbe, an online task-management tool. Since he loves the freedom of being able to work from anywhere, it was only natural that he would build a remote company. He's also a speaker, author of the book *#iPadOnly*, chief editor of *Productive! Magazine*, and a triathlete (https://nozbe.com). His top tip for working remotely: REGULARLY REVIEW THE FUNCTIONALITY OF YOUR HOME OFFICE AND INCREMENTALLY IMPROVE. You can watch the interview, listen to the podcast, or read the transcript at https://collaborationsuperpowers.com/99-curate-your-notifications-for-maximum-productivity.

MARION SMITS is an associate professor and neuroradiologist at Erasmus MC in Rotterdam, the Netherlands. She is also an honorary consultant and reader at University College London Hospital NHS Foundation Trust in London, U.K. She recommends paying for good internet on the road and setting boundaries between work and play (http://marionsmits.net). Marion shares: "I love working while traveling. I love the focus you can get out of a long train ride or plane." You can watch the interview, listen to the podcast, or read the transcript at https://collaborationsuperpowers.com/12-scanning-brains-and-managing-students-remotely-marion-smits.

TEAGUE SODERMAN is the communications lead at NASA, SSERVI. A communications specialist with a background in technical writing and graphic production, he has been writing for the scientific community since 2004. His top tip for working remotely: TRUST ULTIMATELY COMES DOWN TO DELIVERING RESULTS. You can watch the interview, listen to the podcast, or read the transcript at https://collaborationsuperpowers.com/episode-3-collaboration-space-exploration-nasa-sservi.

JEREMY STANTON, senior vice president of engineering at Amino Payments, has been developing software since 1996. He's worked remotely since 2000, when the company he was working for decided to relocate. Their working relationship was such that the new distance between them wasn't an issue (https://www.linkedin.com/in/jeremystanton). His top tip for working remotely: IT'S IMPORTANT TO DEFINE WHAT SUCCESS AND FAILURE LOOK LIKE. You can watch the interview, listen to the podcast, or read the transcript at https://www.collaborationsuperpowers.com/10-being-deliberate-with-onboarding-and-culture-jeremy-stanton.

TIM STOUGH, a long-time data system architect, is currently the applied science program manager for JPL, NASA's Jet Propulsion Laboratory. JPL offers employees a 9/80 flex-time schedule. This means that in a two-week (ten-day) work cycle, an employee can work nine hours per day for nine days and then take the tenth day off. This option was offered in response to wide requests for greater work flexibility. Some people like it because it provides a quiet day at work; some people like the extra day off. And everyone benefits from the option (https://www.linkedin.com/in/timothy-stough-525b08a0). Listen to the podcast or read the transcript at https://www.collaborationsuperpowers.com/58-how-the-980-flextime-schedule-works.

LUIS SUAREZ worked for IBM for seventeen years. He spent the last ten of those years in Gran Canaria, one of Spain's Canary Islands. He first started working remotely after a massive traffic jam motivated him to plead for the option to work from home. He is currently a digital transformation and data analytics adviser for panagenda, a software company that builds solutions for IT collaboration infrastructures (https://www.panagenda.com). His top tip for working remotely: STOP USING EMAIL. INSTEAD, USE SOCIAL NETWORKS TO WORK OUT LOUD AND BE MORE TRANSPARENT TO YOUR COLLEAGUES. You can watch the interview, listen to the podcast, or read the transcript at https://collaborationsuperpowers.com/21-engaging-remotely-with-social-networks-luis-suarez.

EGOR SVIRIDENKO is the managing director for Targetprocess Germany, a tool that virtually visualizes and manages work. Targetprocess deals with teams in Berlin, Buffalo, London, Minsk, and Toronto. Their goal is to zero in on specific focuses, which is sometimes difficult in the face of many teams and many projects (https://targetprocess.com). His top tips for working remotely: VISUALIZE YOUR WORK. KNOW YOUR PEOPLE. CREATE SPACE FOR UNPREDICTABILITY. You can watch the interview, listen to the podcast, or read the transcript at https://collaborationsuperpowers.com/70-visualize-and-manage-your-work-with-targetprocess.

VINCENT TIETZ is a senior consultant and Scrum master at Saxonia Systems in its headquarters, Dresden, Germany. Saxonia Systems has created the ETEO concept: Ein Team Ein Office, a set of best practices for distributed Agile teams. Part of this concept is the eteoBoard—large monitors equipped with cameras, microphones, and a virtual task board set up to simulate face-to-face interaction. The eteoBoard emerged from the need to improve daily stand-ups between teams based in different German cities. eteoBoards have helped teams get to know each other better, build trust, and stay on the same page (http://www.eteoboard.de). You can watch the interview, listen to the podcast, or read the transcript at https://collaborationsuperpowers.com/82-connect-distributed-agile-teams-with-eteo-at-saxonia-systems.

NICK TIMMONS is the director of sales at Personify Inc., where they've developed technology to remove a user's background from their webcam and project the user's image on their screen in real time. When they started, they recruited new hires from the local university. As people grew older, they wanted to move to new locations—and the company wanted to support that. Their company has teams in the United States and Vietnam (http://www.personify.com). His top tip for working remotely: FOR TIME ZONE DIFFERENCES, SHARE THE BURDEN OF LATE OR EARLY MEETINGS. You can watch the interview, listen to the podcast, or read the transcript at https://www.collaborationsuperpowers.com/31-embody-your-team-online-with-personify.

PIERO TOFFANIN is a software developer. A year after he graduated from college, he was working a "normal nine-to-five job" but felt something was missing from his life. He convinced his wife to sell their possessions, start their own business, and hit the road as digital nomads. They traveled the United States in a camper for two years while coding to pay for expenses (http://www.pierotoffanin.com). His top tip for working remotely: BE PATIENT WITH YOURSELF. IT TAKES SOME TIME TO ADAPT. You can watch the interview, listen to the podcast, or read the transcript at https://www.collaborationsuperpowers.com/30-work-as-a-digital-nomad-with-piero-toffanin.

LESLIE TRUEX is a writer, speaker, entrepreneur, social worker, fitness instructor, and mom doing it all from the comfort of her home in Virginia, U.S. Leslie schedules her day according to her energy levels and believes in getting plenty of relaxation time (including taking power naps). She is the author of several books, including *Digital Writer Success: How to Make a Living Blogging, Freelance Writing and Publishing Online*; *The Work-at-Home Success Bible*; and *Jobs Online: How to Find and Get Hired to a Work-at-Home Job.* She offers work-at-home information and resources through her website, https://www.workathomesuccess.com. Her top tips for working remotely: KNOW WHICH HOURS OF THE DAY YOU FUNCTION BEST. CREATE A WORK ENVIRONMENT THAT WORKS FOR YOU. Watch the interview, listen to the podcast, or read the transcript at https://www.collaborationsuperpowers.com/91-be-a-work-at-home-success-with-leslie-truex.

THODORIS TSIRIDIS is the lead software engineer at the Swedish company Spotify. Most teams at Spotify are colocated in Stockholm, but Thodoris's iOS team is an exception: they work from all over the world, with members in Bologna, Boston, Florida, New York City—and Stockholm. Thodoris's team works remotely using Google Hangouts for their daily stand-ups and other meetings. They also use it for pair programming, so senior developers can watch and help junior developers with their coding techniques (https://www.spotify.com). His top tip for working remotely: THE PROCESS OF GOING REMOTE WILL BE DIFFERENT FOR EVERY TEAM AND WILL REQUIRE CONSTANT ADJUSTMENT. SO START, BE AGILE, AND ITERATE. You can read a summary of the interview at https://www.collaborationsuperpowers.com/how-a-team-at-spotify-uses-hangouts-to-work-remotely.

BART VAN LOON is an offshore staffing specialist at Zeropoint. His Belgium-based company brings together businesses from Pakistan, Sri Lanka, and several European countries. One of Zeropoint's secrets to success is offering remote team management training to both the client and the employees being hired (https://zeropoint.it). His top tip for working remotely: CONSIDER THE CULTURAL DIFFERENCES OF YOUR TEAM MEMBERS AND PROACTIVELY ADDRESS THEM. You can watch the interview, listen to the podcast, or read the transcript at https://collaborationsuperpowers.com/28-how-to-hire-offshore-staff-with-bart-van-loon.

RALPH VAN ROOSMALEN calls himself an "innovative Agile enabler." He is the CEO of both Agile Strides, a coaching and consultancy firm (https://agilestrides.com) and Management 3.0, a movement of innovation, leadership, and management (https://management30.com). At the time of this interview, he was managing teams in the Netherlands, Romania, and the United States. He is a staunch advocate of treating teams fairly and equally. His top tip for working remotely: ALWAYS WORK ON IMPROVING YOURSELF. KEEP EXPERIMENTING AND LEARN SOMETHING NEW ALL THE TIME. You can watch the interview, listen to the podcast, or read the transcript at https://collaborationsuperpowers.com/24-managing-three-remote-offices-with-ralph-van-roosmalen.

SHRIKANT VASHISHTHA is the cofounder and Agile coach at Malonus Consulting. He specializes in technology strategy and implementation, distributed Agile, and Agile transformation (https://malonus.in). His top tips for working remotely: GIVE PEOPLE CONTEXT ON THE WORK THEY'RE DOING. SHARE YOUR KNOWLEDGE. DON'T BE AFRAID TO TRY THINGS AND FAIL. You can watch the interview, listen to the podcast, or read the transcript at https://www.collaborationsuperpowers.com/11-bridging-the-gap-on-distributed-agile-teams-shrikant-vashishtha.

ADRIANA VELA is the founder of NanoTecNexus.org. Her team works from all over the United States and Canada in their mission to both transform how individuals learn about nanoscience and inspire K–12 students to pursue STEM education and careers. Adriana's work takes her all over the world, so she works while on the go. She has honed her ability to work from anywhere with tools and creativity (http://nanotecnexus.org). Her top tip for working remotely: CHANGE ENVIRONMENTS TO STIMULATE CREATIVITY. You can watch the interview, listen to the podcast, or read the transcript at https://www.collaborationsuperpowers.com/49-how-to-be-efficient-on-the-road-with-adrian-vela.

GRETCHEN WEGNER is an academic life coach for students and creator of the Anti-Boring Approach to Powerful Studying. As an academic coach she helps students hone the learning process and investigates what is causing any learning interruption. She then teaches new skills and helps the student integrate both the new habits and the ability to problem-solve independently. Gretchen and I also wrote a book together—remotely—for a mutual client (https://gretchenwegner.com). Gretchen shares: "There are two kinds of students who really benefit from coaching: those who have trouble motivating themselves, and the overachievers who do way too much." You can watch the interview, listen to the podcast, or read the transcript at https://www.collaborationsuperpowers.com/19-remote-academic-life-coaching-w-ith-gretchen-wegner.

FREDRIK WIIK is a Management 3.0 facilitator and a consultant and founder of Innoproach. At the time of our interview he was a senior consultant at Knowit Management (https://www.knowit.eu) in Stockholm, Sweden. He specializes in helping companies get more value from their product development efforts, including key aspects like time to market and business agility. He has a special interest in the scaled Agile setup required by organizations of a particular size and complexity (https://innoproach.com). His top tip for working remotely: USE SYSTEMS TO PULL INFORMATION FROM EMPLOYEES INSTEAD OF PUSHING INFORMATION TO THEM. Read a summary of the interview at https://collaborationsuperpowers.com/become-agile-remote-collaboration-fredrik-wiik.

ANDY WILLIS is a facilitator, mentor, speaker, and founding director of Working from Anywhere. His company helps small business operators, managers, and other employees fit "work around their life" rather than "life around their work." Though he lives in the beautiful coastal town of Tathra in New South Wales, Australia, he also spends several months every year cycling and hiking in the French Alps. He lives by the mantra "carpe diem," seizing every moment of every day. As he puts it: "THERE IS NO SUCH THING AS WORK-LIFE BALANCE. THERE IS ONLY LIFE." (https://wfa.life) You can watch the interview, listen to the podcast, or read the transcript at https://www.collaborationsuperpowers.com/132-dont-wait-to-start-living.

PETER WILSON is the managing director of Kinetic Innovative Staffing, a company that connects Australian businesses with talent in the Philippines. The two countries are a natural match. Australia is in the same time zone as the Philippines, and the Philippines has a very large English-speaking population. Since huge traffic jams are common in the Philippines, there is a strong incentive for Filipinos to work from home. And the low cost of living in the Philippines is an attractive cost savings for Australian businesses. All of these factors make for a symbiotic working relationship (http://www.kistaffing.com). His top tips for working with offshore teams: AS A MANAGER, TRY TO VISUALLY CONNECT WITH EMPLOYEES EVERY DAY WITH VIDEO. LEARNING ABOUT EACH OTHER'S CULTURES CAN BE RICH AND REWARDING. You can watch the interview, listen to the podcast, or read the transcript at https://www.collaborationsuperpowers.com/95-how-to-hire-and-onboard-an-offshore-team-with-kistaffing.

ANDREA ZABALA is an information systems engineer from Argentina who focuses on business development and offshore projects. She worked in various management positions at companies in the oil and gas industry before making the decision to go freelance so she could spend more time with her family (https://www.linkedin.com/in/adreavzabala). Her top tip for working remotely: TO BUILD TRUST, BE TRANSPARENT AND BE PERSONAL. You can watch the interview, listen to the podcast, or read the transcript at https://www.collaborationsuperpowers.com/72-maximize-your-time-working-remotely-with-andrea-zabala.

TECHNOLOGY & TOOLS

"People still use the arguments from ten years ago when we talked about remote working for the first time. People tried it and it was a lot of hassle, and they won't try it again. Now all the technical stuff just works. Things are in the cloud. Our devices have plenty of battery life. Remote working can work. And when it does, it's brilliant!"

—TEO HÄRÉN, *creativity expert, interesting.org*[1]

CAVEAT: Since new tools are released all the time, it would be impossible to include a definitive list here. This is simply a collection of tools, gadgets, and resources that have been mentioned in my interviews and virtual communities. Note that the companion page at the Collaboration Superpowers website is updated every week (https://collaborationsuperpowers.com/tools).

POPULAR TOOL SUITES

The ever-informative resource Remote.co surveyed scores of remote companies to learn what suite of tools they use to fulfill their primary responsibilities.[2] The following are those most widely used on a regular or daily basis. (The tools in parentheses are listed in order of popularity.)

- Instant messaging (Slack, Skype, Google Chat)
- Project management (Trello, Pivotal Tracker, Basecamp)
- Team collaboration (Slack, Yammer)
- Phone calls (Skype, cell phones, landlines)

Text within quotation marks indicates the manufacturer's phrasing.

COLLABORATION

Brainstorming & Planning

A Web Whiteboard. "A touch-friendly online whiteboard app that makes drawing, collaboration, and sharing easy." (https://awwapp.com)

Cardboard. "Add cards and organize them into story maps. Once you've added some cards, you can start thinking about where you want to take your customers. Framing customer journeys through a story map helps you visualize user experiences, workflows, or test paths." (https://cardboardit.com)

Coggle. "Produce beautiful notes quickly and easily. Share them with friends and colleagues to work on your ideas together." (https://coggle.it)

Dropbox Paper. "A new type of doc where teams can create together in a single space." (https://www.dropbox.com/paper)

eBeam SmartMarker. "Make your meetings more effective and interactive by streaming your notes in real time. Slip an everyday marker into the sleeve and wherever you go, whatever you write, with whatever device you use, you and your team can collaborate together easily." (http://www.e-beam.com/smartmarker.html)

GroupMap. Customizable brainstorming templates for meetings and workshops that help you think better—together. (https://www.groupmap.com)

IdeaBoardz. Digital sticky-notes on a board help you "brainstorm across oceans, . . . Retrospect, and collaborate." (http://www.ideaboardz.com)

iObeya. "Collaborate visually anywhere in real time from your computer, tablet, or touch display." (http://www.iobeya.com)

Lino. "Colorful collaboration with Lino—a free sticky and canvas service that requires nothing but a web browser." (http://en.linoit.com)

MeetingSphere. "Workshop tools for professionals." MeetingSphere Pro is for subject matter experts and professional facilitators. MeetingSphere One is designed for people who need to get an outcome from the group during a conference call; it is targeted to all types of people who call online meetings but who are not necessarily either subject matter experts or professional facilitators. (https://www.meetingsphere.com)

Mural. "Think and collaborate visually, anywhere." (https://mural.co)

NoteApp. "Sticky notes for your team, in real time." (https://noteapp.com)

Popplet. "A tool for the iPad and web to capture and organize your ideas." (http://www.popplet.com)

Post-it Plus App. "Simply capture your notes, organize, and then share with everyone." (https://www.post-it.com/3M/en_US/post-it/ideas/plus-app)

RealtimeBoard. "Your company-wide normalization layer for notes, media, data, and other inputs—all from different sources and in different formats." (https://realtimeboard.com)

Scribble. "Scribble adds an instant shared whiteboard to any call." (https://scribbletogether.com)

Stormboard. "An online sticky note whiteboard that makes meetings, brainstorms, and creative projects more productive and effective." (https://stormboard.com)

Collaborative Touchscreens

eteoBoard. A digital task board that consists of large monitors equipped with cameras, microphones, and a virtual task board setup to simulate face-to-face interaction as much as possible. (https://www.sogehtsoftware.de/zusammenarbeit-alt/eteoboard) Check out my interview with senior consultant and Scrum Master Vincent Tietz at https://collaborationsuperpowers.com/82-connect-distributed-agile-teams-with-eteo-at-saxonia-systems.

Rentouch. "55-inch touchscreens to boost your Agile efficiency." (http://www.rentouch.ch)

Decision-Making

Conceptboard. "Visual online collaboration for creative and remote teams—helping you get projects from initial idea to final approval." (https://conceptboard.com)

Conteneo. Looks at classes of problems that are collaborative in nature and then designs games to help groups collaboratively solve those problems. (https://conteneo.co) Check out my interview with founder and CEO Luke Hohmann at https://www.collaborationsuperpowers.com/creating-epic-wins-through-collaborative-games-luke-hohmann.

Delegation Poker. "Enables management to clarify delegation and to foster empowerment for both management and workers." (https://management30.com/practice/delegation-board)

Ideaflip. "Ideaflip makes it easy for your team to quickly turn thoughts into ideas, then share and refine them. . . . It's a beautifully simple web app that's perfect for group brainstorms and individual ideas." (https://ideaflip.com)

LOOMIO. "A safe place to have considered discussions and make decisions away from social media." (https://www.loomio.org)

PICKER WHEEL. "A very handy online random decision tool that can spin the wheel and pick a choice from a bunch of inputs." (https://pickerwheel.com/)

WHEEL DECIDE. "If you can't decide, all you need to do is touch the wheel, let go, and let the Wheel Decide." (https://wheeldecide.com/)

SYNTHETRON. "We help engage crowds to get answers to your important questions." (http://www.synthetron.com)

WE THINQ. Idea management software to help companies create an open culture of feedback and innovation. (https://conteneo.co) Check out my interview with director Christian Kreutz at https://www.collaborationsuperpowers.com/76-create-horizontal-organizations-with-wethinq.

YABBU. "Enables teams to make decisions, monitor progress, and discuss topics without having a face-to-face meeting." (https://www.yabbu.com)

Document Editing & Wikis

CONFLUENCE. "Content-collaboration software that changes how modern teams work." (https://www.atlassian.com/software/confluence)

DRAFT. "When you share your document using Draft, any changes your collaborator makes are on their own copy of the document; you can accept or ignore any individual change." (http://docs.withdraft.com)

ETHERPAD. "A highly customizable open-source online editor providing collaborative editing in real-time." (http://etherpad.org)

GOOGLE DOCS. "Create a new document and edit with others at the same time—from your computer, phone, or tablet. Get stuff done with or without an internet connection. Use Docs to edit Word files. Free from Google." (https://www.google.com/docs/about)

GURU. "Capture an answer [in Slack] by using an emoji reaction. Guru will prompt you to create and save that content to a card that can be reused by the whole team." (https://www.getguru.com/solutions/slack)

QUIP. "Combines your team's work and communication in one central hub that's accessible from every device." (https://quip.com)

SMASHDOCs. "Create, review, and produce professional documents with other people through your own web browser." (https://www.smashdocs.net)

TETTRA. "A company wiki that helps Slack teams manage and share organizational knowledge." (https://tettra.co)

Mind Mapping

EDRAW MAX. "An all-in-one diagram software [to] simplify the creation of . . . business presentations, building plans, mind maps, science illustration, fashion designs, UML diagrams, workflows, wireframes, electrical diagrams, p&id diagram, directional maps, database diagrams, and more." (https://www.edrawsoft.com/download-edrawmax.php)

MINDMUP. "Easy to use Mind mapping tool that you can save files to google drive at no cost". (https://www.mindmup.com/)

MINDMEISTER. "Online mind-mapping tool that lets you capture, develop, and share ideas visually." (https://www.mindmeister.com)

MINDNODE. "Visualize your ideas. Start with a central thought and then brainstorm, organize, and share your mind maps." (https://mindnode.com)

SCAPPLE. "Ever scribbled ideas on a piece of paper and drawn lines between related thoughts? Then you already know what Scapple does. It's a virtual sheet of paper that lets you make notes anywhere and connect them using lines or arrows." (https://www.literatureandlatte.com/scapple/overview)

XMIND. Mind-mapping/brainstorming software. (http://www.xmind.net)

COMMUNICATION

According to "7 REMOTE WORK TRENDS IN 2017" from Remoters.net, Skype and Slack are the most popular tools for communication.[3]

Group Chat

FRONT. "The shared in-box for teams. All your emails, apps, and teammates in one collaborative workspace." (https://frontapp.com)

GLIP. "Team messaging, file sharing, and video that you'll fall in love with." (https://glip.com)

Hangouts Chat. "A messaging platform built for teams." (https://gsuite.google.com/products/chat)

Slack. Team conversations in open or private channels. (https://slack.com)

Stride. As of August 2018, Atlassian announced a partnership with Slack; both HipChat Cloud and Stride will be phased out by 2019.[4]

Twist. "Keeps your conversations on-topic and in one place for fewer notifications and more meaningful teamwork." (https://twistapp.com)

WhatsApp. "Simple, secure, reliable messaging." (https://www.whatsapp.com)

Telepresence

Beam. With the Beam you can call in (like with Skype) and drive yourself around using the arrow keys on your keyboard. (https://suitabletech.com) Check out my interview with marketing director Erin Rapacki at https://collaborationsuperpowers.com/47-be-in-two-places-at-once-with-beam-smart-presence.

Kubi. Beam into the Kubi and move yourself from side to side and up and down. Great for meetings where there's only one remote attendee. You can sit at the table with others and turn yourself to see who is speaking or look at the white board. (https://www.revolverobotics.com) Watch my interview with some of the Revolve Robotics team at https://collaborationsuperpowers.com/18-teleport-with-the-kubi-teleconference-robot-revolve-robotics.

Ohmni. "Useful and affordable robots that bring people together. . . . Be there in one click—from anywhere in the world." (https://ohmnilabs.com)

Personify. "Teleport yourself, holographically. For augmented/virtual mixed reality." (https://www.personify.com) Check out my interview with some of the Personify team at https://www.collaborationsuperpowers.com/31-embody-your-team-online-with-personify.

Video Conferencing

Amazon Chime. "Frustration-free online meetings with exceptional audio and video quality." (https://aws.amazon.com/chime)

BlueJeans. "Video, audio, and web conferencing that works with the collaboration tools you use every day." (https://www.bluejeans.com)

Catch. Send quick video messages that expire after twenty-four hours. (https://betalist.com/startups/catch)

COLLABIFY. Online meetings made easy. No registration. No log in. No worries. Just one click. (https://collabify.app)

DISCORD. "All-in-one voice and text chat for gamers that's free, secure, and works on both your desktop and phone." (https://discordapp.com)

GOTOMEETING. "Online meeting software with HD video conferencing." (https://www.gotomeeting.com)

GOOGLE MEET. Real-time meetings by Google. Using your browser, share your video, desktop, and presentations with teammates and customers. (https://meet.google.com)

JITSI MEET. "No downloads required. Jitsi Meet works directly within your browser. Simply share your conference URL with others to get started." (https://meet.jit.si)

JOIN.ME. Free screen sharing, online meetings, and web conferencing. (https://www.join.me)

LOOM. Google Chrome extension that allows you to record and share your screen and webcam. (https://www.useloom.com)

MEETING OWL. Intelligent 360-degree all-in-one video conferencing device. (https://www.owllabs.com/meeting-owl)

ODRO. One-click online video meetings. (http://www.odro.co.uk)

SCREENCASTIFY. Free screen recorder extension for Chrome. Easily "capture, edit, and share your entire desktop, browser tab, or webcam." No software download required. (https://www.screencastify.com)

SHINDIG. Large-scale video chat events that allow you to present to an online audience of up to one thousand people. You can also take questions from the audience, provide audience with chat, and stream to YouTube or Facebook Live. (https://www.shindig.com)

SUPERCARDS. These beautiful Supercards enable you to communicate visually during your online meetings. (https://www.collaborationsuperpowers.com/supercards)

WHEREBY. "Enjoy the freedom to live and work where you thrive with easy video meetings from Whereby." (https://whereby.com)

ZEEN. "Video conferencing that provides the insights and tools to help your teams be effective." (https://zeen.com)

ZOOM. Enterprise video and web conferencing. (https://zoom.us)

Virtual Reality

3D Immersive Collaboration. "Your virtual place for real training, education, collaboration, and more." (https://www.3dicc.com)

rumii. "Virtual reality software for remote teams." (http://www.doghead simulations.com) Check out my interview with Doghead Simulations at https://collaborationsuperpowers.com/151-virtual-reality-for-remote-teams -with-doghead-simulations.

Second Life. "The pioneering virtual world that's been enjoyed by millions of people and seen billions of dollars transacted among users in its economy." (http://secondlife.com)

Voice Conferencing

Discord. "All-in-one voice and text chat for gamers that's free, secure, and works on both your desktop and phone." (https://discordapp.com)

Vail. "Voice + email." (http://danariely.com/resources/vail-voice-email)

Voxer. A walkie-talkie app that offers "secure, real-time communication in one powerful push-to-talk." (https://voxer.com)

MEETINGS

Online Meeting Managers & Accessories

ChromaCam. "A Windows desktop application that works with a standard webcam and all leading video chat apps." (https://www.chromacam.me) Check out my interview with some of the Personify team at https://collabo rationsuperpowers.com/31-embody-your-team-online-with-personify.

Cogsworth. "Lets your customers book time with you when you are available." (https://get.cogsworth.com)

Descript. "From meeting notes to multitrack editing, Descript is the powerful, flexible, and easy to use home for your audio and video." (https:// www.descript.com/use-cases.

Inspirometer. "Bringing the business culture of meetings out of the dark ages…" (https://inspirometer.com/)

Kiryl's Facilitation Toolkit. "An extensive set of templates for different kinds of facilitated online sessions supported with guides and examples." (https://baranoshnik.com)

Lean Coffee Table. "Lean Coffee Table helps distributed teams run effective 'agenda-less' Lean Coffee meetings. Lean Coffee is a wonderfully simple idea developed by Jim Benson and Jeremy Lightsmith." (http://leancoffeetable.com)

Lucid Meetings. "Smart software for great meetings." Helps you schedule times, send calendar reminders, agree on an agenda, log action items, gather user feedback, and use or create your own meeting templates. (https://www.lucidmeetings.com)

Mentimeter. Free tool for interactive presentations, workshops, and meetings—no installation or download required. (https://mentimeter.com)

Parabol. Free online Retrospectives and meetings. "Reflect and improve. Execute and check-in. Share progress." (https://www.parabol.co)

Roti.express. "ROTI = Return on Time Invested. Get instant feedback from your meetings, workshops, and conferences." (https://roti.express)

Slido. Live Q&A, polls, and slides—for team meetings, company meetings, and conferences. (https://www.sli.do)

Vidrio. "Vidrio makes for effortlessly engaging screencasts." (https://vidr.io/)

Stand-Up Meetings/Status Updates

iDoneThis. "Run more effective and productive teams with easy daily check-ins and powerful progress reports." (https://home.idonethis.com)

Stand-Bot. "Run asynchronous stand-up meetings in Slack. Keep your team up-to-date." (https://softwaredevtools.com/stand-bot)

Standup Bot. "Standup Bot collects information from your team, organizes it, and posts it in one easy-to-find place. It keeps teams accountable, allows them to track goals, and removes roadblocks by getting your team back in sync." (https://standupbot.com)

Standuply. "Run asynchronous stand-up meetings via text and audio/video, and track team performance." (https://standuply.com)

Weekdone. "Set structured goals to align activities throughout your organization. Track weekly progress, provide feedback, and move everyone in a unified direction." (https://weekdone.com)

Olaph. "A Slack bot that facilitates daily standups for your team inside of Slack." (https://olaph.io/)

Video Broadcasting

BE LIVE. "Engage your audience on Facebook Live with an amazing live broadcast." (https://belive.tv)

CROWDCAST. "Grow your audience with live video Q&As, interviews, summits, webinars, and more." (https://www.crowdcast.io)

Virtual Icebreakers

DR. CLUE. Virtual and in-person treasure hunts for teams. (https://drclue.com) Check out my interview with Dr. Clue at https://www.collaborationsuperpowers.com/solve-the-puzzles-of-teamwork-with-dr-clue.

KAHOOT. "Create, play, and share learning games." (https://kahoot.com)

MEETING SPICER. A one-minute card game to spice up your meetings. (https://www.meetingspicer.com)

PERSONAL MAPS. A simple mind-mapping technique to help you get to know your remote or colocated team members. (https://management30.com/practice/personal-maps)

PROTOTYPING.WORK. "Get your shot of inspiration for your check-in question." (https://prototyping.work/check-inspiration/)

WORKSTYLE. "Understand how you and your team work best. Build a unique profile of your personality, working style preferences, and values to help people work more effectively with you." (https://www.workstyle.io)

NITTY-GRITTY/LOGISTICS

Password Management

1PASSWORD. "Remembers all [your passwords] for you. Save your passwords and log in to sites with a single click." (https://1password.com)

DASHLANE. "Never forget another password. Manage important account passwords intelligently and automatically." (https://www.dashlane.com)

LASTPASS. "Remembers all your passwords, so you don't have to." (https://www.lastpass.com)

ROBOFORM. "You'll never need to remember or type your passwords again." (https://www.roboform.com)

ZOHO VAULT. "Password manager for teams." (https://www.zoho.eu/vault)

Task & Project Management

> There are too many task- and project-management tools to list them all. For more information, check out https://en.wikipedia.org/wiki/Comparison_of_project_management_software.

AHA! "Roadmap software to manage your products and connect strategy to execution. For PMs who want their mojo back." (https://www.aha.io)

ASANA. "Manage team projects and tasks—easily." (https://asana.com)

BASECAMP. "Basecamp puts everything you need to get work done in one place. It's the calm, organized way to manage projects, work with clients, and communicate company-wide." (https://basecamp.com)

CAGE. "Project management and collaborative software tool for designers, agencies, and teams to share their creative work." (https://cageapp.com/)

CLIO. "All you need to run a law practice from intake to invoice, with powerful tools to manage cases, clients, documents, bills, calendars, time tracking, reporting, and accounting." (https://www.clio.com)

EYLEAN. "Scrum and Kanban desktop software that integrates well into the Office tools and TFS [Team Foundation Server] from the Microsoft product family." (http://www.eylean.com)

FREETER. Freeter helps you to "gather all the things you need for work in one place and have quick access to them." (https://freeter.io)

G SUITE (formerly Google Apps for Work). "Gmail, Docs, Drive, and Calendar for business. All you need to do your best work, together in one package that works seamlessly from your computer, phone, or tablet." (https://gsuite.google.com)

HIBOX. "Task- and project-management, chat, and video calls in a single app." (https://www.hibox.co) Check out my interview with cofounder and COO Spencer Coon at https://collaborationsuperpowers.com/109-capture-productivity-in-one-place-with-hibox.

INSTAGANTT. "Gantt charts for Asana. Manage your schedules, tasks, timelines, and workload like a pro." (https://instagantt.com)

INVISION. "Create context around your projects with Boards—flexible spaces to store, share, and discuss design ideas. Built-in layout options allow you to create visual hierarchy for your ideas." (https://www.invisionapp.com)

Jira. "Plan, track, and manage your Agile and software development projects in Jira. Customize your workflow, collaborate, and release great software." (https://www.atlassian.com/software/jira) Check out my interview with Dom Price, head of R&D and work futurist at Atlassian, at https://www.collaborationsuperpowers.com/evolve-rituals-include-remote-colleagues-2.

Nozbe. "To-do, task-, project-, and time-management application." (https://nozbe.com) Check out my interview with founder Michael Sliwinski at https://www.collaborationsuperpowers.com/99-curate-your-notifications-for-maximum-productivity.

Pivotal Tracker. "The Agile project-management tool of choice for developers around the world for real-time collaboration around a shared, prioritized backlog." (https://www.pivotaltracker.com)

Podio. "With content, conversations, and processes structured and together on one tool, Podio creates the focus and clarity your people need to get their best work done." (https://podio.com)

ProofHub. "All-in-one project-management software for your growing business needs." (https://www.proofhub.com)

Quip. "A Quip doc is your team's collaboration headquarters. Insert Live Apps for calendars, Kanban boards, videos, images, and polls. Or, you can build your own." (https://quip.com)

Redbooth. "Easy-to-use online task- and project-management software to help busy teams get more done." (https://redbooth.com)

Redmine. A flexible cross-platform, cross-database project-management web application using the Ruby on Rails framework. (https://www.redmine.org)

Ring Central. "Take back one-third of your time by replacing unnecessary emails with team messaging, file sharing, tasks, scheduling, and integrations." (https://www.ringcentral.co.uk/teams/overview.html)

Salesforce Chatter. "Share knowledge, files, and data. Connect with experts from across your organization regardless of their role or location." (https://www.salesforce.com/products/chatter/overview)

ScrumDo. "Agile and Kanban software for better work." (https://www.scrumdo.com) Check out my interview with cofounder Marc Hughes at https://www.collaborationsuperpowers.com/64-align-your-remote-team-in-scrumdo-with-marc-hughes.

Scrumile. "No more choosing between Jira and your scrum tools. . . . Supercharge your Agile teams." (https://www.scrumile.com)

SCRUMPOKER. "Play Planning Poker in Confluence to estimate your Jira backlogs." (https://softwaredevtools.com/scrum-poker)

SMARTSHEET. "Plan, track, automate, and report on work; move from idea to impact—fast." (https://www.smartsheet.com)

TALKSPIRIT. "Your own branded enterprise social network solution to share information, encourage modern collaboration, and strengthen company culture." (https://www.talkspirit.com)

TEAMWORK. "Online project-management, help-desk, and team-messaging software designed to maximize your team's productivity, communication, and overall customer happiness." (https://www.teamwork.com)

TRELLO. Trello's boards, lists, and cards help you keep track of everything, from the big picture to the minute details. (https://trello.com)

VIVIFY. "For small Agile teams and large organizations alike. Handle all your projects in one place—from top to bottom." (https://www.vivifyscrum.com)

WORKPLACE BY FACEBOOK. "Make space for teams to share ideas, brainstorm, and achieve more together. More than just a collaboration tool, Workplace by Facebook connects everyone to familiar features and their favorite business tools." (https://www.facebook.com/workplace)

YAMMER. "Connect with people across your organization to make better decisions, faster." (https://www.yammer.com)

ZENHUB. Agile project management for GitHub. "Multi-repo Boards, Epics, and reports—all without ever leaving GitHub." (https://www.zenhub.com)

Time Tracking

CLOCKIFY. A "simple time tracker and timesheet app. Unlimited users, free forever." (https://clockify.me)

CLOCKSPOT. "Track employee time from anywhere. Manage timesheets in real-time. Finish payroll in minutes." (https://www.clockspot.com)

HARVEST. "Time tracking and reporting that let you operate with insight." (https://www.getharvest.com)

RESCUETIME. "Helps you understand your daily habits so you can focus and be more productive." (https://www.rescuetime.com)

TIME DOCTOR. "Employee time-tracking software that helps you and your team get a lot more done each day." (https://www.timedoctor.com)

TOGGL. "Hassle-free time tracking." (https://toggl.com)

Time Zones

EVERY TIME ZONE. "Never warp your brain with time zone math again." (http://everytimezone.com)

THE TIME ZONE CONVERTER. Quickly convert times from one time zone to another. (http://www.thetimezoneconverter.com)

TIMEZONE.IO. "Keep track of when your team is." (https://timezone.io)

WORLD TIME BUDDY. A "world clock, a time zone converter, and an online meeting scheduler." (https://www.worldtimebuddy.com)

WORLD TIME ZONE. A map of all the world's time zones with the current time. (https://www.worldtimezone.com)

Virtual Assistants

TIME ETC. "Gives you a U.S.-based virtual assistant who'll take care of your to-do list for a fraction of the cost of a full-time executive assistant." (https://web.timeetc.com)

VIRTUALEMPLOYEE. "From simple tasks like updating your database to complex ones like VBA coding, our [virtual assistants] can cover every task." (https://www.virtualemployee.com)

ZIRTUAL. "Virtual assistants for entrepreneurs, professionals, and small teams." (https://www.zirtual.com)

Workflow & Process Automation

ASANA. "A home base for all your workflows; . . . create workflows and track your team's work." (https://asana.com/uses/workflow-management)

DOJO. "A progressive framework for modern web apps." (https://dojo.io)

INTEGRIFY. "Improve productivity, efficiency, and customer experience with workflow automation." (https://www.integrify.com/workflow-automation)

KISSFLOW. "A workflow tool and business process workflow management software to automate your workflow process." (https://kissflow.com)

NINTEX. "Compete more effectively in today's digital world with workflows and automated document generation. Use real-time workflow analytics for operational visibility and improve business results." (https://www.nintex.com/workflow-automation)

PROCESSMAKER. Their "intuitive, drag-and-drop interface makes it easy for business analysts to model approval-based workflows." (https://www.processmaker.com)

SKORE. "A cross-team knowledge platform that ties into your workflow and boosts results fast." (http://skore.io)

WEBPROOF. "Workflow software and proofing tools. You upload and share—your clients comment and approve. It's easy to save time." (http://www.webproof.com)

ZAPIER. "Connect your apps and automate workflows." (https://zapier.com)

ZOHO CREATOR. "Design custom workflows that streamline communication and automate routine tasks to efficiently manage your daily work." (https://www.zoho.com/creator/workflow-automation.html)

TEAM BUILDING

Appreciation

BONUSLY. "An engaging recognition and rewards platform that enriches your company culture. Make recognition fun. Love your work." (https://bonus.ly)

Cobudget. "Makes it easy for organizations and groups to allocate funds collaboratively and transparently." (https://cobudget.co)

GROUPGREETING. "Create group eCards in sixty seconds, add photos, and invite others to sign. Then watch as you make someone's day!" (http://www.groupgreeting.com)

HEYTACO! "Sparks conversations and builds stronger relationships with its fun and unique kindness currency: tacos!" (https://www.heytaco.chat)

Kudobox.co. "An easy way to share your thanks." (http://kudobox.co)

Merit Money. "360-degree peer-to-peer recognition." (https://management30.com/practice/merit-money)

KUDOS ON LINKEDIN. "LinkedIn members who are connected to each other can give kudos to each other." (https://www.linkedjetpack.com/linkedin-secrets/linkedin-kudos/)

MO. "A fresh approach to employee recognition that improves employee engagement with a focus on social and peer-to-peer activity." (https://mo.work/)

TINGGLY. "Give stories, not stuff. . . . You choose a gift box, they pick an experience, everyone feels warm and Tinggly." (https://www.tinggly.com)

YOUEARNEDIT. "Real-time, meaningful recognition. Personalized, powerful rewards. Insights and analytics." (https://youearnedit.com)

Feedback

15FIVE. "Unlock the potential of your entire workforce. Makes continuous employee feedback simple." (https://www.15five.com)

ELIN. "Elin finds development areas for the team and proposes action steps for the employees and managers to improve." (https://elin.ai/about/)

OFFICEVIBE. "Equips you with honest feedback from your team to help you proactively turn issues into conversations, and conversations into solutions before problems can form." (https://www.officevibe.com)

SELLEO MERIT MONEY SERVICE. Its "360-degree peer-to-peer feedback enables employees to reward their coworkers with kudos (reward points that may convert to bonuses) as a token of appreciation for their colleagues' efforts, performance, demeanor—anything worth rewarding." (https://selleo.com/portfolios/merit-money-service/?pnt=6067)

TEAM CANVAS. "The business model canvas for teamwork. Organize team alignment meetings to bring members on the same page, resolve conflicts, and build productive culture, fast." (http://theteamcanvas.com)

Retrospectives

AGILE RETROSPECTIVES FOR CONFLUENCE. "Run interactive and engaging Retrospective sessions within Confluence." (https://softwaredevtools.com/retrospectives)

AGILE RETROSPECTIVES FOR JIRA. "Transparency + visibility = increased team accountability. Get on your way to continuous improvement now." (https://softwaredevtools.com/retrospectives/jira)

FUN RETROSPECTIVES. "Activities and ideas for making Agile Retrospectives more engaging." (http://www.funretrospectives.com)

MINDFUL TEAM. "Run health checks and Retrospectives that help your team measure, track, and take action on their productivity and morale." (https://mindful.team) Check out my interview with cofounders Emma Joy Obanye and Irene Francis at https://www.collaborationsuperpowers.com/140-reflect-and-take-action-with-mindful-team.

ONLINE SCRUMS. "Systemized daily Scrums and sprint Retrospectives integrated with powerful reporting." (https://www.onlinescrums.com)

REMOTERETRO. "Elevate your remote team members to first-class citizens and hold better, more productive Agile Retrospective meetings . . . remotely." (https://remoteretro.io)

RETRIUM. "Vote on the best ideas. Prioritize your discussion. Keep your team engaged." (https://www.retrium.com/welcome/lisette-sutherland) Check out my interview with founder and CEO David Horowitz at https://collaboration superpowers.com/37-abolish-the-postmortem-with-david-horowitz.

RETRO TOOL. "Simple, fun, flexible remote Retrospectives." Start with a blank board, or choose from one of three templates: Mad/Sad/Glad, Start/Stop/Continue, or Liked/Learnt/Lacked. (https://retrotool.io)

SCATTERSPOKE. "Retrospectives with the tools you need to improve beyond the last two weeks." (https://www.scatterspoke.com) Check out my interview with cofounder Colleen Johnson at https://collaborationsuperpowers.com/68-manage-the-work-not-the-people-with-colleen-johnson.

TEAMRETRO. "Simple, engaging, and action-focused Retrospectives with customizable templates." (https://www.teamretro.com)

Retreats

COWORKATION. "Inspirational coworking retreats, set in stunning locations around the world." (https://coworkation.com) Check out my interview with consultant Kirsty Thompson at https://collaborationsuperpowers.com/101-coworkation-when-work-meets-vacation.

DR. CLUE. "Solving the puzzles of teamwork." (https://drclue.com) Check out my interview with founder Dave Blum at https://collaborationsuperpowers.com/74-solve-the-puzzles-of-remote-teamwork-with-dr-clue.

REBEL + CONNECT. "Custom retreats for your remote team." (http://www.rebelandconnect.co) Check out my interview with cofounder Charlie Birch at https://collaborationsuperpowers.com/103-retreats-for-remote-teams.

REMOTE-HOW. "Introduces the digital nomad trend to corporate life by organizing remote-work programs for employees. Remote-how is a remote work and travel incentive program, to attract and retain your top talents." (https://www.remote-how.com)

SURF OFFICE. "Let Surf Office be your next offŁsite team building experience. Whether it's for the whole office, or simply a meetup with your remote team, our unique combination of work and play is sure to bring you and your employees closer together." (https://www.thesurfoffice.com/)

Virtual Office

> Working with colleagues in a virtual office can create a surprisingly strong sense of community and connection.

Bisner. "We empower coworking spaces around the globe to communicate and interact better with their community." (https://www.bisner.com)

Complice. "Find people to work with. If there's nobody else in a room, you can still go in it and invite your friends to join." (https://complice.co/rooms)

PukkaTeam. "Bring your remote team together, get real team presence with automated selfie photos, and see their status throughout the day." (https://pukkateam.com)

Sococo. Sococo offers a virtual office with a customizable floor plan. All logged-in workers' avatars are visible, so everyone knows who is working. Includes options for group discussion rooms with video and screen sharing, a virtual water cooler chatting area, and a Do Not Disturb Room. (https://www.sococo.com) Check out my interview with some of the Sococo team at https://collaborationsuperpowers.com/60-be-a-high-functioning-connected-team-in-a-sococo-virtual-office.

Walkabout Workplace. This "award-winning online workplace connects remote teams—seamlessly." (https://www.walkaboutco.com)

MISCELLANEOUS HANDY GADGETS

Chatlight. "The first rechargeable light made specifically for video chatting. Chatlight fits almost all of your devices and has fully adjustable lighting brightness and direction." (https://www.chatlight.com)

Duet Display. "Ex-Apple Engineers turn your iPad into an extra display." (https://www.duetdisplay.com)

Jabra Speak Series. "The entry-level portable USB conference speakerphone." (https://www.jabra.com/business/speakerphones/jabra-speak-series)

Rocketbook. "The magical pen-and-paper notebook designed for our digital world." (https://getrocketbook.co.uk)

Sidecar. "Attach your tablet as a second monitor to your laptop." (http://www.dockem.com/SideCar-by-VenosTech-p/sidecar-wh.htm)

Topo. "Standing . . . done right. The anti-fatigue mat designed specifically for standing desks." (http://ergodriven.com/topo)

FOR FURTHER READING, LISTENING & *Consultation*

GENERAL

FeeBee. "Helps business freelancers and consultants find out what their peers charged for similar projects, and guides companies on how to budget for projects in a specific skill area." (https://www.flexingit.com/feebee)

Freelancers Union. This free-to-join group is "open to freelancers of all kinds, from graphic designers to contractors to entrepreneurs to moonlighters." Freelancers Union offers benefits such as health insurance, local freelance hubs in nearly twenty-five major cities, access to resources, and advocacy for policy change, such as the Freelance Isn't Free campaign to pass city laws mandating timely payment of freelancer invoices. (https://www.freelancersunion.org)

Remote.Co. In addition to their job listings (https://remote.co/remote-jobs) and weekly "Fresh Jobs" newsletter, Remote.co offers a Remote Work Blog (https://remote.co/remote-work-blog) as well as extensive Q&As from both remote workers (https://www.remote.co/remote-workers) and remote-friendly companies (https://remote.co/qa-leading-remote-companies).

BOOKS & GUIDES

For Individuals

Clean Language: Revealing Metaphors and Opening Minds by Wendy Sullivan and Judy Rees. This book teaches how using "clean" language—devoid of assumption and metaphor—can help improve communication. (https://judyrees.co.uk/clean-language-get-the-book)

Digital Nomads: How to Live, Work and Play Around the World by Esther Jacobs. (https://shop.estherjacobs.info/product/digital-nomads-en)

Digital Nomad Survival Guide: How to Successfully Travel the World While Working Remotely by Peter Knudson and Katherine Conaway. (http://www.homsweethom.com/digital-nomad-survival-guide)

Digital Writer Success: How to Make a Living Blogging, Freelance Writing, and Publishing Online by Leslie Truex. (https://digitalwritersuccess.com)

Don't Reply All: 18 Email Tactics That Help You Write Better Emails and Improve Communication with Your Team by Hassan Osman. (http://www.thecouchmanager.com/resources)

Fierce Conversations: Achieving Success at Work and in Life One Conversation at a Time by Susan Scott. (https://www.penguinrandomhouse.com/books/289515/fierce-conversations-by-susan-scott/9780425193372)

The Freelancer's Guide to Getting Paid on Time, which includes a Contract Creator, invoicing advice, and tips on pursuing non-payment claims. An additional tool kit guides U.S. freelancers on how to bring New York City's Freelance Isn't Free Law to your city or state. (https://www.freelancersunion.org/advocacy/guide-to-getting-paid)

How to Become a Digital Nomad: A Step-by-Step Guide for Achieving Location Independence in Your Business or Career by Konrad Waliszewski, Annie Erling Gofus, and Team TripScout. (https://www.amazon.com/dp/B073C4M2BS/ref=sspa_dk_detail_0?psc=1)

Job Escape Plan: The 7 Steps to Build a Home Business, Quit Your Job, and Enjoy the Freedom by Jyotsna Ramachandran. (http://jyotsnaramachandran.com/book)

Jobs Online: How to Find and Get Hired to a Work-at-Home Job by Leslie Truex. (https://www.workathomesuccess.com/about)

Manage Your Job Search by Johanna Rothman. (https://www.jrothman.com/books/manage-your-job-search)

Nature and Well-Being in the Digital World: Practical Activities to Help You Feel Better Without Logging Off by Sue Thomas. (https://suethomasnet.wordpress.com/publications/2017-nature-and-wellbeing-in-the-digital-age-a-beginners-guide-to-technobiophilia)

The Remote Revolution by John Elston. (http://johnelston.com/buy-the-book-more)

Serve No Master: How to Escape the 9–5, Start Up an Online Business, Fire Your Boss and Become a Lifestyle Entrepreneur or Digital Nomad by Jonathan Green. (https://servenomaster.com/book)

Skip the Commute: The Ultimate Guide to 150+ Careers from Home by Alison Moxley. (https://www.amazon.com/Skip-Commute-Ultimate-Guide-Careers-ebook/dp/B00TJ44KIQ)

The Smarter Home Office: 8 Simple Steps to Increase Your Income, Inspiration, and Comfort by Linda Varone. (http://www.lindavarone.com/feng-shui-resources)

Stuck? Unhappy? Become the CEO of Your Own Life! by Beat Bühlmann. (https://cuvillier.de/uploads/preview/public_file/10367/9783736994980_Inhaltsverzeichnis.pdf)

The Suitcase Entrepreneur: Create Freedom in Business and Adventure in Life by Natalie Sisson. (https://suitcaseentrepreneur.com/book)

Technobiophilia: Nature and Cyberspace by Sue Thomas. (https://suethomasnet.wordpress.com/whatistechnobiophilia/technobiophilia)

The Work-at-Home Success Bible: A Complete Guide for Women by Leslie Truex. (https://www.workathomesuccess.com/about)

The Year Without Pants: WordPress.com and the Future of Work by Scott Berkun. (http://scottberkun.com/books)

ZAPIER'S REMOTE WORK SURVIVAL GUIDE. "Nine do's and don'ts every remote worker needs to know." (https://zapier.com/blog/survival-guide-to-remote-work)

For Teams and Managers

Agile and Lean Program Management: Scaling Collaboration Across the Organization by Johanna Rothman. (https://www.jrothman.com/books/agile-and-lean-program-management-scaling-collaboration-across-the-organization)

Better Remote Work: Do It Right, and Reap the Benefits by Jarkko Oksanen. (Amazon)

Building & Managing Virtual Teams by Chris Lema. (http://chrislema.com/product/building-managing-virtual-teams)

Can You Hear Me Now? Working with Global, Distributed, Virtual Teams by Jesse Fewell. (http://jessefewell.com)

Clean Language: Revealing Metaphors and Opening Minds by Wendy Sullivan and Judy Rees. This book teaches how using "clean" language—devoid of assumption and metaphor—can help improve communication. (https://judyrees.co.uk/clean-language-get-the-book)

The Collaborative Organization: A Strategic Guide to Solving Your Internal Business Challenges Using Emerging Social and Collaborative Tools by Jacob Morgan. (https://thefutureorganization.com/books)

*CTRL Shift: 50 Games for 50 ****ing Days Like Today* by Mike Bonifer and Jessie Shternshus. This book offers fifty original improv games tailored to help you and your team bond over whatever frustrating **** you happen to be dealing with at the time. (http://improveffect.com/#book)

The Distance Manager: A Hands-On Guide to Managing Off-Site Employees and Virtual Teams by Kimball Fisher and Mareen Fisher. (http://www.kimballfisher.com/books)

The Diversity Bonus: How Great Teams Pay Off in the Knowledge Economy by Scott E. Page. (https://sites.lsa.umich.edu/scottepage/; https://www.amazon.com/Diversity-Bonus-Knowledge-Compelling-Interests/dp/0691176884)

Don't Reply All: 18 Email Tactics That Help You Write Better Emails and Improve Communication with Your Team by Hassan Osman. (http://www.thecouchmanager.com/resources)

The Employee Experience Advantage: How to Win the War for Talent by Giving Employees the Workspaces They Want, the Tools They Need, and a Culture They Can Celebrate by Jacob Morgan. (https://thefutureorganization.com/books)

Fierce Conversations: Achieving Success at Work and in Life One Conversation at a Time by Susan Scott. (https://www.penguinrandomhouse.com/books/289515/fierce-conversations-by-susan-scott/9780425193372)

50 Digital Team-Building Games: Fast, Fun Meeting Openers, Group Activities and Adventures using Social Media, Smart Phones, GPS, Tablets, and More by John Chen. (Wiley)

The Future of Work: Attract New Talent, Build Better Leaders, and Create a Competitive Organization by Jacob Morgan. (https://thefutureorganization.com/books)

Getting Value Out of Agile Retrospectives: A Toolbox of Retrospective Exercises by Ben Linders and Luis Gonçalves. (https://www.benlinders.com/getting-value-out-of-agile-retrospectives)

Global Teams: How the Best Teams Achieve High Performance by Jo Owen. (http://www.pearson.com.au/products/O-R-Owen-Jo/Global-Teams-How-the-best-teams-achieve-high-performance/9781292171913?R=9781292171913)

Hiring Geeks That Fit by Johanna Rothman. (https://www.jrothman.com/books/hiring-geeks-that-fit)

How to Embrace Remote Work. Trello's "ultimate guide of tried-and-tested strategies, from the world's leading companies for remote work." Includes sections on Dispelling Myths and Providing Tips, Communication and Collaboration, Digital Tools, Company Culture, and Jobs and Hiring. (https://info.trello.com/hubfs/Trello-Embrace-Remote-Work-Ultimate-Guide.pdf)

How to Get Prepared For Managing a Remote Team by Hugo Messer. (http://hugomesser.com/books)

How to Not Screw Up When Managing a Remote Team by Hugo Messer. (http://hugomesser.com/books)

Influencing Virtual Teams: 17 Tactics That Get Things Done with Your Remote Employees by Hassan Osman. (https://ldpges.leadpages.co/ivtbook4)

#iPadOnly: How to Use Only Your iPad to Work, Play, and Everything in Be tween by Augusto Pinaud and Michael Sliwinski. (http://ipadonly.com/start)

Leading Effective Virtual Teams: Overcoming Time and Distance to Achieve Exceptional Results by Nancy M. Settle-Murphy. (https://guidedinsights.com/leading-effective-virtual-teams)

The Long-Distance Leader: Rules for Remarkable Remote Leadership by Kevin Eikenberry and Wayne Turmel. (https://www.bkconnection.com/books/title/The-Long-Distance-Leader)

Management 3.0: Leading Agile Developers, Developing Agile Leaders by Jurgen Appelo. (https://management30.com/product/management30)

Manager's Guide to Virtual Teams by Kimball Fisher and Mareen Fisher. (http://www.kimballfisher.com/books)

A Manager's Guide to Virtual Teams by Yael Zofi. (http://www.yaelzofi.com/book-products)

Managing for Happiness: Games, Tools, and Practices to Motivate Any Team by Jurgen Appelo. (https://management30.com/product/managing-for-happiness)

Need to Manage a Virtual Team? Theory and Practice in a Nutshell by Beat Bühlmann. (Amazon)

Practical Remote Team Leadership: Methods, Tools and Templates for Virtual Leaders by Emanucla Giangregorio. (http://www.aikaizen.com/leading_remote_teams)

Remote: Office Not Required by Jason Fried and David Heinemeier Hansson. (https://basecamp.com/books/remote)

Rework by Jason Fried and David Heinemeier Hansson. (https://basecamp.com/books/rework)

The 7 Habits of Highly Effective Virtual Teams by Paul F. Alexander. (http://booklaunch.io/paulfrederickalexander/7highlyeffectivehabits)

Social Technologies in Business: Connect | Share | Lead by Isabel De Clercq. (https://www.diekeure.be/nl-be/professional/8077/social-technologies-in-business)

Virtual Culture: The Way We Work Doesn't Work Anymore—A Manifesto by Bryan Miles. (https://virtualculturebook.com)

Virtual Freedom: How to Work with Virtual Staff to Buy More Time, Become More Productive, and Build Your Dream Business by Chris Ducker. (http://www.virtualfreedombook.com)

Virtual Leadership: Learning to Lead Differently by Ghislaine Caulat. (https://www.black-gazelle.com/index.php?option=com_content&view=article&id=24&Itemid=147)

Virtual Leadership: Practical Strategies for Getting the Best Out of Virtual Work and Virtual Teams by Dr. Penny Pullen. (http://www.makingprojectswork.co.uk/penny-pullan)

The Virtual Manager Collection by Harvard Business Review. "With the Virtual Manager Collection (3 books + tools), you will be well equipped with the knowledge and tools to be more productive than ever in a virtual world. This set offers practical advice, sample language, and countless tips for the modern employee—whether you're managing a team, a project, or just your own work." (https://hbr.org/product/the-virtual-manager-collection-3-books-tools/10122E-KND-ENG)

Virtual Teams: Mastering Communication and Collaboration in the Digital Age by Terri R. Kurtzberg. (https://www.amazon.com/Virtual-Teams-Mastering-Communication-Collaboration/dp/1440828377)

Who Is Agile? A Book of Personal Reflections on the Journeys of People Who Stumbled on Agile by Yves Hanoulle. (https://leanpub.com/WhoIsAgile)

Why Managing Sucks and How to Fix It: A Results-Only Guide to Taking Control of Work, Not People by Jody Thompson and Cali Ressler. (https://wiley.com)

Work Without Walls: An Executive's Guide to Attention Management, Productivity, and the Future of Work by Maura Thomas. (https://maurathomas.com/books/work-without-walls)

On Working with Other Cultures

MyLifeElsewhere. "A collaborative site that allows you to compare and contrast the country you live in with other countries around the world, [offering] various statistics that differentiate your country from others, including cost of living, geographic size, and more. If you had been born in another country, what would your life have been like?" (http://www.mylifeelsewhere.com)

IfItWereMyHome.com. Similar to MyLifeElsewhere, this site notes it is a "gateway to understanding life outside your home," and offers statistical comparisons between your country and others. You can also use their visualization tool to help understand the impact of a disaster. Each week they feature a different country. (http://www.ifitweremyhome.com)

Cultural Intelligence: A Guide to Working with People from Other Cultures by Brooks Peterson. "Cultivating cultural intelligence is a skill that can be learned, and Brooks Peterson tells you how." (https://www.amazon.com/Cultural-Intelligence-Working-People-Cultures/dp/1931930007)

The Difference: How the Power of Diversity Creates Better Groups, Firms, Schools, and Societies by Scott E. Page. A "landmark book [that] redefines the way we understand ourselves in relation to one another." (https://press.princeton.edu/titles/8757.html)

Global Dexterity: How to Adapt Your Behavior Across Cultures without Losing Yourself in the Process by Andy Molinsky. The author's site offers a free e-book—"Cheat Sheet to 10 Cultural Codes from Around the World"—namely: Asia (China, India, Japan, Korea), Europe (France, Germany, Great Britain), and the Americas (Brazil, Mexico, U.S.). (www.andymolinsky.com)

Kiss, Bow, or Shake Hands: The Bestselling Guide to Doing Business in More Than 60 Countries by Terri Morrison and Wayne A. Conaway. (http://www.simonandschuster.com/books/Kiss-Bow-Or-Shake-Hands/Terri-Morrison/Kiss-Bow-or-Shake-Hands/9781593373689)

When Cultures Collide: Leading Across Cultures by Richard D. Lewis. This expanded edition offers chapters on Colombia, Iraq, Israel, Pakistan, Serbia, and Venezuela. (https://books.google.com/books?id=9yyfDAAAQBAJ)

Working Across Cultures by John Hooker. This book illustrates how to thrive in unfamiliar cultures; includes a reading list for more than one hundred countries. (https://www.sup.org/books/title/?id=4505)

COMMUNITIES

Freelancers Union. This free-to-join group is "open to freelancers of all kinds, from graphic designers to contractors to entrepreneurs to moonlighters." Freelancers Union offers benefits such as health insurance, local freelance hubs in nearly twenty-five major cities, access to resources, and advocacy for policy change, such as the Freelance Isn't Free campaign to pass city laws mandating timely payment of freelancer invoices. (https://www.freelancersunion.org)

Management 3.0 Supporters Community. A professional happiness association that connects like-minded people and organizations and offers access to practical, insightful, and tangible resources geared toward happiness, job satisfaction, and professional development. The goal: productive and fulfilling lives in meaningful work environments. (Note: I am a proud sponsor and member of this community.) (https://management30.com/happiness-at-work/)

Dynamite Circle. "The Dynamite Circle is a paid membership, private community exclusively for location independent entrepreneurs with established businesses. Membership is available through application only." (https://www.tropicalmba.com/dc/)

Nomad Projects. "A platform for digital nomads who want to start a side project. Connect with other nomads so ideas don't stay ideas, but grow into a side project with diverse expertise". (https://nomadprojects.io/)

Remotive. "The community of remote workers. Where 700+ 'cool kids' in remote work hang out." (https://remotive.io/community)

Virtual Team Talk. "A Slack group of people talking about remote teams and experimenting with new tools and ideas together. We virtually cowork together in a virtual office, plan online conferences, and play a lot. Join us!" (I am a proud member of this community.) (https://virtualteamtalk.com)

CONSULTANTS

Academic Life Coaching

Gretchen Wegner is an internationally recognized academic life coach who inspires students to uncover their true identities as capable, clever, and creative learners in school and life. She does this with her Anti-Boring Approach to Powerful Studying—her unique system for time management, organization, and studying. (https://gretchenwegner.com)

Agile Coaching

Ben Linders is a trainer, coach, and advisor based in Tilburg, the Netherlands. With Luis Gonçalves he cowrote—remotely—*Getting Value Out of Agile Retrospectives: A Toolbox of Retrospective Exercises.* (https://www.benlinders.com)

Fernando Garrido Vaz is a freelance product manager from Brazil with experience managing distributed teams with multiple nationalities and time zones. Fernando says: "It's interesting to have people with different backgrounds and slightly different views of things thinking about the same problems. You're likely going to get more innovative and creative suggestions than if your team were more homogeneous." (http://blog.garridovaz.com)

Jesse Fewell, a writer, coach, and trainer in innovation and Agile methods, is the founder and principal coach at Fewell Innovation in Washington, DC, U.S. He also founded the PMI Agile Community of Practice and cocreated the PMI ACP Agile certification. He wrote a MiniBük called *Can You Hear Me Now? Working with Global, Distributed, Virtual Teams.* (http://jessefewell.com)

Johanna Rothman is a management consultant for software managers and leaders. She is also the author of many books, most recently *Agile and Lean Program Management: Scaling Collaboration Across the Organization.* (http://www.jrothman.com)

Luis Gonçalves is a management consultant, author, speaker, and blogger based in Munich, Germany. He is also founder of Evolution4All, a management consulting firm that helps executives of medium-sized companies become more effective, efficient, and rewarded. With Ben Linders he cowrote—remotely—*Getting Value Out of Agile Retrospectives: A Toolbox of Retrospective Exercises.* (http://lmsgoncalves.com)

Mario Lucero is an Agile coach and Scrum Master based in Santiago, Chile. He has extensive experience with team leadership, continuous integration, architecture, and automation tools. He develops high-level solutions for companies in the technology, billing, and financial sectors. (https://cl.linkedin.com/in/luceromet)

Ralph van Roosmalen is CEO of both Agile Strides and Management 3.0. He has experience simultaneously managing teams in the Netherlands, Romania, and the United States. (https://agilestrides.com)

Yves Hanoulle is a creative collaboration agent at PairCoaching.net in Gent, Belgium. He is also the author of *Who Is Agile? A Book of Personal Reflections on the Journeys of People Who Stumbled on Agile*. (http://www.hanoulle.be)

Communication

Jessie Shternshus is the founder of Improv Effect and the coauthor of *CTRL Shift: 50 Games for 50 ****ing Days Like Today*, a book with fifty original improv games tailored to the kind of ****ing day you're having. She also uses improv (virtually and in person) to help software teams with onboarding, communication, and team building. Improv is a great tool for learning about and accepting each other's uniqueness, thinking on the spot, and being self-aware. It can also help teams find similarities with each other and solve problems creatively. (http://www.improveffect.com)

Judy Rees. A former journalist and media executive based in London, U.K., Judy is now known worldwide as a practical implementer of the inquiry methodology Clean Language. She is also the coauthor of the best-selling book on the topic, *Clean Language: Revealing Metaphors and Opening Minds*. She works as an online facilitator, trainer, and coach and is an Agile enthusiast. (http://judyrees.co.uk)

Outsourcing

Bart Van Loon is an offshore staffing specialist at Zeropoint, which brings together businesses from Europe, Pakistan, and Sri Lanka. One of Zeropoint's secrets to success is offering remote team management training to both the client and to the employees being hired. (https://zeropoint.it)

Brandon Brown calls himself the Swiss Army Knife kind of virtual assistant. His goal is to make his clients forget what they're stressed about. (https://www.upwork.com/o/profiles/users/_~0170815817e346823a)

Dave Hecker, a cofounder at SourceSeek, is a seasoned tech executive, speaker, and author who focuses on distributed team software delivery. He emphasizes the importance of spending time with potential clients in order to build a successful long-term relationship. (http://www.sourceseek.com)

Dirk-Jan Padmos is an HR interim manager/HR consultant with special expertise in the technical wholesale, ICT, and health care branches. He advises owner-managed businesses on how to structure and implement HR policies. (https://www.linkedin.com/in/dirkjanpadmos)

Hugo Messer is a distributed Agile expert with more than ten years' expertise acting as an intermediary between companies in the Netherlands and employees in Ukraine and India. He is the founder of both Bridge Global, an IT solutions provider; and Ekipa, an Agile training and coaching agency. He has coauthored six books on "lessons learned in offshoring and nearshoring." The most recent, Book 6 of the Art of Managing Remote Teams series, is *How to Manage People in Your Remote Team.* (www.ekipa.co, and www.ekipa.co.id)

Peter Wilson is managing director of Kinetic Innovative Staffing, a company that connects Australian businesses with talent in the Philippines. (http://www.kistaffing.com)

Podcasting

Podcasting consultant Nick Jaworski shares: "My eclectic background as a trained musician, licensed teacher, military band member, nonprofit leader, and audio producer means that I offer unique expertise to help you communicate your ideas to the public." (http://www.podcastmonster.com)

Reputation/Personal Development

Stephan Dohrn helps high-performing entrepreneurs unlock the full potential of remote work and lead a free and self-determined life. With his support, clients become emotionally fit, learn to organize their lives, and experience greater well-being—while keeping their professional edge. (www.sdohrn.com)

Per Frykman is reputation advisor at Your Professional Reputation in Stockholm, Sweden. He helps people discover their potential so they can find jobs they love. (https://perfrykman.com)

Taxes

Greenback Expat Tax Services. Greenback helps Americans living abroad stay compliant with their U.S. taxes while living overseas. (https://www.greenbacktaxservices.com)

Transitioning

Virtual not Distant. "At Virtual not Distant, we help managers and leaders of colocated teams make the transition to a remote setup, so that team members can work from where they work best. We also help organizations introduce 'Agile working.'" (https://www.virtualnotdistant.com)

COWORKING

Breather. "Breather creates modern workspaces you can keep for hours, days, or months—all to yourself." (https://breather.com)

Croissant. "Croissant is a platform that helps connects entrepreneurs, freelancers, and remote teams to over 700 coworking spaces worldwide with one monthly pass." (https://www.getcroissant.com/)

CoWorking.Coffee. "The best workplaces with coffee and Wi-Fi, curated by the community, all around the world." (https://www.coworking.coffee)

Desk Surfing. "Desksurfing is coworking at any given place. Find your favorite workspot—and change it whenever the surf feels right. Offer a desk at your office—and share your spot with creative professionals." (http://www.desksurfing.net)

Global Coworking Map. A map of coworking spaces around the world. (https://coworkingmap.org)

Hoffice. "Come and work at someone's home." (http://hoffice.nu)

Kitchin Table. "To be part of a greater community of women, stop by a Kitchin Table or host one of your own." (https://www.kitchintable.com)

ShareDesk. "On-demand workspace, when you need it. Book a coworking space, business center, or shared office space nearby. Discover spaces to rent by the hour, day, or month." (https://www.sharedesk.net)

Workfrom. "Find and share local places to work, meet, and study in every city. [Offers] hard-to-find insights about coffee shops, cafés, coworking spaces, and other non-traditional workspaces." (https://workfrom.co)

HR CONCERNS

Budgeting and Hiring

FeeBee. "Helps business freelancers and consultants find out what their peers charged for similar projects, and guides companies on how to budget for projects in a specific skill area." (https://www.flexingit.com/feebee)

Flexing It. "A curated discovery and market-making platform that connects organizations to professionals on an on-demand basis for projects, consulting assignment, advisory roles, and part-time resource needs." (https://www.flexingit.com)

Health, Disability, and Life Insurance for Remote Teams

Benify. "Our cloud-based portal visualizes your total employee offer worldwide, illustrates your values and culture, and inspires active participation in all aspects of work life—all while helping you manage administration, costs, and risks." (https://www.benify.com)

Lumity. "Your benefits consultant in-a-box." (https://lumity.com)

TriNet. "Small- and midsized-business solutions." (https://www.trinet.com)

Zenefits. "Efficiently manage your HR solutions from anywhere in the world, wherever work takes you." (https://www.zenefits.com)

Remote-Working Policies

Basecamp Employee Handbook. "This is where we'll try to share what's worth knowing about Basecamp the company, our culture, our process, and our history." (https://github.com/basecamp/handbook)

Owl Labs Remote Work, Flexible Schedule, and Working from Home Policy Templates. (https://www.owllabs.com/offers/remote-work-policy-templates)

GitLab's Handbook for Spending Company Money. This resource offers guidelines for fair, timely, on-the-job expenditures. (https://about.gitlab.com/handbook/spending-company-money)

ONLINE WORK SITES

Fivrr. "Freelance services, on demand." (https://www.fiverr.com)

FlexJobs. "The best remote and flexible jobs, and a better way to find them." (https://www.flexjobs.com)

Freelancer. "Hire expert freelancers for any job, online." (https://www.freelancer.com)

Guru. "Makes it easy for quality employers and freelancers to connect, collaborate, and get work done flexibly and securely." (https://www.guru.com)

Landing Jobs. "Don't just look for a tech job. Find the one that fits you." (https://landing.jobs)

letsworkremotely. "Find the best remote jobs and remote talent from anywhere." (https://www.letsworkremotely.com)

Remote.co. "Hand-recruited list in the most recruited categories." (https://remote.co/remote-jobs)

Remote OK. "Find a job you can do anywhere." (https://remoteok.io)

Remote Talent. Specializes in recruiting "the best full-time remote workers around the world." (http://remotetalent.co)

SKIP THE DRIVE. A free service to help job seekers find remote employment—no registration required. (https://www.skipthedrive.com)

STACK OVERFLOW. Jobs for developers. (https://stackoverflow.com/jobs)

UPWORK. "Find jobs. Find freelancers." (https://www.upwork.com)

WE WORK REMOTELY. "The best place to find and list jobs that aren't restricted by commutes or a particular geographic area." (https://weworkremotely.com)

WORK-AT-HOME SUCCESS. "Providing free telecommuting job leads, home business tips and information, WAHS newsletter, scam alerts, and more." (https://www.workathomesuccess.com)

PODCASTS

21ST-CENTURY WORK LIFE. "The world of work is changing. Our attitudes about work are changing. The *21st-Century Work Life* podcast with Pilar Orti looks at different ways of earning a living, of using technology at work, and of managing teams." (https://www.virtualnotdistant.com/podcasts)

COLLABORATION SUPERPOWERS. "Lisette Sutherland interviews people and companies doing great things remotely. The interviews are packed with stories and tips for those whose business models depend on successfully bridging distance in order to accomplish knowledge work." (https://www.collaborationsuperpowers.com/podcasts)

THE FUTURE OF WORK PODCAST. In this weekly show Jacob Morgan "has in-depth discussions with senior executives and business leaders around the world on the future of work." (https://thefutureorganization.com/future-work-podcast/)

DISTRIBUTED.BLOG. "The cofounder of WordPress and CEO of Automattic embarks on a journey to understand the future of work. Having built his own 900-person company with no offices and employees scattered across 68 countries, Mullenweg examines the benefits and challenges of distributed work and recruiting talented people around the globe." (https://distributed.blog/podcast/)

VIRTUAL FRONTIER. "A podcast about virtual teams created by a virtual team." (https://virtualfrontier.simplecast.fm)

YONDER. "Yonder advocates for remote work and we're building a movement to create more distributed companies and change the future of work." (https://www.yonder.io)

WORK TOGETHER ANYWHERE

Workshop

Available both online and in person, this four-part workshop walks you through the most critical aspects of working on a virtual team.

SET EXPECTATIONS FOR HOW TO WORK TOGETHER—
CREATING A TEAM AGREEMENT covers:

- How to establish guidelines for working on a remote team
- Common communication protocols for remote working
- Tools for capturing team agreements

SIMULATE THE OFFICE ONLINE covers:

- How to create a high-bandwidth workspace
- Tools that enable reliable communication
- Techniques for keeping everyone on the same page

FACILITATE ONLINE MEETINGS LIKE A PRO covers:

- How to choose and effectively use online-meeting technology
- How to facilitate interaction and participation while minimizing distractions and multitasking
- Common communication protocols for effective remote meetings

GIVE AND RECEIVE FEEDBACK covers:

- How to set up 360-degree feedback systems
- How to conduct remote Retrospectives
- Techniques for rapid, continuous feedback
- Tools for showing appreciation

HTTPS://COLLABORATIONSUPERPOWERS.COM/ANYWHEREWORKSHOP

About the Authors

LISETTE SUTHERLAND is a German-born American who is totally jazzed by the fact that it's possible to work from anywhere. In fact, it's not just possible; it's completely, productively workable—if you do it right. She is the director of Collaboration Superpowers, a company that shares just how to do it right in a variety of formats:

- Speaking engagements and webinars
- Work Together Anywhere workshops
- Weekly podcasts featuring interviews with remote-working experts
- Bimonthly newsletter
- Guest appearances on Pilar Orti's *21st-Century Work Life* podcasts

Lisette has given presentations at a wide range of events, from conferences and Meetups all over the world to a TEDx talk—Theme: Unbox the Future—in Kaunas, Lithuania. Her workshop and webinar clients include Air France, CrossKnowledge (a Wiley Brand), Ericsson, IKEA, ING, Rabobank, Saint-Gobain, and Volvo. In January 2018, both the *Collaboration Superpowers* podcast and the *21st-Century Work Life* podcast series were deemed among the Best Remote Work Podcasts by Workplaceless. I WAS the remote team manager up until Jan 2020. And the company changed names from Happy Melly to Management 3.0 (which has a much stronger brand recognition and is also the title of one of Wiley's books). She also cofounded Virtual Team Talk (https://www.virtualteamtalk.com), an online community of 500 virtual team enthusiasts. She lives in the Netherlands and works anywhere there's a digital connection. Contact her via lisette@lisettesutherland.com.

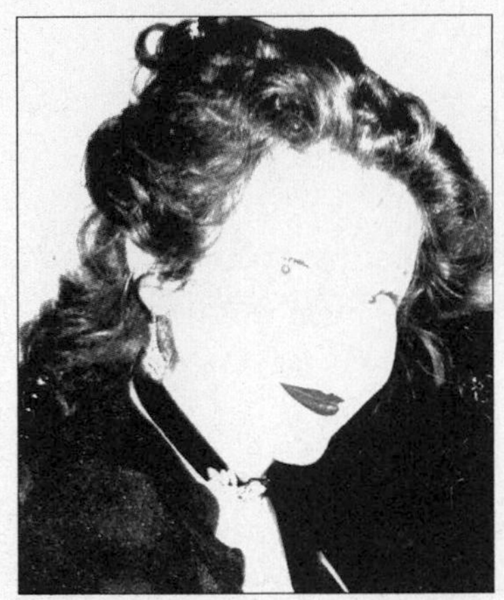

KIRSTEN JANENE-NELSON is a freelance editor and consultant with more than twenty-five years' experience in book publishing. Based in San Francisco, California, she met Lisette on San Juan Island in 2000 by challenging her to an arm wrestle. Though just 5'3" to Lisette's 5'10", Kirsten won the wrestle; they have been friends ever since. Visit her website at www.the-editrice.com.

NOTES

CHAPTER 1. WHY ARE INDIVIDUALS GOING REMOTE?

1. Pilar Orti, "Humanize Remote Work," interview by Lisette Sutherland, 3 November 2014, https://collaborationsuperpowers.com/4-humanizing-remote-work-pilar-orti.

2. GlobalWorkplaceAnalytics.com, "Latest Telecommuting Statistics," updated June 2017, http://globalworkplaceanalytics.com/telecommuting-statistics. Global Workplace Analytics provides statistics on the work-at-home/telework population in the U.S. based on an analysis of 2005–2015 American Community Survey (U.S. Census Bureau) data.

3. Upwork and Freelancers Union, "Freelancing in America: 2017," Results Deck, slide 65, 28 September 2017, https://www.upwork.com/i/freelancing-in-america/2017.

4. Upwork and Freelancers Union, "Freelancing in America: 2017," 28 September 2017, https://www.upwork.com/i/freelancing-in-america/2017.

5. *The Payoneer Freelancer Income Survey 2018*, https://explore.payoneer.com/freelancer-income-survey-2018.

6. *2017 State of Telecommuting in the U.S. Employee Workforce*, Global Work-place Analytics and FlexJobs, https://flexjobs.com/2017-State-of-Telecommuting-US.

7. Brie Weiler Reynolds, "Workers Are More Productive at Home: Here Are 25 Companies Hiring for Remote Jobs," FlexJobs, 21 August 2017, https://www.flexjobs.com/blog/post/productive-working-remotely-top-companies-hiring.

8. Brie Weiler Reynolds, "Workers Are More Productive at Home."

9. Brie Weiler Reynolds, "Working Parents in 2017: What They Want at Work," FlexJobs, 11 August 2017, https://www.flexjobs.com/blog/post/what-working-parents-want-at-work.

10. Leslie Truex, "Be a Work-at-Home Success with Leslie Truex," interview by Lisette Sutherland, Collaboration Superpowers, podcast audio, video, and transcript, 20 April 2016, https://www.collaborationsuperpowers.com/91-be-a-work-at-home-success-with-leslie-truex.

11. Brie Weiler Reynolds, "Communicate Proactively and Build Culture," inter-

view by Lisette Sutherland, Collaboration Superpowers, podcast audio, video, and transcript, 5 August 2015, https://collaborationsuperpowers.com/56-communicate-proactively-and-build-culture-with-brie-reynolds.

12. Upwork and Freelancers Union, "Freelancing in America: 2017," Results Deck, slides 38, 39, and 5, 28 September 2017, https://upwork.com/i/freelancing-in-america/2017.

13. Upwork, "Fortune 500 Enterprises Shift Their Contingent Workforce to Upwork Platform Saving Both Time and Money," press release, 6 February 2018, https://www.upwork.com/press/2018/02/06/fortune-500-enterprises.

14. Jeremy Stanton, "Being Deliberate with Onboarding and Culture with Jeremy Stanton," interview by Lisette Sutherland, Collaboration Superpowers, podcast audio, video, and transcript, 17 November 2014, https://collaborationsuperpowers.com/10-being-deliberate-with-onboarding-and-culture-jeremy-stanton.

15. Leslie Truex, "Be a Work-at-Home Success with Leslie Truex," interview by Lisette Sutherland, Collaboration Superpowers, podcast audio, video, and transcript, 20 April 2016, https://www.collaborationsuperpowers.com/91-be-a-work-at-home-success-with-leslie-truex.

16. Dave Hecker, "Effectively Managing Remote Teams with Dave Hecker," interview by Lisette Sutherland, Collaboration Superpowers, podcast audio, video, and transcript, 20 April 2016, https://www.collaborationsuperpowers.com/93-manage-expectations-on-distributed-teams-with-dave-hecker.

17. "2016 Global Telework Survey," 27 July 2016, https://www.pgi.com/blog/2016/06/2016-global-telework-survey.

18. Brie Weiler Reynolds, "Communicate Proactively and Build Culture," interview by Lisette Sutherland, Collaboration Superpowers, podcast audio, video, and transcript, 5 August 2015, https://collaborationsuperpowers.com/56-communicate-proactively-and-build-culture-with-brie-reynolds.

19. Brie Weiler Reynolds, "Workers Are More Productive at Home: Here Are 25 Companies Hiring for Remote Jobs," FlexJobs, 21 August 2017, https://www.flexjobs.com/blog/post/productive-working-remotely-top-companies-hiring.

20. Leslie Truex, "Be a Work-at-Home Success with Leslie Truex," interview by Lisette Sutherland, Collaboration Superpowers, podcast audio, video, and transcript, 20 April 2016, https://www.collaborationsuperpowers.com/91-be-a-work-at-home-success-with-leslie-truex.

21. Andrea Loubier, "Benefits of Telecommuting for the Future of Work," *Forbes*, 20 July 2017, https://www.forbes.com/sites/andrealoubier/2017/07/20/benefits-of-telecommuting-for-the-future-of-work/#16e712ec16c6.

22. Nicholas Bloom, "To Raise Productivity, Let More Employees Work from Home," *Harvard Business Review*, January–February 2014, https://hbr.org/2014/01/to-raise-productivity-let-more-employees-work-from-home.

23. "Remote Work Isn't Working for IBM," *The American Interest*, 22 March 2017, https://www.the-american-interest.com/2017/03/22/remote-work-isnt-working-for-ibm.

24. Dave Nevogt, "Are Remote Workers More Productive? We've Checked All the Research So You Don't Have To," Hubstaff, 25 July 2016, https://blog.hubstaff.com/remote-workers-more-productive. Hubstaff cites: ConnectSolutions [now CoSo Cloud] Remote Collaborative Worker Survey, "CoSo Cloud Survey Shows Working Remotely Benefits Employers and Employees," CoSo, 17 February 2015, http://www.cosocloud.com/press-release/connectsolutions-survey-shows-working-remotely-benefits-employers-and-employees; Gallup, "State of the American Workplace" report, http://news.gallup.com/reports/199961/state-american-workplace-report-2017.aspx; Scott Edinger, "Why Remote Workers Are More (Yes, More) Engaged," *Harvard Business Review*, 24 August 2012, https://hbr.org/2012/08/are-you-taking-your-people-for; GlobalWorkplaceAnalytics.com, "Latest Telecommuting Statistics," based on an analysis of 2005–2015 American Community Survey (U.S. Census Bureau) data, http://globalworkplaceanalytics.com/telecommuting-statistics; Remote.co, "How Do You Measure the Productivity of Remote Workers?," https://remote.co/qa-leading-remote-companies/how-do-you-measure-productivity-of-remote-workers.

25. Teo Härén, "Work Where You Are Most Productive," interview by Lisette Sutherland, Collaboration Superpowers, podcast audio, video, and transcript, 16 March 2015, https://www.collaborationsuperpowers.com/29-work-where-you-are-most-productive-with-teo-hren.

26. Nick Timmons, "Embody Your Team Online with Personify," interview by Lisette Sutherland, Collaboration Superpowers, podcast audio, video, and transcript, 30 March 2015, https://www.collaborationsuperpowers.com/31-embody-your-team-online-with-personify.

27. Abraham Heward, 9 August 2013 (21:39), comment on Lisette Sutherland, "Is a Hybrid Model an Ideal Scenario for Remote Working?," LisetteSutherland.com,

9 August 2013, http://www.lisettesutherland.com/2013/08/is-a-hybrid-model-an-ideal-scenario-for-remote-working.

28. Yegor Bugayenko, "Extreme Results-Oriented Working with Yegor Bugayenko," interview by Lisette Sutherland, Collaboration Superpowers, podcast audio, video, and transcript, 10 November 2014, https://collaborationsuperpowers.com/extreme-results-oriented-working-yegor-bugayenko.

29. Abraham Heward, 9 August 2013 (21:39), comment on Lisette Sutherland, "Is a Hybrid Model an Ideal Scenario for Remote Working?," LisetteSutherland.com, 9 August 2013, http://www.lisettesutherland.com/2013/08/is-a-hybrid-model-an-ideal-scenario-for-remote-working.

30. Teo Härén, "Work Where You Are Most Productive," interview by Lisette Sutherland, Collaboration Superpowers, podcast audio, video, and transcript, 16 March 2015, https://www.collaborationsuperpowers.com/29-work-where-you-are-most-productive-with-teo-hren.

31. Troy Gardner, 6 March 2014 (07:22), comment on Lisette Sutherland, "Guilty Pleasures of Working from Home," LisetteSutherland.com, 27 February 2014, http://www.lisettesutherland.com/2014/02/guilty-pleasures-working-from-home.

32. Eric Severson, "Forget Work-Life Balance—It's All About Work-Life Integration," interview by Jacob Morgan, *The Future of Work Podcast*, podcast audio, 18 August 2015, https://thefutureorganization.com/forget-work-life-balance-its-all-about-work-life-integration.

33. Laura Rooke, "Remote Technical Support," interview by Lisette Sutherland, Collaboration Superpowers, podcast audio, video, and transcript, 1 December 2014, https://www.collaborationsuperpowers.com/14-remote-technical-support-laura-rooke.

34. Eric Severson, "Forget Work-Life Balance—It's All About Work-Life Integration," interview by Jacob Morgan, *The Future of Work Podcast*, podcast audio, 18 August 2015, https://thefutureorganization.com/forget-work-life-balance-its-all-about-work-life-integration.

35. Stephan Dohrn, "Get Ready for the Future of Work," interview by Lisette Sutherland, Collaboration Superpowers, podcast audio, video, and transcript, 30 November 2015, https://www.collaborationsuperpowers.com/66-what-it-takes-to-be-a-great-virtual-team-leader-with-stephan-dohrn.

36. Yegor Bugayenko, "Extreme Results-Oriented Working with Yegor Bugay-

enko," interview by Lisette Sutherland, Collaboration Superpowers, podcast audio, video, and transcript, 10 November 2014, https://collaborationsuperpowers.com/extreme-results-oriented-working-yegor-bugayenko.

37. Mark Kilby, "Facilitating Distributed Agile Teams," interview by Lisette Sutherland, Collaboration Superpowers, podcast audio, video, and transcript, 12 November 2014, https://www.collaborationsuperpowers.com/9-coaching-distributed-agile-teams-mark-kilby.

38. Gerard Beaulieu, "Virtual Icebreakers with Gerard Beaulieu," interview by Lisette Sutherland, Collaboration Superpowers, podcast audio, video, and transcript, 24 August 2015, https://www.collaborationsuperpowers.com/52-virtual-icebreakers-with-gerard-beaulieu.

39. Eric Severson, "Forget Work-Life Balance—It's All About Work-Life Integration," interview by Jacob Morgan, *The Future of Work Podcast*, podcast audio, 18 August 2015, https://thefutureorganization.com/forget-work-life-balance-its-all-about-work-life-integration.

40. Pam Ross, "2014: The Year of Workplace Reinvention," *HuffPost*, 4 January 2014, https://www.huffingtonpost.com/pam-ross/workplace-reinvention_b_4541805.html.

41. Jake Goldman, "10up Inc. Remote Company Q&A," interview by Remote.co, June 2015, https://remote.co/company/10up-inc.

42. Jamie Nichol, "Pros and Cons of a Results-Only Work Environment (ROWE)," CultureIQ, https://cultureiq.com/results-only-work-environment-rowe.

43. Brie Weiler Reynolds, "Workers Are More Productive at Home: Here Are 25 Companies Hiring for Remote Jobs," FlexJobs, 21 August 2017, https://www.flexjobs.com/blog/post/productive-working-remotely-top-companies-hiring.

CHAPTER 2. HOW REMOTE WORKING BENEFITS EMPLOYERS

1. Lucius Bobikiewicz, "Powerful Online Collaboration with Simple Spreadsheets," interview by Lisette Sutherland, Collaboration Superpowers, podcast audio, video, and transcript, 6 July 2015, https://www.collaborationsuperpowers.com/45-powerful-collaboration-with-simple-spreadsheets.

2. Eurofound and the International Labour Office (2017), *Working Anytime, Anywhere: The Effects on the World of Work*, Publications Office of the European Union, Luxembourg, and the International Labour Office, Geneva, 2017.

3. Gallup, "State of the American Workplace" report, 2017, http://news.gallup

.com/reports/199961/7.aspx?utm_source=gbj&utm_campaign=StateofAmerican Workplace-Launch&utm_medium=copy&utm_content=20170315.

4. Ariane Hegewisch and Janet C. Gornick, *Statutory Routes to Workplace Flexibility in Cross-National Perspective*, Institute for Women's Policy Research, 31 December 2007. See also Emma Plumb, "Work Flexibility Legislation Worldwide," 1 Million for Work Flexibility blog, 4 September 2014, https://workflexibility.org /work-flexibility-legislation-worldwide.

5. Martin Fowler, "Remote Versus Co-located Work," MartinFowler.com, 19 October 2015, https://martinfowler.com/articles/remote-or-co-located.html.

6. Robert Rogge, "An Interview with Managing Virtual Teams," interview by Lisette Sutherland, Collaboration Superpowers, podcast audio, video, and transcript, 12 June 2014, https://collaborationsuperpowers.com/interview-managing -virtual-teams.

7. Brie Weiler Reynolds, "Workers Are More Productive at Home: Here Are 25 Companies Hiring for Remote Jobs," FlexJobs, 21 August 2017, https://www .flexjobs.com/blog/post/productive-working-remotely-top-companies-hiring.

8. Heather Boushey and Sarah Jane Glynn, "There Are Significant Business Costs to Replacing Employees," Center for American Progress, 16 November 2012, https://www.americanprogress.org/wp-content/uploads/2012/11/CostofTurn over.pdf; Jason Hesse, "The True Cost of Hiring an Employee? Much More Than Their Salary," *Forbes*, 30 October 2014, https://www.forbes.com/sites/jasonhesse /2014/10/30/here-is-the-true-cost-of-hiring-an-employee/#1ebe13c76326; Julie Kantor, "High Turnover Costs Way More Than You Think," *HuffPost*, 11 February 2016, updated 11 February 2017, http://www.huffingtonpost.com/julie-kantor/ high-turnover-costs-way-more-than-you-think_b_9197238.html; "Why Retaining Current Employees is Cheaper Than Hiring New Ones," infographic by Mind Flash.com using information provided by Society for Human Resource Management, SHRM.org. Included in Matthew Gates, "Cost of Keeping Employees vs. Hiring New Employees," Confessions of the Professions, http://www.confessions oftheprofessions.com/keeping-employees-infographic.

9. Hugo Messer, "Managing Remote Teams," interview by Lisette Sutherland, Collaboration Superpowers, podcast audio, video, and transcript, 26 November 2014, https://collaborationsuperpowers.com/13-managing-remote-teams-hugo-messer.

10. Fernando Garrido Vaz, "Build Reputation in the Freelance Economy with Fernando Garrido Vaz," interview by Lisette Sutherland, Collaboration Super-

powers, podcast audio, video, and transcript, 2 March 2016, https://collaborationsuperpowers.com/89-build-reputation-in-the-freelance-economy-with-fernando-garrido-vaz.

11. Adriana Vela, "How to Be Efficient on the Road with Adriana Vela," interview by Lisette Sutherland, Collaboration Superpowers, video and transcript, 3 August 2015, https://www.collaborationsuperpowers.com/49-how-to-be-efficient-on-the-road-with-adrian-vela.

12. Hassan Osman, "Influence Your Virtual Team," interview by Lisette Sutherland, Collaboration Superpowers, podcast audio, video, and transcript, 3 November 2013, https://www.collaborationsuperpowers.com/5-managing-your-virtual-team-hassan-osman.

13. Karen Mattison and Emma Stewart, Timewise, *The Timewise Flexible Jobs Index 2017*, http://timewise.co.uk/wp-content/uploads/2015/05/Timewise_Flexible_Jobs_Index.pdf.

14. Luis Suarez, "Engaging Remotely with Social Networks," interview by Lisette Sutherland, Collaboration Superpowers, podcast audio, video, and transcript, 19 January 2015, https://www.collaborationsuperpowers.com/21-engaging-remotely-with-social-networks-luis-suarez.

15. Chris Ridgewell, "Implement Flexible Working," interview by Lisette Sutherland, Collaboration Superpowers, podcast audio, video, and transcript, 22 October 2014, https://www.collaborationsuperpowers.com/episode-1-implement-flexible-working-chris-ridgewell.

16. Jeremy Stanton, "Being Deliberate with Onboarding and Culture with Jeremy Stanton," interview by Lisette Sutherland, Collaboration Superpowers, podcast audio, video, and transcript, 17 November 2014, https://www.collaborationsuperpowers.com/10-being-deliberate-with-onboarding-and-culture-jeremy-stanton.

17. Laura Rooke, "Remote Technical Support," interview by Lisette Sutherland, Collaboration Superpowers, podcast audio, video, and transcript, 1 December 2014, https://www.collaborationsuperpowers.com/14-remote-technical-support-laura-rooke.

18. Yegor Bugayenko, "Extreme Results-Oriented Working with Yegor Bugayenko," interview by Lisette Sutherland, Collaboration Superpowers, podcast audio, video, and transcript, 10 November 2014, https://collaborationsuperpowers.com/extreme-results-oriented-working-yegor-bugayenko.

19. Heather Boushey and Sarah Jane Glynn, "There Are Significant Business Costs to Replacing Employees," Center for American Progress, 16 November 2012, https://

www.americanprogress.org/wp-content/uploads/2012/11/CostofTurnover.pdf; Jason Hesse, "The True Cost of Hiring an Employee? Much More Than Their Salary," *Forbes*, 30 October 2014, https://www.forbes.com/sites/jasonhesse/2014/10/30/here-is-the-true-cost-of-hiring-an-employee/#1ebe13c76326; Julie Kantor, "High Turnover Costs Way More Than You Think," *HuffPost*, 11 February 2016, updated 11 February 2017, http://www.huffingtonpost.com/julie-kantor/high-turnover-costs-way-more-than-you-think_b_9197238.html; "Why Retaining Current Employees is Cheaper Than Hiring New Ones," infographic by Mind Flash.com using information provided by Society for Human Resource Management, SHRM.org. Included in Matthew Gates, "Cost of Keeping Employees vs. Hiring New Employees," Confessions of the Professions, http://www.confessionsoftheprofessions.com/keeping-employees-infographic.

20. Jeremy Stanton, "Being Deliberate with Onboarding and Culture with Jeremy Stanton," interview by Lisette Sutherland, Collaboration Superpowers, podcast audio, video, and transcript, 17 November 2014, https://www.collaborationsuperpowers.com/10-being-deliberate-with-onboarding-and-culture-jeremy-stanton.

21. Mario Lucero, "Create Big Results with Small Changes," interview by Lisette Sutherland, Collaboration Superpowers, podcast audio, video, and transcript, 2 February 2015, https://www.collaborationsuperpowers.com/23-create-big-results-small-changes-mario-lucero.

22. Victor Ingalls, VP, world service, "American Express Remote Company Q&A," interview with Remote.co, January 2016, https://remote.co/team/american-express.

23. Chris Ridgewell, "Implement Flexible Working," interview by Lisette Sutherland, Collaboration Superpowers, podcast audio, video, and transcript, 22 October 2014, https://www.collaborationsuperpowers.com/episode-1-implement-flexible-working-chris-ridgewell.

24. Tiziano Perrucci, "A Remote Team Perspective with StarterSquad," interview by Lisette Sutherland, Collaboration Superpowers, podcast audio, video, and transcript, 16 February 2015, https://www.collaborationsuperpowers.com/25-a-remote-team-perspective-with-startersquad.

25. Larry Alton, "Are Remote Workers More Productive Than In-Office Workers?," *Forbes*, 7 March 2017, https://www.forbes.com/sites/larryalton/2017/03/07/are-remote-workers-more-productive-than-in-office-workers/2/#77544c4f78f5.

26. Global Workplace Analytics, "Costs and Benefits," http://globalworkplaceanalytics.com/resources/costs-benefits.

27. Global Workplace Analytics, "Pros and Cons," http://www.globalworkplace analytics.com/pros-cons.

28.Chris Ridgewell, "Implement Flexible Working," interview by Lisette Sutherland, Collaboration Superpowers, podcast audio, video, and transcript, 22 October 2014, https://www.collaborationsuperpowers.com/episode-1-implement-flexible -working-chris-ridgewell.

29. Judy Rees, "Discover a Common Language," interview by Lisette Sutherland, Collaboration Superpowers, podcast audio, video, and transcript, 13 April 2015, https://www.collaborationsuperpowers.com/33-discover-a-common-language -with-judy-rees.

30. Marcus Rosenthal, "Teleport with the Kubi Teleconference Robot (Revolve Robotics)," interview by Lisette Sutherland, Collaboration Superpowers, podcast audio, video, and transcript, 29 December 2014, https://collaborationsuperpowers .com/18-teleport-with-the-kubi-teleconference-robot-revolve-robotics.

31. Chris Ridgewell, "Implement Flexible Working," interview by Lisette Sutherland, Collaboration Superpowers, podcast audio, video, and transcript, 22 October 2014, https://www.collaborationsuperpowers.com/episode-1-implement-flexible -working-chris-ridgewell.

32. Peter Wilson, "How to Hire and Onboard an Offshore Team with KIStaffing," interview by Lisette Sutherland, Collaboration Superpowers, podcast audio, video, and transcript, 20 June 2016, https://collaborationsuperpowers.com/95-how -to-hire-and-onboard-an-offshore-team-with-kistaffing.

33. Marissa Lang, "Employers Can Collect Reams of Worker Data Through Electronic Tracking," *San Francisco Chronicle*, 17 October 2017, updated 19 October 2017, https://www.sfchronicle.com/business/article/Employers-can-collect-reams -of-worker-data-12282997.php.

34. Piero Toffanin, "Work as a Digital Nomad," interview by Lisette Sutherland, Collaboration Superpowers, podcast audio, video, and transcript, 23 March 2015, https://www.collaborationsuperpowers.com/30-work-as-a-digital-nomad-with -piero-toffanin.

35. Bart Van Loon, "How to Hire Offshore Staff," interview by Lisette Sutherland, Collaboration Superpowers, podcast audio, video, and transcript, 9 March 2015, https://collaborationsuperpowers.com/28-how-to-hire-offshore-staff-with -bart-van-loon.

36. Brie Weiler Reynolds, "Communicate Proactively and Build Culture," interview by Lisette Sutherland, Collaboration Superpowers, podcast audio, video, and

transcript, 5 August 2015, https://collaborationsuperpowers.com/56-communicate-proactively-and-build-culture-with-brie-reynolds.

37. "Why Appreciation Matters So Much," *Harvard Business Review*, 23 January 2012, https://hbr.org/2012/01/why-appreciation-matters-so-mu.html; and Gallup (2017), "State of the Global Workplace" report, Washington, DC.

38. Pilar Orti, "Humanize Remote Work," interview by Lisette Sutherland, 3 November 2014, https://collaborationsuperpowers.com/4-humanizing-remote-work-pilar-orti.

39. Marc Hughes, "Align Your Remote Team in ScrumDo," interview by Lisette Sutherland, Collaboration Superpowers, podcast audio, video, and transcript, 16 November 2015, https://collaborationsuperpowers.com/64-align-your-remote-team-in-scrumdo-with-marc-hughes.

40. Karolina Szczur, "Building Remote-First Teams," Medium, 3 May 2016, https://medium.com/@fox/building-remote-first-teams-a98bf8581db.

41. Christina Ng, "Validate Your Work from Home Excuses," interview by Lisette Sutherland, Collaboration Superpowers, podcast audio, video, and transcript, 7 August 2015, https://www.collaborationsuperpowers.com/51-validate-your-work-from-home-excuses-with-christina-ng.

42. AgileBill Krebs, "Collaborating in Virtual Worlds," interview by Lisette Sutherland, Collaboration Superpowers, podcast audio, video, and transcript, 8 December 2014, https://www.collaborationsuperpowers.com/15-collaborating-in-virtual-worlds-agilebill-krebs.

43. Sumant Kowshik, "Embody Your Team Online with Personify," interview by Lisette Sutherland, Collaboration Superpowers, podcast audio, video, and transcript, 30 March 2015, https://www.collaborationsuperpowers.com/31-embody-your-team-online-with-personify.

44. Vanessa Shaw, "Helping You Tech Better," interview by Lisette Sutherland, Collaboration Superpowers, podcast audio, video, and transcript, 7 September 2015, https://www.collaborationsuperpowers.com/54-helping-you-tech-better-with-vanessa-shaw.

45. Andrew Montalenti, CTO, "Parse.ly Remote Company Q&A," interview with Remote.co, July 2016, https://remote.co/company/parse-ly.

46. Ryan Baker, founder and CEO, "Timely Remote Company Q&A," interview with Remote.co, February 2016, https://remote.co/company/timely.

47. Chris Ridgewell, "Implement Flexible Working," interview by Lisette Sutherland, Collaboration Superpowers, podcast audio, video, and transcript, 22 October

2014, https://www.collaborationsuperpowers.com/episode-1-implement-flexible-working-chris-ridgewell.

48. Jeremy Stanton, "Being Deliberate with Onboarding and Culture with Jeremy Stanton," interview by Lisette Sutherland, Collaboration Superpowers, podcast audio, video, and transcript, 17 November 2014, https://www.collaborationsuperpowers.com/10-being-deliberate-with-onboarding-and-culture-jeremy-stanton.

49. Howard B. Esbin, "Tuning Your Virtual Team," interview by Lisette Sutherland, Collaboration Superpowers, podcast audio, video, and transcript, 22 October 2014, https://www.collaborationsuperpowers.com/episode-2-tuning-virtual-team-howard-esbin.

50. Maarten Koopmans, "How to Eat an Elephant," interview by Lisette Sutherland, Collaboration Superpowers, 5 February 2013, https://www.collaborationsuperpowers.com/hire-right-people-remote-working-Maarten-koopmans.

51. Jeremy Stanton, "Being Deliberate with Onboarding and Culture with Jeremy Stanton," interview by Lisette Sutherland, Collaboration Superpowers, podcast audio, video, and transcript, 17 November 2014, https://www.collaborationsuperpowers.com/10-being-deliberate-with-onboarding-and-culture-jeremy-stanton.

52. Dirk-Jan Padmos, "Management Is a Skill, Not a Job," interview by Lisette Sutherland, Collaboration Superpowers, 23 April 2013, https://www.collaborationsuperpowers.com/management-skill-job-dirk-jan-padmos.

53. Ralph van Roosmalen, "How to Manage Three Remote Offices," interview by Lisette Sutherland, Collaboration Superpowers, podcast audio, video, and transcript, 9 February 2015, https://www.collaborationsuperpowers.com/24-managing-three-remote-offices-with-ralph-van-roosmalen.

54. Remote.co, "What Advice Would You Give to a Team Considering to Go Remote?," https://remote.co/qa-leading-remote-companies/what-advice-would-you-give-to-a-company-considering-to-go-remote.

55. Deven Bhagwandin, "Managing Cultural and Language Divides Within Your Remote Team," Workafar.com, 22 November 2015, http://www.workafar.com/managing-cultural-and-language-divides-within-your-remote-team.

Frequently Asked Questions

1. Morgan Legge, Slack message to author, 2 February 2018.

2. Brie Weiler Reynolds, "Working Parents in 2017: What They Want at Work, FlexJobs, 11 August 2017, https://flexjobs.com/blog/post/what-working-parents-want-at-work.

3. Global Workplace Analytics, "Costs and Benefits," http://globalworkplace analytics.com/resources/costs-benefits.

4. Upwork and Freelancers Union, "Freelancing in America: 2017," Results Deck, slide 43, 28 September 2017, https://www.upwork.com/i/freelancing-in -america/2017.

5. Pew Research Center, www.pewinternet.org/2016/11/17/gig-work-online -selling-and-home-sharing.

6. Upwork, "Fortune 500 Enterprises Shift their Contingent Workforce to Upwork Platform Saving Both Time and Money," press release, 6 February 2018, https://www.upwork.com/press/2018/02/06/fortune-500-enterprises.

7. Remoters.net, "7 Remote Work Trends in 2017," http://remoters.net/remote-work-trends-2017.

8. "Global Survey of 24,000+ Workers Unearths the 'Need' for Flexibility in the Workplace in Order for Businesses to Thrive," 20 March 2017, Polycom Inc., http://www.polycom.com/company/news/press-releases/2017/20170321.html.

9. ConnectSolutions [now CoSo Cloud] Remote Collaborative Worker Survey, "CoSo Cloud Survey Shows Working Remotely Benefits Employers and Employees," CoSo, 17 February 2015, http://cosocloud.com/press-release/connectsolutions -survey-shows-working-remotely-benefits-employers-and-employees.

10. Rieva Lesonsky, "Is Your Work-at-Home Policy Spurring Jealousy?," Small Business Trends, 1 November 2017, https://smallbiztrends.com/2013/10/work-at -home-policy-jealousy.html.

11. Global Workplace Analytics, "Pros and Cons," http://www.globalworkplace analytics.com/pros-cons.

12. Rachel Jay, "When Your Coworkers Don't Support Your Remote Work," FlexJobs, 29 May 2017, https://www.flexjobs.com/blog/post/coworkers-dont-support -remote-work.

13. Brie Weiler Reynolds, "Workers Are More Productive at Home: Here Are 25 Companies Hiring for Remote Jobs," FlexJobs, 21 August 2017, https://www .flexjobs.com/blog/post/productive-working-remotely-top-companies-hiring.

14. "Remote Work Isn't Working for IBM," *The American Interest*, 22 March 2017, https://www.the-american-interest.com/2017/03/22/remote-work-isnt-working -for-ibm.

15. Remote.co, "How Do You Measure the Productivity of Remote Workers?," https://remote.co/qa-leading-remote-companies/how-do-you-measure-productivity -of-remote-workers.

16. Heather Boushey and Sarah Jane Glynn, "There Are Significant Business Costs to Replacing Employees," Center for American Progress, 16 November 2012, https://www.americanprogress.org/wp-content/uploads/2012/11/CostofTurnover.pdf; Jason Hesse, "The True Cost of Hiring an Employee? Much More Than Their Salary," *Forbes*, 30 October 2014, https://www.forbes.com/sites/jasonhesse/2014/10/30/here-is-the-true-cost-of-hiring-an-employee/#1ebe13c76326; Julie Kantor, "High Turnover Costs Way More Than You Think," *HuffPost*, 11 February 2016, updated 11 February 2017, http://www.huffingtonpost.com/julie-kantor/high-turnover-costs-way-more-than-you-think_b_9197238.html; "Why Retaining Current Employees is Cheaper Than Hiring New Ones," infographic by MindFlash.com using information provided by Society for Human Resource Management, SHRM.org. Included in Matthew Gates, "Cost of Keeping Employees vs. Hiring New Employees," Confessions of the Professions, http://www.confessionsoftheprofessions.com/keeping-employees-infographic.

17. PGi, "2015 PGi Global Telework Survey," http://go.pgi.com/gen-genspec-15telesur-SC1129.

18. Dave Nevogt, "Are Remote Workers More Productive? We've Checked All the Research So You Don't Have To," Hubstaff, 25 July 2016, https://blog.hubstaff.com/remote-workers-more-productive. Hubstaff cites: ConnectSolutions [now CoSo Cloud] Remote Collaborative Worker Survey, "CoSo Cloud Survey Shows Working Remotely Benefits Employers and Employees," CoSo, 17 February 2015, http://www.cosocloud.com/press-release/connectsolutions-survey-shows-working-remotely-benefits-employers-and-employees; Gallup, "State of the American Workplace" report, http://news.gallup.com/reports/199961/state-american-workplace-report-2017.aspx; Scott Edinger, "Why Remote Workers Are More (Yes, More) Engaged," *Harvard Business Review*, 24 August 2012, https://hbr.org/2012/08/are-you-taking-your-people-for; GlobalWorkplaceAnalytics.com, "Latest Telecommuting Statistics," based on an analysis of 2005–2015 American Community Survey (U.S. Census Bureau) data, http://globalworkplaceanalytics.com/telecommuting-statistics; Remote.co, "How Do You Measure the Productivity of Remote Workers?," https://remote.co/qa-leading-remote-companies/how-do-you-measure-productivity-of-remote-workers.

19. Victor Ingalls, VP, world service, American Express, company Q&A interview with Remote.co, January 2016, https://remote.co/team/american-express.

20. Pilar Orti and Lisette Sutherland, "WLP126: Are Virtual Teams Dysfunc-

tional?," 15 June 2017, *21st-Century Work Life*, Virtual Not Distant, https://www.virtualnotdistant.com/podcasts/dysfunctional-team.

21. Patrick Lencioni, "Virtual Teams Are Worse Than I Thought," The Hub, May 2017, https://tablegroup.com/hub/post/05/21/2017/virtual-teams-are-worse-than-i-thought. See also Patrick Lencioni, *The Five Dysfunctions of a Team: A Leadership Fable* (San Francisco: Jossey-Bass, 2002).

22. "Global Survey of 24,000+ Workers Unearths the 'Need' for Flexibility in the Workplace in Order for Businesses to Thrive," 20 March 2017, Polycom Inc., http://www.polycom.com/company/news/press-releases/2017/20170321.html.

23. Jason Fried, *Remote: Office Not Required* (New York: Crown Business, 2013), back cover.

24. "Why Appreciation Matters So Much," *Harvard Business Review*, 23 January 2012, https://hbr.org/2012/01/why-appreciation-matters-so-mu.html.

25. Larry Alton, "Are Remote Workers More Productive Than In-Office Workers?," *Forbes*, 7 March 2017, https://www.forbes.com/sites/larryalton/2017/03/07/are-remote-workers-more-productive-than-in-office-workers/2/#77544c4f78f5.

26. Eric Severson, "Forget Work-Life Balance—It's All About Work-Life Integration," interview by Jacob Morgan, *The Future of Work Podcast*, podcast audio, 18 August 2015, https://thefutureorganization.com/forget-work-life-balance-its-all-about-work-life-integration.

27. Fredrik Wiik, "Become More Agile with Remote Collaboration with Fredrik Wiik," interview by Lisette Sutherland, Collaboration Superpowers, 28 November 2013, https://collaborationsuperpowers.com/become-agile-remote-collaboration-fredrik-wiik.

28. Nick Timmons, "Embody Your Team Online with Personify," interview by Lisette Sutherland, Collaboration Superpowers, podcast audio, video, and transcript, 30 March 2015, https://www.collaborationsuperpowers.com/31-embody-your-team-online-with-personify.

29. ConnectSolutions [now CoSo Cloud] Remote Collaborative Worker Survey, "CoSo Cloud Survey Shows Working Remotely Benefits Employers and Employees," CoSo Cloud LLC, 17 February 2015, http://www.cosocloud.com/press-release/connectsolutions-survey-shows-working-remotely-benefits-employers-and-employees.

30. Global Workplace Analytics, "Pros and Cons," http://www.globalworkplaceanalytics.com/pros-cons.

PART II OPENER

1. Jesse Fewell, "Let Go of Old Habits with Jesse Fewell," interview by Lisette Sutherland, Collaboration Superpowers, podcast audio, video, and transcript, 26 January 2016, https://www.collaborationsuperpowers.com/80-let-go-of-old-habits-with-jesse-fewell.

CHAPTER 3. REMOTE WORKING 101: GETTING STARTED

1. Lisette Sutherland, "Work Together Anywhere," TEDx talk for Theme: Unbox the Future, 19 November 2017, Kaunas, Lithuania, http://lisettesutherland.com/tedx.

2. Meghan M. Biro, "Telecommuting Is the Future of Work," *Forbes*, 12 January 2014, https://www.forbes.com/sites/meghanbiro/2014/01/12/telecommuting-is-the-future-of-work/#175008543c86.

3. Dirk-Jan Padmos, "Management Is a Skill, Not a Job," interview by Lisette Sutherland, Collaboration Superpowers, 23 April 2013, https://www.collaborationsuperpowers.com/management-skill-job-dirk-jan-padmos.

4. Kathryn Ottinger, "Intridea/Mobomo Remote Company Q&A," interview with Remote.co, July 2015, https://remote.co/company/intrideamobomo.

5. Ben Linders, "Writing a Book Together Remotely," interview by Lisette Sutherland, Collaboration Superpowers, video and transcript, 14 April 2014, https://www.collaborationsuperpowers.com/interview-with-ben-linders-and-luis-goncalves.

6. AgileBill Krebs, "Collaborating in Virtual Worlds," interview by Lisette Sutherland, Collaboration Superpowers, podcast audio, video, and transcript, 8 December 2014, https://www.collaborationsuperpowers.com/15-collaborating-in-virtual-worlds-agilebill-krebs.

7. "A Highly Scientific Post About Lighting Zoom Meetings," 12 February 2015, Zoom blog, https://blog.zoom.us/wordpress/2015/02/12/scientific-lighting-zoom-meetings-will-ever-read. See also G. C. Brainard, J. P. Hanifin, J. M. Greeson, B. Byrne, G. Glickman, E. Gerner, and M. D. Rollag, "Action Spectrum for Melatonin Regulation in Humans: Evidence for a Novel Circadian Photoreceptor," *The Journal of Neuroscience* 21, no. 16, 15 August 2001, http://jneurosci.org/content/21/16/6405.long.

8. AgileBill Krebs, "Collaborating in Virtual Worlds," interview by Lisette Sutherland, Collaboration Superpowers, podcast audio, video, and transcript, 8

December 2014, https://www.collaborationsuperpowers.com/15-collaborating-in-virtual-worlds-agilebill-krebs.

9. Eurofound and the International Labour Office (2017), *Working Anytime, Anywhere: The Effects on the World of Work*, Publications Office of the European Union, Luxembourg, and the International Labour Office, Geneva; GlobalWorkplaceAnalytics.com, http://globalworkplaceanalytics.com/telecommuting-statistics; and 2017 Modern Families Index, http://docplayer.net/32438346-The-modern-families-index-2017.html.

10. Jesse Fewell, "Let Go of Old Habits with Jesse Fewell," interview by Lisette Sutherland, Collaboration Superpowers, podcast audio, video, and transcript, 26 January 2016, https://collaborationsuperpowers.com/80-let-go-of-old-habits-with-jesse-fewell.

11. Vanessa Shaw, "Helping You Tech Better," interview by Lisette Sutherland, Collaboration Superpowers, podcast audio, video, and transcript, 7 September 2015, https://www.collaborationsuperpowers.com/54-helping-you-tech-better-with-vanessa-shaw.

12. David Horowitz, "Make Remote Retrospectives Easy," interview by Lisette Sutherland, Collaboration Superpowers, podcast audio, video, and transcript, 11 May 2015, https://collaborationsuperpowers.com/37-abolish-the-postmortem-with-david-horowitz.

13. Adriana Vela, "How to Be Efficient on the Road with Adriana Vela," interview by Lisette Sutherland, Collaboration Superpowers, video and transcript, 3 August 2015, https://collaborationsuperpowers.com/49-how-to-be-efficient-on-the-road-with-adrian-vela.

CHAPTER 4. REMOTE WORKING 201: PERFECTING YOUR GAME

1. Maarten Koopmans, "How to Eat an Elephant," interview by Lisette Sutherland, Collaboration Superpowers, 5 February 2013, https://collaborationsuperpowers.com/hire-right-people-remote-working-Maarten-koopmans.

2. Ben Linders, "Writing a Book Together Remotely," interview by Lisette Sutherland, Collaboration Superpowers, video and transcript, 14 April 2014, https://www.collaborationsuperpowers.com/interview-with-ben-linders-and-luis-goncalves.

3. Andrea Zabala, "Maximize Your Time Working Remotely," interview by Lisette Sutherland, Collaboration Superpowers, podcast audio, video, and transcript,

11 January 2016, https://www.collaborationsuperpowers.com/72-maximize-your-time-working-remotely-with-andrea-zabala.

4. Maarten Koopmans, "How to Eat an Elephant," interview by Lisette Sutherland, Collaboration Superpowers, 5 February 2013, https://collaborationsuperpowers.com/hire-right-people-remote-working-Maarten-koopmans.

5. Maarten Koopmans, "How to Eat an Elephant."

6. Adam Gorlick, "Media Multitaskers Pay Mental Price, Stanford Study Shows," Stanford News Service, 24 August 2009, https://news.stanford.edu/2009/08/24/multitask-research-study-082409.

7. Paul Minors, "10 Reasons Why Asana Is the Best Project Management Tool, PaulMinors.com, 13 March 2017, https://paulminors.com/10-reasons-why-asana-is-the-best-project-management-tool.

8. Jim Benson, "Introduction to Personal Kanban," PersonalKanban.com, http://personalkanban.com/pk/personal-kanban-101. For example, David Rock offers the following: "Picturing something you have not yet seen is going to take a lot of energy and effort. This partly explains why people spend more time thinking about problems (things they have seen) than solutions (things they have never seen). This of course also explains why prioritizing is so hard. Prioritizing involves imagining and then moving around concepts of which you have no direct experience. What's more, prioritizing involves every function . . . understanding new ideas, as well as making decisions, remembering, and inhibiting, all at once. It's like the triathlon of mental tasks." David Rock, *Your Brain at Work: Strategies for Overcoming Distraction, Regaining Focus, and Working Smarter All Day Long* (New York: Harper Collins, 2009), 13.

9. Benson, "Introduction to Personal Kanban," http://personalkanban.com/pk/personal-kanban-101.

10. Ed Erwin, 4 March 2014 (17:41), comment on Lisette Sutherland, "Guilty Pleasures of Working from Home," LisetteSutherland.com, 27 February 2014, http://www.lisettesutherland.com/2014/02/guilty-pleasures-working-from-home.

11. Derek Scruggs, "Use Tools and Increase Productivity," interview by Lisette Sutherland, Collaboration Superpowers, podcast audio, video, and transcript, 23 February 2015, https://www.collaborationsuperpowers.com/26-using-tools-and-increasing-productivity-with-derek-scruggs.

12. Francesco Cirillo, "The Pomodoro Technique," CirilloCompany.de, https://cirillocompany.de/pages/pomodoro-technique/book.

13. Linda Varone, "Home Office Design," Smarter Home Office, www.thesmart erhomeoffice.com/home-office-design.

14. Marion Smits, "Scan Brains and Manage Students Remotely," interview by Lisette Sutherland, Collaboration Superpowers, podcast audio, video, and transcript, 24 November 2014, https://collaborationsuperpowers.com/12-scanning-brains-and-managing-students-remotely-marion-smits.

15. Yves Hanoulle, "Welcome People and Develop Trust While Walking with Yves Hanoulle," interview by Lisette Sutherland, Collaboration Superpowers, podcast audio, video, and transcript, 12 January 2015, https://www.collaborationsuperpowers.com/20-welcome-people-and-develop-trust-while-walking-yves-hanoulle.

16. Jeremy Stanton, "Being Deliberate with Onboarding and Culture with Jeremy Stanton," interview by Lisette Sutherland, Collaboration Superpowers, podcast audio, video, and transcript, 17 November 2014, https://www.collaborationsuperpowers.com/10-being-deliberate-with-onboarding-and-culture-jeremy-stanton.

17. Leslie Truex, "Be a Work-at-Home Success with Leslie Truex," interview by Lisette Sutherland, Collaboration Superpowers, podcast audio, video, and transcript, 20 April 2016, https://www.collaborationsuperpowers.com/91-be-a-work-at-home-success-with-leslie-truex.

18. Genevieve N. Healy, Elisabeth A. H. Winkler, Neville Owen, Satyamurthy Anuradha, and David W. Dunstan, "Replacing Sitting Time with Standing or Stepping: Associations with Cardio-Metabolic Risk Biomarkers," *European Heart Journal* 36, no. 39: 2643–2649, 14 October 2015, https://doi.org/10.1093/eurheartj/ehv308.

19. Phil Montero, "Apply the Right Technology," interview by Lisette Sutherland, Collaboration Superpowers, video and transcript, 5 August 2014, https://www.collaborationsuperpowers.com/apply-right-technology-phil-montero.

20. Carrie Rice, COO, and Nita Tune, director of project management, "Site-Pen Remote Company Q&A," interview with Remote.co, October 2015; and Tom Sepper, COO, "World Wide Web Hosting Remote Company Q&A," interview with Remote.co, September 2015, both at https://remote.co/qa-leading-remote-companies/what-traits-do-you-look-for-in-candidates-for-a-remote-job.

21. Andy Willis, "Don't Wait to Start Living," interview by Lisette Sutherland, Collaboration Superpowers, podcast audio, video, and transcript, 6 March 2017, https://www.collaborationsuperpowers.com/132-dont-wait-to-start-living.

22. Jeffry Hesse, "How to Be a Self-Organizing Remote Team," interview by Lisette Sutherland, Collaboration Superpowers, podcast audio, video, and tran-

script, 25 May 2015, https://www.collaborationsuperpowers.com/39-how-to-be-a-self-organizing-remote-team.

23. Iwein Fuld, "Build a Company of Entrepreneurs," interview by Lisette Sutherland, Collaboration Superpowers, podcast audio, video, and transcript, 5 November 2014, https://collaborationsuperpowers.com/build-a-company-of-entrepreneurs-iwein-fuld.

24. Mark Kilby, "Facilitating Distributed Agile Teams," interview by Lisette Sutherland, Collaboration Superpowers, podcast audio, video, and transcript, 12 November 2014, https://collaborationsuperpowers.com/9-coaching-distributed-agile-teams-mark-kilby.

25. Ralph van Roosmalen, "How to Manage Three Remote Offices," interview by Lisette Sutherland, Collaboration Superpowers, podcast audio, video, and transcript, 9 February 2015, https://www.collaborationsuperpowers.com/24-managing-three-remote-offices-with-ralph-van-roosmalen.

26. Chris Ridgewell, "Implement Flexible Working," interview by Lisette Sutherland, Collaboration Superpowers, podcast audio, video, and transcript, 22 October 2014, https://www.collaborationsuperpowers.com/episode-1-implement-flexible-working-chris-ridgewell.

27. Peter Hilton, "The Need for Face-to-Face on Virtual Teams," interview by Lisette Sutherland, Collaboration Superpowers, podcast audio, video, and transcript, 22 December 2014, https://collaborationsuperpowers.com/17-the-need-for-face-to-face-on-virtual-teams-peter-hilton.

28. Fernando Garrido Vaz, "Build Reputation in the Freelance Economy with Fernando Garrido Vaz," interview by Lisette Sutherland, Collaboration Superpowers, podcast audio, video, and transcript, 2 March 2016, https://www.collaborationsuperpowers.com/89-build-reputation-in-the-freelance-economy-with-fernando-garrido-vaz.

29. Ben Linders, "Writing a Book Together Remotely," interview by Lisette Sutherland, Collaboration Superpowers, video and transcript, 14 April 2014, https://www.collaborationsuperpowers.com/interview-with-ben-linders-and-luis-goncalves.

30. Per Frykman, "Manage Your Reputation Remotely," interview by Lisette Sutherland, Collaboration Superpowers, podcast audio, video, and transcript, 26 January 2015, https://www.collaborationsuperpowers.com/22-managing-your-reputation-remotely-per-frykman.

31. Michael Sliwinski, "Curate Your Notifications for Maximum Productiv-

ity," interview by Lisette Sutherland, Collaboration Superpowers, podcast audio, video, and transcript, 1 July 2016, https://www.collaborationsuperpowers.com/99-curate-your-notifications-for-maximum-productivity.

32. Phil Montero, "Apply the Right Technology," interview by Lisette Sutherland, Collaboration Superpowers, video and transcript, 5 August 2014, https://www.collaborationsuperpowers.com/apply-right-technology-phil-montero.

33. Dave Blum, "Team Building Adventures with Dr. Clue," interview by Lisette Sutherland, Collaboration Superpowers, podcast audio, video, and transcript, 8 December 2015, https://www.collaborationsuperpowers.com/74-solve-the-puzzles-of-remote-teamwork-with-dr-clue.

34. Andrea Zabala, "Maximize Your Time Working Remotely," interview by Lisette Sutherland, Collaboration Superpowers, podcast audio, video, and transcript, 11 January 2016, https://www.collaborationsuperpowers.com/72-maximize-your-time-working-remotely-with-andrea-zabala.

35. Pilar Orti, "Humanize Remote Work," interview by Lisette Sutherland, 3 November 2014, https://www.collaborationsuperpowers.com/4-humanizing-remote-work-pilar-orti.

36. Vanessa Shaw, "Helping You Tech Better," interview by Lisette Sutherland, Collaboration Superpowers, podcast audio, video, and transcript, 7 September 2015, https://www.collaborationsuperpowers.com/54-helping-you-tech-better-with-vanessa-shaw.

37. Lauren Moon, "Avoid the Seagull Effect: The 30/60/90 Framework for Feedback," Trello Blog, 4 June 2018, https://blog.trello.com/avoid-the-seagull-effect-30/60/90-feedback-framework.

38. Claire Drumond, "Kill the Triad—Long Live the TEAM," 23 August 2017, https://medium.com/smells-like-team-spirit/why-my-team-is-killing-our-triad-86946b099b.

39. Lauren Moon, "Avoid the Seagull Effect: The 30/60/90 Framework for Feedback," Trello Blog, 4 June 2018, https://blog.trello.com/avoid-the-seagull-effect-30/60/90-feedback-framework.

40. Hassan Osman, "Influence Your Virtual Team," interview by Lisette Sutherland, Collaboration Superpowers, podcast audio, video, and transcript, 3 November 2013, https://www.collaborationsuperpowers.com/5-managing-your-virtual-team-hassan-osman.

41. Fernando Garrido Vaz, "Build Reputation in the Freelance Economy with

Fernando Garrido Vaz," interview by Lisette Sutherland, Collaboration Superpowers, podcast audio, video, and transcript, 2 March 2016, https://www.collaborationsuperpowers.com/89-build-reputation-in-the-freelance-economy-with-fernando-garrido-vaz.

42. Vanessa Shaw, "Helping You Tech Better," interview by Lisette Sutherland, Collaboration Superpowers, podcast audio, video, and transcript, 7 September 2015, https://www.collaborationsuperpowers.com/54-helping-you-tech-better-with-vanessa-shaw.

43. Jeffry Hesse, "How to Be a Self-Organizing Remote Team," interview by Lisette Sutherland, Collaboration Superpowers, podcast audio, video, and transcript, 25 May 2015, https://www.collaborationsuperpowers.com/39-how-to-be-a-self-organizing-remote-team.

QUESTIONNAIRE FOR INDIVIDUALS

1. Kristi DePaul, "7 Tips for Getting Ready to Work Remotely," Remote.co, 4 October 2016, https://remote.co/7-tips-for-getting-ready-to-work-remotely.

2. "17 Non-Tech Fully Remote Jobs," Remote.co, 24 March 2017, updated 6 February 2018, https://remote.co/non-tech-fully-remote-jobs.

CONVINCING YOUR BOSS (OR TEAM)

1. Meghan M. Biro, "Telecommuting Is the Future of Work," *Forbes*, 12 January 2014, https://www.forbes.com/sites/meghanbiro/2014/01/12/telecommuting-is-the-future-of-work/#175008543c86.

2. Brie Weiler Reynolds, "Workers Are More Productive at Home: Here Are 25 Companies Hiring for Remote Jobs," FlexJobs, 21 August 2017, https://www.flexjobs.com/blog/post/productive-working-remotely-top-companies-hiring.

SEEKING REMOTE EMPLOYMENT

1. Leslie Truex, "Be a Work-at-Home Success with Leslie Truex," interview by Lisette Sutherland, Collaboration Superpowers, podcast audio, video, and transcript, 20 April 2016, https://www.collaborationsuperpowers.com/91-be-a-work-at-home-success-with-leslie-truex.

2. "17 Non-Tech Fully Remote Jobs," Remote.co, 24 March 2017, updated 6 February 2018, https://remote.co/non-tech-fully-remote-jobs. [Slack later bought Stride.]

3. Luis Suarez, "Engaging Remotely with Social Networks," interview by Lisette Sutherland, Collaboration Superpowers, podcast audio, video, and transcript, 19

January 2015, https://www.collaborationsuperpowers.com/21-engaging-remotely-with-social-networks-luis-suarez.

4. Fernando Garrido Vaz, "Build Reputation in the Freelance Economy with Fernando Garrido Vaz," interview by Lisette Sutherland, Collaboration Superpowers, podcast audio, video, and transcript, 2 March 2016, https://www.collaborationsuperpowers.com/89-build-reputation-in-the-freelance-economy-with-fernando-garrido-vaz.

FLEXJOBS LIST: 100 TOP COMPANIES WITH REMOTE JOBS IN 2018

1. FlexJobs, "100 Top Companies with Remote Jobs in 2020," 12 January 2020, https://www.flexjobs.com/blog/post/100-top-companies-with-remote-jobs-2020/.

PART III. SUCCESSFUL REMOTE TEAMS 101

1. Tabitha Colie, director of operations, "Seeq Remote Company Q&A," interview with Remote.co, April 2016, https://remote.co/company/seeq. This was in answer to the question: "What advice would you give to a team considering [going] remote?"

2. Alex Turnbull, founder and CEO, "Groove Remote Company Q&A," interview with Remote.co, July 2015, https://remote.co/company/groove. This was in answer to the question: "What advice would you give to a team considering [going] remote?"

3. Gabrielle Pitre, recruiter, "Coalition Technologies Remote Company Q&A," interview with Remote.co, July 2017, https://remote.co/company/coalition-technologies. This was in answer to the question: "What advice would you give to a team considering [going] remote?"

CHAPTER 5 TRANSITIONING TOWARD THE REMOTE OPTION

1. Ka Wai Cheung, "A Remote First Approach to the Workplace," The Done-Done Blog, 11 June 2014, https://www.getdonedone.com/remote-first-approach-workplace.

2. Ka Wai Cheung, "A Remote First Approach to the Workplace."

3. Adapted from Balki Kodarapu, "How We Created a Remote-First Manifesto," Medium.com, 13 September 2017, https://medium.com/@balki.io/how-we-created-a-remote-first-manifesto-e7dd6add2b3b; republished on LinkedIn.com,

31 October 2017, https://www.linkedin.com/pulse/how-we-created-remote-first-manifesto-balki-kodarapu. [Note: the named tool HipChat later became Slack.]

4. Jesse Fewell, "Let Go of Old Habits with Jesse Fewell," interview by Lisette Sutherland, Collaboration Superpowers, podcast audio, video, and transcript, 26 January 2016, https://www.collaborationsuperpowers.com/80-let-go-of-old-habits-with-jesse-fewell.

5. Alari Aho, founder and CEO, "Toggl Remote Company Q&A," interview with Remote.co, June 2015, https://remote.co/company/toggl.

6. Ade Olonoh, "Focus on Process, Not Tools, with Ade Olonoh," interview by Lisette Sutherland, Collaboration Superpowers, podcast audio, video, and transcript, 22 February 2016, https://www.collaborationsuperpowers.com/78-focus-on-process-not-tools-with-ade-olonoh.

7. Cris Hazzard, partner, "Sanborn Remote Company Q&A," interview with Remote.co, April 2016, https://remote.co/company/sanborn-media-factory.

8. Carrie Rice, COO, and Nita Tune, director of project management, "SitePen Remote Company Q&A," interview with Remote.co, October 2015, https://remote.co/company/sitepen.

9. Pilar Orti, "Humanize Remote Work," interview by Lisette Sutherland, 3 November 2014, https://www.collaborationsuperpowers.com/4-humanizing-remote-work-pilar-orti.

10. "15 Things to Look For When Hiring Remote Employees," Job Monkey, http://www.jobmonkey.com/employer-insights/remote-employees-characteristics.

11. "What Were Your Biggest Fears in Managing Remote Workers?," Remote.co, https://remote.co/qa-leading-remote-companies/what-were-your-biggest-fears-in-managing-remote-workers. Note that they've continued interviewing companies past the 135 companies noted herein. As of July 2018 that figure had reached 138.

12. Brian Patterson, partner, "Go Fish Digital Remote Company Q&A," interview with Remote.co, July 2015, https://remote.co/company/go-fish-digital.

13. Chris Byers, CEO, "Formstack Remote Company Q&A," interview with Remote.co, September 2015, https://remote.co/company/formstack.

14. Jon Lay, founder, "Hanno Remote Company Q&A," interview with Remote.co, January 2016, https://remote.co/company/hanno.

15. "What Were Your Biggest Fears in Managing Remote Workers?," Remote.co, https://remote.co/qa-leading-remote-companies/what-were-your-biggest-fears-in-managing-remote-workers; and "What Is the Hardest Part about Managing a

Remote Workforce?," Remote.co, https://remote.co/qa-leading-remote-companies/what-is-the-hardest-part-about-managing-a-remote-workforce.

Chapter 6. Hiring Remote Workers and Teams

1. Carrie McKeegan, "Build a Global, Virtual Business with Greenback Expat Tax Services," interview by Lisette Sutherland, Collaboration Superpowers, podcast audio, video, and transcript, 2 November 2015, https://collaborationsuperpowers.com/62-build-a-global-virtual-business-with-carrie-mckeegan-of-greenback-expat-tax-services.

2. Adriana Vela, "How to Be Efficient on the Road with Adriana Vela," interview by Lisette Sutherland, Collaboration Superpowers, video and transcript, 3 August 2015, https://www.collaborationsuperpowers.com/49-how-to-be-efficient-on-the-road-with-adrian-vela.

3. Dirk-Jan Padmos, "Management Is a Skill, Not a Job," interview by Lisette Sutherland, Collaboration Superpowers, 23 April 2013, https://www.collaborationsuperpowers.com/management-skill-job-dirk-jan-padmos.

4. Sources referenced include Angela Crist, "12 Qualities to Look For When Hiring Remote Workers," RemoteJobs.com, 21 June 2016, https://remotejobs.com/12-qualities-remote-workers; Brenda Do, "Grow Smart: 4 Traits to Look For When Hiring Remote Workers," Upwork.com, 11 July 2016, https://www.upwork.com/hiring/startup/4-traits-hiring-remote-workers); Rachel Go, "Hiring Remote Workers? Look For These 5 Qualities (Infographic)," https://www.15five.com/blog/hiring-remote-workers-infographic; "What to Look For When Hiring Remote Workers," Hivedesk.com (https://www.hivedesk.com/blog/what-to-look-for-when-hiring-remote-workers); Jessica Howington, "What Employers Look For When Hiring Remote Workers," FlexJobs.com, 11 May 2014, https://www.flexjobs.com/blog/post/employers-look-hiring-remote-workers; "15 Things to Look For When Hiring Remote Employees," Job Monkey (http://www.jobmonkey.com/employer-insights/remote-employees-characteristics); Anna Johansson, "6 Characteristics of Successful Remote Employees," Entrepreneur.com, 17 February 2017, https://www.entrepreneur.com/article/289370; Dunja Lazic, "5 Traits to Look For in Remote Employees," Remote.co, 19 August 2015, https://remote.co/5-traits-to-look-for-in-remote-employees; Siofra Pratt, "5 Essential Qualities to Look For in a Remote Worker," SocialTalent.com, 14 April 2016, https://www.socialtalent.com/blog/recruitment/5-essential-qualities-to-look-for-in-a-remote-worker; Brie Reynolds,

"5 Traits to Look For When Hiring Remote Workers," Recruiter.com, 24 September 2015, https://www.recruiter.com/i/5-traits-to-look-for-when-hiring-remote-workers; Lance Walley, "Hiring & Firing for Small Business Success: 25 Years, 130 People," Chargify.com, 12 January 2016, https://www.chargify.com/blog/hiring-firing-success)—plus the additional eighty-eight companies who responded to Remote.co's question: "What Traits Do You Look For in Candidates for a Remote Job?" (https://remote.co/qa-leading-remote-companies/what-traits-do-you-look-for-in-candidates-for-a-remote-job).

5. Siofra Pratt, "5 Essential Qualities to Look For in a Remote Worker," SocialTalent, 14 April 2016, https://www.socialtalent.com/blog/recruitment/5-essential-qualities-to-look-for-in-a-remote-worker.

6. Jeremy Stanton, "Being Deliberate with Onboarding and Culture with Jeremy Stanton," interview by Lisette Sutherland, Collaboration Superpowers, podcast audio, video, and transcript, 17 November 2014, https://www.collaborationsuperpowers.com/10-being-deliberate-with-onboarding-and-culture-jeremy-stanton.

7. Carrie McKeegan, "Build a Global, Virtual Business with Greenback Expat Tax Services," interview by Lisette Sutherland, Collaboration Superpowers, podcast audio, video, and transcript, 2 November 2015, https://collaborationsuperpowers.com/62-build-a-global-virtual-business-with-carrie-mckeegan-of-greenback-expat-tax-services.

8. Lance Walley, "Hiring & Firing for Small Business Success: 25 Years, 130 People," Chargify: The Bullring Blog, 12 January 2016, https://www.chargify.com/blog/hiring-firing-success.

9. "What Challenges Have You Encountered Building a Remote Team?," Remote.co, https://remote.co/qa-leading-remote-companies/what-challenges-have-you-encountered-building-remote-company.

10. Sara Tiffany, VP of product, "AirTreks Remote Company Q&A," interview with Remote.co, May 2017, https://remote.co/company/airtreks.

11. "What Were Your Biggest Fears in Managing Remote Workers?," Remote.co, https://remote.co/qa-leading-remote-companies/what-were-your-biggest-fears-in-managing-remote-workers.

12. Sources referenced include Angela Crist, "12 Qualities to Look For When Hiring Remote Workers," RemoteJobs.com, 21 June 2016, https://remotejobs.com/12-qualities-remote-workers; Brenda Do, "Grow Smart: 4 Traits to Look For When Hiring Remote Workers," Upwork.com, 11 July 2016, https://www.upwork.com

/hiring/startup/4-traits-hiring-remote-workers); Rachel Go, "Hiring Remote Workers? Look For These 5 Qualities (Infographic)," https://www.15five.com/blog/hiring-remote-workers-infographic; "What to Look For When Hiring Remote Workers," Hivedesk.com (https://www.hivedesk.com/blog/what-to-look-for-when-hiring-remote-workers); Jessica Howington, "What Employers Look For When Hiring Remote Workers," FlexJobs.com, 11 May 2014, https://www.flexjobs.com/blog/post/employers-look-hiring-remote-workers; "15 Things to Look For When Hiring Remote Employees," Job Monkey (http://www.jobmonkey.com/employer-insights/remote-employees-characteristics); Anna Johansson, "6 Characteristics of Successful Remote Employees," Entrepreneur.com, 17 February 2017, https://www.entrepreneur.com/article/289370; Dunja Lazic, "5 Traits to Look For in Remote Employees," Remote.co, 19 August 2015, https://remote.co/5-traits-to-look-for-in-remote-employees; Siofra Pratt, "5 Essential Qualities to Look For in a Remote Worker," SocialTalent.com, 14 April 2016, https://www.socialtalent.com/blog/recruitment/5-essential-qualities-to-look-for-in-a-remote-worker; Brie Reynolds, "5 Traits to Look For When Hiring Remote Workers," Recruiter.com, 24 September 2015, https://www.recruiter.com/i/5-traits-to-look-for-when-hiring-remote-workers; Lance Walley, "Hiring & Firing for Small Business Success: 25 Years, 130 People," Chargify.com, 12 January 2016, https://www.chargify.com/blog/hiring-firing-success)—plus the additional eighty-eight companies who responded to Remote.co's question: "What Traits Do You Look For in Candidates for a Remote Job?" (https://remote.co/qa-leading-remote-companies/what-traits-do-you-look-for-in-candidates-for-a-remote-job).

13. David Horowitz, "Make Remote Retrospectives Easy," interview by Lisette Sutherland, Collaboration Superpowers, podcast audio, video, and transcript, 11 May 2015, https://collaborationsuperpowers.com/37-abolish-the-postmortem-with-david-horowitz.

14. Lance Walley, "Hiring & Firing for Small Business Success: 25 Years, 130 People," Chargify: The Bullring Blog, 12 January 2016, https://www.chargify.com/blog/hiring-firing-success.

15. Sara Tiffany, VP of product, "AirTreks Remote Company Q&A," interview with Remote.co, May 2017, https://remote.co/company/airtreks.

16. Kate Harvey, 1 August 2016 (8:56), comment on Dave Nevogt, "Are Remote Workers More Productive? We've Checked All the Research So You Don't Have To," Hubstaff, 25 July 2016, https://blog.hubstaff.com/remote-workers-more-productive.

17. Derek Scruggs, "Use Tools and Increase Productivity," interview by Lisette Sutherland, Collaboration Superpowers, podcast audio, video, and transcript, 23 February 2015, https://www.collaborationsuperpowers.com/26-using-tools-and-increasing-productivity-with-derek-scruggs.

18. Carrie McKeegan, "Build a Global, Virtual Business with Greenback Expat Tax Services," interview by Lisette Sutherland, Collaboration Superpowers, podcast audio, video, and transcript, 2 November 2015, https://collaborationsuperpowers.com/62-build-a-global-virtual-business-with-carrie-mckeegan-of-greenback-expat-tax-services.

19. Remote.co, "How Do You Conduct Interviews for Remote Jobs?," https://remote.co/qa-leading-remote-companies/how-do-you-conduct-interviews-for-remote-jobs.

20. Sheila Murphy, cofounder and partner, "FlexProfessionals Remote Company Q&A," interview with Remote.co, November 2015, https://remote.co/company/flexprofessionals-llc.

21. Ann MacDonald, director of content strategy, "Love to Know Remote Company Q&A," interview with Remote.co, June 2015, https://remote.co/company/lovetoknow-corp.

22. Jeremy Stanton, "Being Deliberate with Onboarding and Culture with Jeremy Stanton," interview by Lisette Sutherland, Collaboration Superpowers, podcast audio, video, and transcript, 17 November 2014, https://www.collaborationsuperpowers.com/10-being-deliberate-with-onboarding-and-culture-jeremy-stanton.

23. Jeremy Stanton, "Being Deliberate with Onboarding and Culture with Jeremy Stanton."

24. Jessie Shternshus, "Make Shift Happen with Jessie Shternshus," interview by Lisette Sutherland, Collaboration Superpowers, podcast audio, video, and transcript, 28 January 2016, https://collaborationsuperpowers.com/85-make-shift-happen-with-jessie-shternshus.

25. Yves Hanoulle, "Welcome People and Develop Trust While Walking with Yves Hanoulle," interview by Lisette Sutherland, Collaboration Superpowers, podcast audio, video, and transcript, 12 January 2015, https://www.collaborationsuperpowers.com/20-welcome-people-and-develop-trust-while-walking-yves-hanoulle.

26. Sara Rosso, marketing manager, and Lori McLeese, head of HR, "Automattic Remote Company Q&A," interview with Remote.co, June 2015, https://remote.co/company/automatic.

27. Paula Strozak, chief business officer, "Bitovi Remote Company Q&A," interview with Remote.co, September 2017, https://remote.co/company/bitovi.

28. Remote.co, "What is the Hardest Part About Managing a Remote Workforce?," https://www.remote.co/qa-leading-remote-companies/what-is-the-hardest-part-about-managing-a-remote-workforce. (Note that as of this printing Allie Schwartz is director of people operations at Healthify.)

HIRING CHEAT SHEET

1. John Lee Dumas, "1: John Lee Dumas of EntrepreneurOnFire," *Entrepreneur on Fire*, https://www.eofire.com/podcast/podcast-interview-with-entrepreneur-john-lee-dumas-of-entrepreneur-on-fire.

REMOTE-ONLY MANIFESTO

1. John Northrup, "Remote-Only Manifesto" GitLab, June 2016, https://www.remoteonly.org.

PART IV. SUCCESSFUL REMOTE TEAMS 201

1. Phil Montero, "Apply the Right Technology," interview by Lisette Sutherland, Collaboration Superpowers, video and transcript, 5 August 2014, https://www.collaborationsuperpowers.com/apply-right-technology-phil-montero.

2. Jon Lay, founder, "Hanno Remote Company Q&A," interview with Remote.co, January 2016, https://remote.co/company/hanno.

CHAPTER 7. COMMIT AND LEAD, TRUST AND SUCCEED

1. Luis Suarez, "Engaging Remotely with Social Networks," interview by Lisette Sutherland, Collaboration Superpowers, podcast audio, video, and transcript, 19 January 2015, https://www.collaborationsuperpowers.com/21-engaging-remotely-with-social-networks-luis-suarez.

2. Meghan M. Biro, "Telecommuting Is the Future of Work," *Forbes*, 12 January 2014, https://www.forbes.com/sites/meghanbiro/2014/01/12/telecommuting-is-the-future-of-work/#175008543c86.

3. AgileBill Krebs, "Collaborating in Virtual Worlds," interview by Lisette Sutherland, Collaboration Superpowers, podcast audio, video, and transcript, 8 December 2014, https://www.collaborationsuperpowers.com/15-collaborating-in-virtual-worlds-agilebill-krebs.

4. Maarten Koopmans, "How to Eat an Elephant," interview by Lisette Suther-

land, Collaboration Superpowers, 5 February 2013, https://collaborationsuperpowers.com/hire-right-people-remote-working-Maarten-koopmans.

5. "Global Survey of 24,000+ Workers Unearths the 'Need' for Flexibility in the Workplace in Order for Businesses to Thrive," 20 March 2017, Polycom Inc., http://www.polycom.com/company/news/press-releases/2017/20170321.html.

6. Nick Timmons, "Embody Your Team Online with Personify," interview by Lisette Sutherland, Collaboration Superpowers, podcast audio, video, and transcript, 30 March 2015, https://www.collaborationsuperpowers.com/31-embody-your-team-online-with-personify.

7. Sumant Kowshik, "Embody Your Team Online with Personify," interview by Lisette Sutherland, Collaboration Superpowers, podcast audio, video, and transcript, 30 March 2015, https://www.collaborationsuperpowers.com/31-embody-your-team-online-with-personify.

8. "A Highly Scientific Post About Lighting Zoom Meetings," 12 February 2015, Zoom blog, https://blog.zoom.us/wordpress/2015/02/12/scientific-lighting-zoom-meetings-will-ever-read. See also G. C. Brainard, J. P. Hanifin, J. M. Greeson, B. Byrne, G. Glickman, E. Gerner, and M. D. Rollag, "Action Spectrum for Melatonin Regulation in Humans: Evidence for a Novel Circadian Photoreceptor," *The Journal of Neuroscience* 21, no. 16, 15 August 2001, http://www.jneurosci.org/content/21/16/6405.long.

9. Ricky Guest, "Collaboration in Space Exploration NASA/SSERVI," interview by Lisette Sutherland, Collaboration Superpowers, podcast audio, video, and transcript, 22 October 2014, https://www.collaborationsuperpowers.com/episode-3-collaboration-space-exploration-nasa-sservi.

10. Alice Hendricks, CEO, "Jackson River Remote Company Q&A," interview with Remote.co, July 2015, https://remote.co/company/jackson-river.

11. Ricky Guest, "Collaboration in Space Exploration NASA/SSERVI," interview by Lisette Sutherland, Collaboration Superpowers, podcast audio, video, and transcript, 22 October 2014, https://www.collaborationsuperpowers.com/episode-3-collaboration-space-exploration-nasa-sservi.

12. Lucius Bobikiewicz, "Powerful Online Collaboration with Simple Spreadsheets," interview by Lisette Sutherland, Collaboration Superpowers, podcast audio, video, and transcript, 6 July 2015, https://www.collaborationsuperpowers.com/45-powerful-collaboration-with-simple-spreadsheets.

13. Ryan Baker, founder and CEO, "Timely Remote Company Q&A," interview with Remote.co, February 2016, https://remote.co/company/timely.

14. Phil Montero, "Apply the Right Technology," interview by Lisette Sutherland, Collaboration Superpowers, video and transcript, 5 August 2014, https://www.collaborationsuperpowers.com/apply-right-technology-phil-montero.

15. Phil Montero, "Apply the Right Technology."

16. Mark Kilby, "Facilitating Distributed Agile Teams," interview by Lisette Sutherland, Collaboration Superpowers, podcast audio, video, and transcript, 12 November 2014, https://collaborationsuperpowers.com/9-coaching-distributed-agile-teams-mark-kilby.

17. Luis Suarez, "Engaging Remotely with Social Networks," interview by Lisette Sutherland, Collaboration Superpowers, podcast audio, video, and transcript, 19 January 2015, https://www.collaborationsuperpowers.com/21-engaging-remotely-with-social-networks-luis-suarez.

18. Felix Dubinsky, cofounder, "SimpleTexting Remote Company Q&A," interview with Remote.co, May 2016, https://remote.co/company/simple-texting.

CHAPTER 8. FACILITATE THEIR SUCCESS . . .

1. Lance Walley, "Hiring & Firing for Small Business Success: 25 Years, 130 People," Chargify: The Bullring Blog, 12 January 2016, https://www.chargify.com/blog/hiring-firing-success.

2. AgileBill Krebs, "Collaborating in Virtual Worlds," interview by Lisette Sutherland, Collaboration Superpowers, podcast audio, video, and transcript, 8 December 2014, https://www.collaborationsuperpowers.com/15-collaborating-in-virtual-worlds-agilebill-krebs.

3. Howard B. Esbin, "Tuning Your Virtual Team," interview by Lisette Sutherland, Collaboration Superpowers, podcast audio, video, and transcript, 22 October 2014, https://www.collaborationsuperpowers.com/episode-2-tuning-virtual-team-howard-esbin.

4. Tom Sepper, COO, "World Wide Web Hosting Remote Company Q&A," interview with Remote.co, September 2015, https://remote.co/company/world-wide-web-hosting.

5. Liz Peterson, operations manager, "ezhome Remote Company Q&A," interview with Remote.co, July 2017, https://remote.co/company/ezhome.

6. Sieva Kozinsky, CEO, "StudySoup Remote Company Q&A," interview with Remote.co, January 2016, https://remote.co/company/studysoup.

7. James Law, HR director, "Envato Remote Company Q&A," interview with Remote.co, May 2016, https://remote.co/team/envato.

8. Cris Hazzard, partner, "Sanborn Remote Company Q&A," interview with Remote.co, April 2016, https://remote.co/company/sanborn-media-factory.

9. Fred Perrotta, CEO, "Tortuga Remote Company Q&A," interview with Remote.co, June 2017, https://remote.co/company/Tortuga.

10. Magnus Karlsson, "A Management System for Innovation," interview by Lisette Sutherland, Collaboration Superpowers, 4 March 2015, https://collaborationsuperpowers.com/ideaboxes-a-management-system-for-innovation-magnus-karlsson.

11. Noelle Daley, "What Colocated Teams Can Learn from Remote Teams," Medium.com, 9 June 2018, https://medium.com/@elnoelle/what-colocated-teams-can-learn-from-remote-teams-f48bb4a708d1.

12. Teague Soderman, "Collaboration in Space Exploration NASA/SSERVI," interview by Lisette Sutherland, Collaboration Superpowers, podcast audio, video, and transcript, 22 October 2014, https://www.collaborationsuperpowers.com/episode-3-collaboration-space-exploration-nasa-sservi.

13. Ryan Chartrand, from video "Slack Tips Tuesday: How to Not Look Like a Slacker on Slack" on "The 5 Most Important Things We Do As a Remote Company," X-Team, 10 July 2015, https://x-team.com/blog/5-important-things-remote-company.

14. Tish Briseno, "Celebrating 2 Years at Automattic," 1 June 2017, https://tish.blog/2017/06/01/2-years-at-automattic; see also https://wordpress.org/themes/p2.

15. Mario Peshev, founder and WordPress architect, "DevriX Remote Company Q&A," interview with Remote.co, July 2016, https://remote.co/company/devrix.

16. Pierre Veyrat, "Check Out 10 Examples of OKRs and See How This Methodology Works," Heflo.com, 23 December 2016, https://www.heflo.com/blog/business-management/examples-of-okrs.

17. Jurgen Appelo, "The Peer-to-Peer Bonus System," *Forbes*, 8 July 2015, https://www.forbes.com/sites/jurgenappelo/2015/07/08/the-peer-to-peer-bonus-system/#6e1b96594329.

18. Louise Brace, email message to the author, 8 February 2015.

19. ShriKant Vashishtha, "Bridging the Gap on Distributed Agile Teams," interview by Lisette Sutherland, Collaboration Superpowers, podcast audio, video, and transcript, 19 November 2014, https://www.collaborationsuperpowers.com/11-bridging-the-gap-on-distributed-agile-teams-shrikant-vashishtha.

20. AgileBill Krebs, "Collaborating in Virtual Worlds," interview by Lisette

Sutherland, Collaboration Superpowers, podcast audio, video, and transcript, 8 December 2014, https://www.collaborationsuperpowers.com/15-collaborating-in-virtual-worlds-agilebill-krebs.

21. Howard B. Esbin, "Tuning Your Virtual Team," interview by Lisette Sutherland, Collaboration Superpowers, podcast audio, video, and transcript, 22 October 2014, https://www.collaborationsuperpowers.com/episode-2-tuning-virtual-team-howard-esbin.

22. ShriKant Vashishtha, "Bridging the Gap on Distributed Agile Teams," interview by Lisette Sutherland, Collaboration Superpowers, podcast audio, video, and transcript, 19 November 2014, https://www.collaborationsuperpowers.com/11-bridging-the-gap-on-distributed-agile-teams-shrikant-vashishtha.

23. Thodoris Tsiridis, "How to Use Hangouts as a Virtual Office with Spotify," interview by Lisette Sutherland, Collaboration Superpowers, 28 November 2013, https://collaborationsuperpowers.com/how-a-team-at-spotify-uses-hangouts-to-work-remotely.

24. Mark Kilby, "Facilitating Distributed Agile Teams," interview by Lisette Sutherland, Collaboration Superpowers, podcast audio, video, and transcript, 12 November 2014, https://collaborationsuperpowers.com/9-coaching-distributed-agile-teams-mark-kilby.

25. Luis Suarez, "Engaging Remotely with Social Networks," interview by Lisette Sutherland, Collaboration Superpowers, podcast audio, video, and transcript, 19 January 2015, https://www.collaborationsuperpowers.com/21-engaging-remotely-with-social-networks-luis-suarez.

26. Tom Howlett, "Build Trust on Remote Teams Through Pair Collaboration," interview by Lisette Sutherland, Collaboration Superpowers, podcast audio, video, and transcript, 2 March 2015, https://www.collaborationsuperpowers.com/27-build-trust-on-remote-teams-through-pair-collaboration.

27. Mandy Ross, "Be a High-Functioning Connected Team in a Sococo Virtual Office," interview by Lisette Sutherland, Collaboration Superpowers, podcast audio, video, and transcript, 19 October 2015, https://collaborationsuperpowers.com/60-be-a-high-functioning-connected-team-in-a-sococo-virtual-office.

28. Carrie Kuempel, "Be a High-Functioning Connected Team in a Sococo Virtual Office," interview by Lisette Sutherland, Collaboration Superpowers, podcast audio, video, and transcript, 19 October 2015, https://collaborationsuperpowers.com/60-be-a-high-functioning-connected-team-in-a-sococo-virtual-office.

29. Howard B. Esbin, "Tuning Your Virtual Team," interview by Lisette Sutherland, Collaboration Superpowers, podcast audio, video, and transcript, 22 October 2014, https://www.collaborationsuperpowers.com/episode-2-tuning-virtual-team-howard-esbin.

30. Mandy Ross, "Be a High-Functioning Connected Team in a Sococo Virtual Office," interview by Lisette Sutherland, Collaboration Superpowers, podcast audio, video, and transcript, 19 October 2015, https://collaborationsuperpowers.com/60-be-a-high-functioning-connected-team-in-a-sococo-virtual-office.

31. Anna Danes, "An Interview with Managing Virtual Teams," interview by Lisette Sutherland, Collaboration Superpowers, podcast audio, video, and transcript, 12 June 2014, https://www.collaborationsuperpowers.com/interview-managing-virtual-teams.

32. Jeremy Stanton, "Being Deliberate with Onboarding and Culture with Jeremy Stanton," interview by Lisette Sutherland, Collaboration Superpowers, podcast audio, video, and transcript, 17 November 2014, https://www.collaborationsuperpowers.com/10-being-deliberate-with-onboarding-and-culture-jeremy-stanton.

33. Brie Weiler Reynolds, "Communicate Proactively and Build Culture," interview by Lisette Sutherland, Collaboration Superpowers, podcast audio, video, and transcript, 5 August 2015, https://collaborationsuperpowers.com/56-communicate-proactively-and-build-culture-with-brie-reynolds.

34. Carrie McKeegan, "Build a Global, Virtual Business with Greenback Expat Tax Services," interview by Lisette Sutherland, Collaboration Superpowers, podcast audio, video, and transcript, 2 November 2015, https://collaborationsuperpowers.com/62-build-a-global-virtual-business-with-carrie-mckeegan-of-greenback-expat-tax-services.

35. Robert Rogge, "An Interview with Managing Virtual Teams," interview by Lisette Sutherland, Collaboration Superpowers, podcast audio, video, and transcript, 12 June 2014, https://collaborationsuperpowers.com/interview-managing-virtual-teams.

36. Ralph van Roosmalen, "How to Manage Three Remote Offices," interview by Lisette Sutherland, Collaboration Superpowers, podcast audio, video, and transcript, 9 February 2015, https://www.collaborationsuperpowers.com/24-managing-three-remote-offices-with-ralph-van-roosmalen.

37. Ryan Baker, founder and CEO, "Timely Remote Company Q&A," interview with Remote.co, February 2016, https://remote.co/company/timely.

38. Pilar Orti, "Humanize Remote Work," interview by Lisette Sutherland, 3 November 2014, https://www.collaborationsuperpowers.com/4-humanizing-remote-work-pilar-orti.

39. Pilar Orti, "Humanize Remote Work."

40. "Retrospective Plans," http://retrospectivewiki.org/index.php?title=Retrospective_Plans.

41. David Horowitz, "Make Remote Retrospectives Easy," interview by Lisette Sutherland, Collaboration Superpowers, podcast audio, video, and transcript, 11 May 2015, https://collaborationsuperpowers.com/37-abolish-the-postmortem-with-david-horowitz.

42. Henrik Kniberg, "Squad Health Check Model: Visualizing What to Improve," Spotify Labs, 16 September 2014, https://labs.spotify.com/2014/09/16/squad-health-check-model.

43. Susan Scott, *Fierce Conversations: Achieving Success at Work and in Life One Conversation at a Time* (New York: New America Library/Berkley, 2004), 189.

44. Kristin Kanger, VP of talent management, "Working Solutions Remote Company Q&A," interview with Remote.co, https://remote.co/team/working-solutions.

CHAPTER 9 TUNE YOUR TEAM WITH A TEAM AGREEMENT

1. Robert Rogge, "An Interview with Managing Virtual Teams," interview by Lisette Sutherland, Collaboration Superpowers, podcast audio, video, and transcript, 12 June 2014, https://collaborationsuperpowers.com/interview-managing-virtual-teams.

2. Hugo Messer, "Managing Remote Teams," interview by Lisette Sutherland, Collaboration Superpowers, podcast audio, video, and transcript, 26 November 2014, https://collaborationsuperpowers.com/13-managing-remote-teams-hugo-messer.

3. Howard B. Esbin, "Tuning Your Virtual Team," interview by Lisette Sutherland, Collaboration Superpowers, podcast audio, video, and transcript, 22 October 2014, https://www.collaborationsuperpowers.com/episode-2-tuning-virtual-team-howard-esbin.

4. Derek Scruggs, "Use Tools and Increase Productivity," interview by Lisette Sutherland, Collaboration Superpowers, podcast audio, video, and transcript, 23 February 2015, https://www.collaborationsuperpowers.com/26-using-tools-and-increasing-productivity-with-derek-scruggs.

5. Frances Frei and Anne Morriss, "Culture Takes Over When the CEO Leaves

the Room," *Harvard Business Review*, 10 May 2012, https://hbr.org/2012/05/culture-takes-over-when-the-ce.

6. Ade Olonoh, "Focus on Process, Not Tools, with Ade Olonoh," interview by Lisette Sutherland, Collaboration Superpowers, podcast audio, video, and transcript, 22 February 2016, https://www.collaborationsuperpowers.com/78-focus-on-process-not-tools-with-ade-olonoh.

7. Hugo Messer, "Managing Remote Teams," interview by Lisette Sutherland, Collaboration Superpowers, podcast audio, video, and transcript, 26 November 2014, https://collaborationsuperpowers.com/13-managing-remote-teams-hugo-messer.

8. Mark Kilby, "Facilitating Distributed Agile Teams," interview by Lisette Sutherland, Collaboration Superpowers, podcast audio, video, and transcript, 12 November 2014, https://collaborationsuperpowers.com/9-coaching-distributed-agile-teams-mark-kilby.

9. Peter Hilton, "The Need for Face-to-Face on Virtual Teams," interview by Lisette Sutherland, Collaboration Superpowers, podcast audio, video, and transcript, 22 December 2014, https://collaborationsuperpowers.com/17-the-need-for-face-to-face-on-virtual-teams-peter-hilton.

10. Pilar Orti, "Humanize Remote Work," interview by Lisette Sutherland, 3 November 2014, https://www.collaborationsuperpowers.com/4-humanizing-remote-work-pilar-orti.

11. Tom Howlett, "Build Trust on Remote Teams Through Pair Collaboration," interview by Lisette Sutherland, Collaboration Superpowers, podcast audio, video, and transcript, 2 March 2015, https://www.collaborationsuperpowers.com/27-build-trust-on-remote-teams-through-pair-collaboration.

12. Luis Gonçalves, "Writing a Book Together Remotely," interview by Ben Linders, Collaboration Superpowers, video and transcript, 14 April 2014, https://www.collaborationsuperpowers.com/interview-with-ben-linders-and-luis-goncalves.

13. Paul-Andrea Berry-Breanna, "Communication Tips for Global Virtual Teams," *Harvard Business Review*, 30 October 2014, https://hbr.org/2014/10/communication-tips-for-global-virtual-teams.

14. Cris Hazzard, partner, "Sanborn Remote Company Q&A," interview with Remote.co, April 2016, https://remote.co/company/sanborn-media-factory.

15. Scott Hoppe, "Prioritize Happiness and Profit," interview by Lisette Sutherland, Collaboration Superpowers, podcast audio, video, and transcript, 18 September 2017, https://collaborationsuperpowers.com/160-prioritize-happiness-and-profit-with-scott-hoppe.

16. Nita Tune, email message to the authors, 12 June 2018.

17. AgileBill Krebs, "Collaborating in Virtual Worlds," interview by Lisette Sutherland, Collaboration Superpowers, podcast audio, video, and transcript, 8 December 2014, https://www.collaborationsuperpowers.com/15-collaborating-in-virtual-worlds-agilebill-krebs.

18. Peter Hilton, "The Need for Face-to-Face on Virtual Teams," interview by Lisette Sutherland, Collaboration Superpowers, podcast audio, video, and transcript, 22 December 2014, https://collaborationsuperpowers.com/17-the-need-for-face-to-face-on-virtual-teams-peter-hilton.

19. Laura Rooke, "Remote Technical Support," interview by Lisette Sutherland, Collaboration Superpowers, podcast audio, video, and transcript, 1 December 2014, https://www.collaborationsuperpowers.com/14-remote-technical-support-laura-rooke.

20. Mark Kilby, "Facilitating Distributed Agile Teams," interview by Lisette Sutherland, Collaboration Superpowers, podcast audio, video, and transcript, 12 November 2014, https://collaborationsuperpowers.com/9-coaching-distributed-agile-teams-mark-kilby.

21. Happy Melly team, Sample Team Agreement Etiquette for Slack, 2018.

22. Howard B. Esbin, "Tuning Your Virtual Team," interview by Lisette Sutherland, Collaboration Superpowers, podcast audio, video, and transcript, 22 October 2014, https://www.collaborationsuperpowers.com/episode-2-tuning-virtual-team-howard-esbin.

23. Patrick Sarnacke, "Visualizing Time Zone Challenges for Distributed Teams," Mingle blog, 13 June 2016, https://www.thoughtworks.com/mingle/scaled-agile/2016/06/13/visualizing-time-zones.html.

24. Sebastian Göttschkes, VP of platform, "Blossom Remote Company Q&A," interview with Remote.co, April 2016, https://remote.co/company/blossom.

25. Pablo Hoffman, director, "ScrapingHub Remote Company Q&A," interview with Remote.co, June 2015, https://remote.co/company/scrapinghub.

26. Paul-Andrea Berry-Breanna, "Communication Tips for Global Virtual Teams," *Harvard Business Review*, 30 October 2014, https://hbr.org/2014/10/communication-tips-for-global-virtual-teams.

27. Vanessa Shaw, "Helping You Tech Better," interview by Lisette Sutherland, Collaboration Superpowers, podcast audio, video, and transcript, 7 September 2015, https://www.collaborationsuperpowers.com/54-helping-you-tech-better-with-vanessa-shaw.

28. Ralph van Roosmalen, "How to Manage Three Remote Offices," interview by Lisette Sutherland, Collaboration Superpowers, podcast audio, video, and transcript, 9 February 2015, https://www.collaborationsuperpowers.com/24-managing-three-remote-offices-with-ralph-van-roosmalen.

29. Fernando Garrido Vaz, "Build Reputation in the Freelance Economy with Fernando Garrido Vaz," interview by Lisette Sutherland, Collaboration Superpowers, podcast audio, video, and transcript, 2 March 2016, https://www.collaborationsuperpowers.com/89-build-reputation-in-the-freelance-economy-with-fernando-garrido-vaz.

30. Hugo Messer, "Managing Remote Teams," interview by Lisette Sutherland, Collaboration Superpowers, podcast audio, video, and transcript, 26 November 2014, https://www.collaborationsuperpowers.com/13-managing-remote-teams-hugo-messer.

31. Hugo Messer, "Managing Remote Teams."

32. Scott E. Page, "#52 Raising the Bar," interview by Alex Goldman, *Reply All*, GimletMedia.com, 20 January 2016, https://gimletmedia.com/episode/52-raising-the-bar. See also Scott E. Page, *The Difference: How the Power of Diversity Creates Better Groups, Firms, Schools, and Societies* (Princeton: Princeton University Press, 2007).

33. Tiziano Perrucci, "A Remote Team Perspective with StarterSquad," interview by Lisette Sutherland, Collaboration Superpowers, podcast audio, video, and transcript, 16 February 2015, https://www.collaborationsuperpowers.com/25-a-remote-team-perspective-with-startersquad.

34. Paul-Andrea Berry-Breanna, "Communication Tips for Global Virtual Teams," *Harvard Business Review*, 30 October 2014, https://hbr.org/2014/10/communication-tips-for-global-virtual-teams.

35. Deven Bhagwandin, "Managing Cultural and Language Divides Within Your Remote Team," Workafar.com, 22 November 2015, http://workafar.com/managing-cultural-and-language-divides-within-your-remote-team.

36. Silvina Martínez, "An Interview with Managing Virtual Teams," interview by Lisette Sutherland, Collaboration Superpowers, podcast audio, video, and transcript, 12 June 2014, https://collaborationsuperpowers.com/interview-managing-virtual-teams.

37. John Rampton, "10 Tips for Overcoming the Language Barrier When Expanding Overseas," *Fast Company*, 10 March 2015, https://www.fastcompany

.com/3043336/10-tips-for-overcoming-the-language-barrier-when-expanding-overseas. For more, visit https://www.johnrampton.com.

38. "5 Tips for Overcoming the Language Barrier on a Distributed Team," Sococo blog, https://www.sococo.com/blog/5-tips-overcoming-language-barrier-distributed-team.

39. Lucius Bobikiewicz, "Powerful Online Collaboration with Simple Spreadsheets," interview by Lisette Sutherland, Collaboration Superpowers, podcast audio, video, and transcript, 6 July 2015, https://www.collaborationsuperpowers.com/45-powerful-collaboration-with-simple-spreadsheets.

40. Jeremy Stanton, "Being Deliberate with Onboarding and Culture with Jeremy Stanton," interview by Lisette Sutherland, Collaboration Superpowers, podcast audio, video, and transcript, 17 November 2014, https://www.collaborationsuperpowers.com/10-being-deliberate-with-onboarding-and-culture-jeremy-stanton.

CHAPTER 10. BRING IT ALL TOGETHER

1. Emily Klein, "The World of Work in 2018: How the Workplace Will Evolve," Flexwork Global.com, 18 January 2018, http://flexworkglobal.com/world-work-2018-workplace-will-evolve.

2. Mark Kilby, "Facilitating Distributed Agile Teams," interview by Lisette Sutherland, Collaboration Superpowers, podcast audio, video, and transcript, 12 November 2014, https://collaborationsuperpowers.com/9-coaching-distributed-agile-teams-mark-kilby.

3. Sally French, "Ten Rules of Etiquette for Videoconferencing," *The Wall Street Journal*, 13 March 2016, https://www.wsj.com/articles/ten-rules-of-etiquette-for-videoconferencing-1457921535.

4. *The Wall Street Journal*, 21 December 2016, https://www.wsj.com/articles/everybody-unmute-its-time-for-the-virtual-office-christmas-party-1482334506. (Photo by Lisette Sutherland.)

5. Dean Anderson, "Great Meeting Facilitation Technique," 27 March 2011, http://changeleadersnetwork.com/great-meeting-facilitation-technique; "E.L.M.O.: How a Muppet Can Save Your Meetings . . . and Your Sanity!," The Persimmon Group blog, 20 May 2016, https://www.thepersimmongroup.com/e-l-m-o-how-a-muppet-can-save-your-meetings-and-your-sanity; Tom Richert, "Enough Let's Move On: ELMO," Lean Project, 12 August 2016, www.leanproject.com/news/enough-lets-move-on-elmo.

6. Melinda Wenner, "Smile! It Could Make You Happier," *Scientific American*, 1 September 2009, https://www.scientificamerican.com/article/smile-it-could-make-you-happier.

7. Soulaima Gourani, CEO, "Trade Conductor Remote Company Q&A," interview with Remote.co, January 2017, https://remote.co/company/tradeconductor.

8. Victor Lipman, "66% of Employees Would Quit If They Feel Unappreciated," Forbes.com, 15 April 2017, https://www.forbes.com/sites/victorlipman/2017/04/15/66-of-employees-would-quit-if-they-feel-unappreciated/#4fa5103f6897.

9. Vernon Gunnarson, "4 Reasons to Praise Employees' Effort, Not Talent," *The Muse*, https://www.themuse.com/advice/4-reasons-to-praise-employees-effort-not-talent; see also Carol S. Dweck, "The Secret to Raising Smart Kids," *Scientific American*, December 2007, https://www.scientificamerican.com/article/the-secret-to-raising-smart-kids.

10. Ralph van Roosmalen, "How to Manage Three Remote Offices," interview by Lisette Sutherland, Collaboration Superpowers, podcast audio, video, and transcript, 9 February 2015, https://www.collaborationsuperpowers.com/24-managing-three-remote-offices-with-ralph-van-roosmalen.

11. Allie VanNest, head of communications, "Parse.ly Remote Company Q&A," interview with Remote.co, July 2016, https://remote.co/company/parse-ly.

12. Erin Davidson, recruiting coordinator, "Appirio Remote Company Q&A," interview with Remote.co, December 2016, https://remote.co/team/appirio.

13. Chris Arnold, partner, "Authentic Form & Function Remote Company Q&A," interview with Remote.co, April 2016, https://www.remote.co/company/authentic-form-function.

14. Claire O'Connell, director of people & culture, "Canonical Remote Company Q&A," interview with Remote.co, September 2015, https://www.remote.co/company/canonical.

15. Jeremy Stanton, "Being Deliberate with Onboarding and Culture with Jeremy Stanton," interview by Lisette Sutherland, Collaboration Superpowers, podcast audio, video, and transcript, 17 November 2014, https://www.collaborationsuperpowers.com/10-being-deliberate-with-onboarding-and-culture-jeremy-stanton.

16. "What Is Agile? What Is Scrum?," cPrime, https://www.cprime.com/resources/what-is-agile-what-is-scrum.

17. "What Has Changed About How Your Remote Team Operates?," Remote.co, https://remote.co/qa-leading-remote-companies/what-has-changed-about-how-your-remote-team-operates.

18. Sieva Kozinsky, CEO, "StudySoup Remote Company Q&A," interview with Remote.co, January 2016, https://remote.co/company/studysoup.

19. Nathaniel Manning, COO, "Ushahidi Remote Company Q&A," interview with Remote.co, May 2016, https://remote.co/company/ushahidi.

20. "What Is the Hardest Part About Managing a Remote Workforce?," Remote.co, https://remote.co/qa-leading-remote-companies/what-is-the-hardest-part-about-managing-a-remote-workforce.

21. Casey Cobb, partner/developer, "Project Ricochet Remote Company Q&A," interview with Remote.co, July 2016, https://remote.co/company/project-ricochet.

22. Frazier Miller, COO, "Articulate Inc. Remote Company Q&A," interview with Remote.co, August 2015, https://remote.co/company/articulate-inc.

23. Coby Chapple, product designer, "GitHub Inc. Remote Company Q&A," interview with Remote.co, June 2015 https://remote.co/company/github-inc.

24. Stella Garber, VP of marketing, "Trello Remote Company Q&A," interview with Remote.co, June 2015, https://remote.co/company/trello.

25. Kristin Kanger, VP of talent management, "Working Solutions Remote Company Q&A," interview with Remote.co, December 2015, https://remote.co/team/working-solutions.

26. Fred Perrotta, CEO, "Tortuga Remote Company Q&A," interview with Remote.co, June 2017, https://remote.co/company/Tortuga.

27. Kristin Kanger, VP of talent management, "Working Solutions Remote Company Q&A," interview with Remote.co, December 2015, https://remote.co/team/working-solutions.

28. Alex Frison, co-owner and project manager, "Inpsyde GmbH Remote Company Q&A," interview with Remote.co, June 2016, https://remote.co/company/inpsyde-gmbh.

29. Martin Van Ryswyk, EVP of engineering, "DataStax Remote Company Q&A," interview with Remote.co, October 2015, https://remote.co/company/datastax.

30. Paul Jun, content marketer, "Help Scout Remote Company Q&A," interview with Remote.co, November 2015, https://remote.co/company/help-scout.

GLOSSARY

1. "2016 Global Telework Survey," 27 July 2016, https://www.pgi.com/blog/2016/06/2016-global-telework-survey.

2. Paul R. Niven and Ben Lamorte, *Objectives and Key Results: Driving Focus,*

Alignment, and Engagement with OKRs (Hoboken, NJ: John Wiley *&* Sons, 2016), 6.

3. Terrence Metz, "How to Manage Your Meeting Parking Lot and Assign Action Items," MG Rush, *FAST Facilitation Leadership Monthly*, https://mgrush.com/blog/2011/08/04/meeting-parking-lot.

4. Eurofound and the International Labour Office (2017), *Working Anytime, Anywhere: The Effects on the World of Work*, Publications Office of the European Union, Luxembourg, and the International Labour Office, Geneva.

5. Ward Cunningham, "Front Page," Content Creation Wiki, 23 December 2014, http://wiki.c2.com/?FrontPage.

TECHNOLOGY & TOOLS

1. Teo Härén, "Work Where You Are Most Productive," interview by Lisette Sutherland, Collaboration Superpowers, podcast audio, video, and transcript, 16 March 2015, https://www.collaborationsuperpowers.com/29-work-where-you-are-most-productive-with-teo-hren.

2. "17 Non-Tech Fully Remote Jobs," Remote.co, 24 March 2017, updated 6 February 2018, https://remote.co/non-tech-fully-remote-jobs.

3. Remoters.net, "7 Remote Work Trends in 2017," http://remoters.net/remote-work-trends-2017.

4. Udit Agarwal, "Atlassian Invests in Slack, Kills HipChat and Stride," *Tech Story*, 27 July 2018, https://techstory.in/atlassian-invests-in-slack-kills-hipchat-and-stride.

INDEX

Note that all interviewees appear in the "Interviewees" section; interviewees quoted in the book also appear in the index. * All tool *categories* included in "Technology & Tools" also appear in the index. Specific tools in "Technology & Tools" appear in the index only if they are discussed to some degree. * No glossary definitions are included in the index.

If you have benefited from this book, please consider donating one or more copies of the print edition to your local library and/or coworking space. (For guidelines and templates for doing so, visit https://collaborationsuperpowers.com/donate-a-book.) The more of us who learn how to successfully work together from anywhere, the more we have to offer and the greater good we can do. Together, we can make the world a better place. Join us!